THE COMPLETE GUIDE TO
PRUNING
AND TRAINING
PLANTS

DAVID JOYCE

TECHNICAL CONSULTANT: CHRISTOPHER BRICKELL,
DIRECTOR-GENERAL OF THE ROYAL HORTICULTURAL SOCIETY
FOREWORD BY ELVIN MCDONALD

SIMON AND SCHUSTER

NEW YORK   LONDON   TORONTO   SYDNEY   TOKYO   SINGAPORE

SIMON AND SCHUSTER
Simon & Schuster Building
Rockefeller Center
1230 Avenue of the Americas
New York, New York 10020

Edited and designed by
Mitchell Beazley Publishers,
part of Reed International Books,
Michelin House,
81 Fulham Road,
London SW3 6RB.

Senior Art Editor Eljay Yildirim
Senior Editor Robert Saxton
Designer Geoff Fennell
Editors Simon Ryder, Lydia Segrave
Editorial Assistant Jaspal Bhangra
Production Sarah Schuman
American Editor Marjorie Dietz
Commissioned Photography Andrew Lawson
Commissioned Artwork Elsa Godfrey
Picture Research Brigitte Arora, Ellen Root, Liz Fowler

Typeset in Optima by Litho Link Ltd., Welshpool, Powys, Wales
Color Reproduction by Mandarin Offset Ltd., Hong Kong
Printed in Germany by Mohndruck GmbH, Gütersloh

10 9 8 7 6 5 4 3 2 1

Library of Congress Cataloging in Publication Data

Joyce, David,
    The complete guide to pruning and training plants/David Joyce:
    technical consultant, Christopher Brickell: foreword by Elvin McDonald.
        p.   cm.
        Includes index.
        ISBN 0-671-73842-9
    1. Pruning. 2. Plants – Training. 3. Pruning – Pictorial works.
    4. Plants – Training – Pictorial works. I. Brickell, Christopher.
    II. Title.
SB125.J84   1991
635.004--dc20
                                                        91-30134
                                                        CIP
ISBN: 0-671-73842-9

The publishers have made every effort to ensure that all instructions given in this book are accurate and safe, but they cannot accept liability for any resulting injury, damage or loss to either person or property whether direct or consequential and howsoever arising. The author and publishers will be grateful for any information which will assist them in keeping future editions up to date.

Author's Acknowledgments
The author gratefully acknowledges the generous help given by many people in the preparation of this book and especially by the gardening and administrative staff at the Royal Horticultural Society Garden, Wisley, England, the editorial and design staff at Mitchell Beazley, the book's technical consultant, Christopher Brickell, and the following specialists, Harry Baker, Mark Burleton, A. M. Clevely, Jim Gardiner, Michael Gibson, and Ray Waite.

Photographs
Right: Hedge and topiary of box. Contents: climbing roses on pergolas and box topiary. Foreword: laburnum tunnel.

CONTENTS

FOREWORD

Christopher Brickell is a leading world authority on horticulture who says he'd most like to be remembered as a gardener. In this book we are permitted to look over his shoulder as, with David Joyce, he demonstrates the steps necessary to pruning and training plants, arguably the most difficult of gardening practices to learn. Because many pruning and training activities are done only once a year, and some, such as thinning of certain shrubs, only every two or three, the pruner is always in need of brushing up before going out to practice.

Although gardening may seem to be an inexact science, the techniques having to do with the pruning and training of plants have been refined by gardeners through the ages. Today they are essentially the same for any given plant in any climate, any garden and in any language. Sound technique as set out by David Joyce and a gardener of Christopher Brickell's breadth of experience is sound technique. Since pruning, like transplanting, can stimulate a plant or kill it, practice can only make perfect if it is in fact based on sound technique applied at the right time to the right plant.

Pruning and training are inherently hopeful activities, the same as planting seeds or harvesting vegetables from one's own garden. If you have more than a few plants, there is usually something that can be pruned or trained to benefit at any season and any morning, noon or evening of the year when a dose of plants as therapy might be in order for the gardener. Just remember, never squeeze the handles of your clippers until all fingers are accounted for; and make haste with deliberate slowness.

Several years ago it was my pleasure as a career gardening journalist to work a season as if I were one of the professional gardeners at the Brooklyn Botanic Garden. Early on a Friday morning at the end of April, Bernard Currid, the gardener I'd been assisting that week, stopped in his tracks as we came up into the garden proper from the nether world of the potting shed. In my "as if" position, I stopped too, and realized that he was pausing to worship the beauty all around. As my eyes followed his into the distant flowering tree branches I saw how generations of gardeners had pruned and trained in order to produce what was at once horticulturally sound and esthetically pleasing. In succeeding weeks, as I was assigned to assist first one gardener and then another, it also became apparent that when minutes of gardening are spent well, they have an amazing way of yielding hours of pleasure.

"God is in the details" is a currently popular expression that seems readily applicable to pruning and training plants. In order to discipline the plant, it is necessary first to discipline the mind. If you find yourself actually "thinking" as you are gardening, stewing over something having nothing to do with what you are doing, stop. Every act of pruning and training requires us to be in the moment. In other words, do in the garden but don't think. Otherwise, you run the risk of robbing the garden of its ageless and miraculous ability to bring peace and physical sustenance. Fortunately this book gives us lots of practical and exciting things to do. Savor the practice, enjoy the rewards.

Elvin McDonald

INTRODUCTION

Controlling the growth of plants and shaping them by pruning and training are often considered the most puzzling aspects of gardening. Sadly, many gardeners content themselves with a policy of random snipping or savage butchery rather than acquiring the relatively uncomplicated skills that can be so important in the successful cultivation of plants.

Those who have participated in the making of this book hope that the straightforward explanation of pruning and training procedures offered here, based on their professional experience, will encourage more gardeners to acquire these valuable skills. As well as explaining in text, diagrams, and photographs the major techniques of pruning and training, the book presents the specific requirements of ornamentals, tree fruits, and soft fruits, with particular reference to those grown in the temperate parts of the world.

The diagrams and photographs are seen as an important amplification of the text, but it must be recognized when using them as a guide that there can be considerable differences between individual specimens of plants. The age of wood is often a significant factor in pruning and therefore different tones of green have been used in the diagrams to distinguish one year's growth from another.

Many, indeed most, of the operations described in this book can be carried out by home gardeners, provided that they are equipped with the right tools. Large pruning cuts are dealt with in more detail on pages 43-5, but it is necessary to warn non-professionals against undertaking almost all forms of tree surgery. Experienced and qualified tree surgeons should be employed to remove all large limbs and to undertake any major pruning requiring the use of power tools and ladders.

Pruning, training, and plant growth

In pruning a shoot or branch the gardener is interfering with the plant's own mechanism for controlling its development. On most woody plants each shoot ends in a terminal or apical bud, below which other buds are arranged in a pattern characteristic of the species, the position of the buds determining where branches will form. The arrangement may be alternate, opposite, spiral or whorled.

The apical bud is the growing point of the shoot and asserts its dominance by producing a chemical that inhibits growth of the buds below it. If the terminal bud is removed, whether pruned, pinched out (sometimes known as stopping), or broken off, the supply of the growth-retarding substance is interrupted. The relatively rapid growth of lateral shoots, known as "breaking", is quickly discernible in the case of a sub-shrub such as a fuchsia which has had its leading shoot pinched out. The same response, resulting in bushy growth, is produced by the frequent removal of terminal buds in hedge clipping.

In practice many pruning cuts are made to a specific bud or pair of buds below the tip of the shoot. Selecting a bud that will grow in the desired direction, usually out

Right: The techniques of pruning and training are relevant to plants grown under glass as well as to those grown in the open garden. This standard of the fuchsia 'Flying Cloud' has been formed by training a single leader vertically and then pinching out the topmost laterals to make a bushy head.

Right: Apples and pears grown as fans and other restricted forms need careful initial training and then regular summer pruning by the Modified Lorette System (see pp. 145-47).

from the center of the plant, and cutting back to just above it is the key to the skilful shaping of most ornamentals and fruit-bearing bushes and trees. All cuts must be made with sharp clean tools (see pp. 214-15), for bruised or crushed stems and ragged edges can be points of entry for disease.

It is worth mentioning that woody plants compartmentalize wounds, including pruning cuts, as a defense against infection. It is now recognized that the old practice of flush cutting when removing limbs from trees and large shrubs destroys the plants' own lines of defense, and may lead to serious infection even when a wound forms a callus.

The severity of cutting back is another factor influencing plant growth. As a rule, pruning stimulates growth, and this is particularly true of pruning carried out in winter. It is an important point to grasp, and an apparent contradition, that weak growth can be stimulated to grow vigorously by hard cutting back and that vigorous growth is best checked by light pruning. Repeated savage pruning of a problem plant that keeps outgrowing its space will simply encourage it to be more vigorous.

Another key fact that explains many pruning and training techniques is the tendency of stems near the horizontal to grow more slowly than those that are upright, but this check to growth stimulates the production of flower buds. This is exploited in the training of some ornamentals (rambling roses, for example, flower best with their stems trained laterally) and many fruit trees.

The reasons for pruning and training

It is sometimes argued that as plants in the wild are not pruned there is no need to prune them in the garden. In fact a wild plant is normally undergoing a continuous process of renewal, in which flowers, leaves, and twigs fall and, less frequently, branches are shed. Furthermore, the garden is not simply an unaltered segment of the natural world, but a managed environment in which selected plants are grown for specific ornamental effects or to produce crops.

Even when pruning is recognized as a necessity, it is often thought that its purpose is limited to reducing the size of plants that have grown too large, an idea that is sometimes associated with a vague notion that at some time in the year all plants need to be tidied up. Cutting back shoots and branches simply to keep a plant within an allotted space or to impose an arbitrary order is, however, a relatively crude use of pruning techniques. Although many plants may need occasional trimming of unruly growth and some plants are cut back regularly for special effects (as when eucalypts such as *Eucalyptus gunnii* are maintained in the juvenile form because of their attractive foliage), most plants that need hard cutting back to contain them are inappropriate for the position in which they are planted. Because pruning stimulates growth, the problem very often proves self-perpetuating.

The need for drastic surgery can be avoided by sensible planting. When choosing trees and shrubs, select cultivars according to their vigor as well as their ornamental value. When choosing fruit trees, consider the rootstock, which will determine the plant's vigor, as well as the merits of particular cultivars. The main aim of pruning and training, in contrast to the largely negative intention when plants are cut back in size, is to realize the maximum ornamental effect or to obtain the optimum yield of a crop. Many trees and shrubs,

Left: Many ornamental shrubs and trees, including the flowering cherries (*Prunus*), produce impressive displays with little pruning. Because of the risk of silver leaf infection through wounds, pruning should be kept to a minimum.

Right: The pruning of fruit trees maintains a balance between vegetative and flowering wood in order to ensure sustainable crops.

including some fruit trees, will give the desired results with only minor pruning once mature. Even these, however, generally require some initial training to form a well balanced framework.

Pruning cuts on young plants heal quickly and in many cases a framework of well spaced branches can be formed simply by removing a few poorly placed or weak growths. When growths are young and pliant, before they lignify, is also the time to train climbers and wall shrubs. Some forms of fruit trees may need long-term staking. Ornamental trees, however, should only be staked for the first year or two using a low stake, so that there is enough movement to promote the natural strengthening of the trunk as it grows.

The more restricted the form in which a plant is grown, the more rigorous the early training must be. It may take more than four or five years to build up the framework of an espaliered apple or a fan-trained peach and even longer to create a mature hedge, topiary specimen, or avenue of pleached lindens. A standard or pyramid of a sub-shrub such as a fuchsia can be built up much more quickly, but the speed of growth has to be matched by the frequency with which the growing points are pinched out. Restricted forms generally require regular pruning even in maturity. For example, apples and pears grown as cordons or other restricted forms need annual summer pruning. Hedges and topiary require clipping once and sometimes several times in a growing season.

Even most unrestricted forms of tree fruits and soft fruits require annual pruning to remain healthy and productive. Annual cutting out of old wood is also necessary to get the best results from a number of ornamentals, including most roses, which bloom more freely and produce flowers of larger size on young wood. The same principle applies to some shrubs grown for their foliage or their brightly colored stems. At its most

basic, renewal pruning can consist of annual trimming of plants such as lavenders and santolinas, which as a result remain compact and youthful.

Maintaining the health of plants must be an underlying principle of all pruning. Dead, damaged, and diseased shoots and branches should be cut back to sound wood and destroyed. This removes possible reservoirs of disease from the garden and a clean cut made in the correct position offers the plant the best chance of healing quickly and resisting infection.

Correct pruning is not in itself enough to keep a plant healthy, for vigorous growth can only be made when there are adequate supplies of nutrients and water. A plant's preference for sun or shade and damp or dry soil are also relevant. Regular feeding and watering are particularly important for plants that are pruned hard each year.

Some measures may also be necessary to control pests and diseases. The value of one measure that was strongly advocated in the past, the application of wound paints to all cuts more than 6in (15cm) in diameter, is now doubted except as a protection against specific diseases such as silver leaf.

Timing

Although some plants can be pruned at almost any time of the year, in general this is far from being the case and often timing is critical if a desired result is to be achieved. The main pruning period for many plants, including

Left: The wisterias are vigorous climbers that need directing when trained on buildings or other structures such as pergolas. Flowering is improved by annual spur pruning.

Right: Hard pruning in spring can enhance the foliage effect of many variegated and purple-leaved shrubs. The purple-leaved filbert *Corylus maxima* 'Purpurea' will bear nuts, but is often grown purely for its foliage.

roses, soft fruits, and many tree fruits, is the dormant season, from late autumn to early spring. However, winter pruning stimulates growth whereas summer pruning checks it. Most of the pruning to form the spur systems of restricted forms of fruit trees, such as cordons and espaliers, is carried out in summer to avoid promoting unmanageable growth, the Modified Lorette System being the most widely used for apples and pears.

The full ornamental potential of many plants can only be realized by pruning at an appropriate time and must take account of the age of the wood that bears flowers, the most decorative foliage, or the most vividly colored stems. Many shrubs that flower in the spring, forsythias among them, do so most prolifically on one-year-old wood. Cutting out the oldest wood immediately after flowering will encourage the development of replacement shoots that will flower the following year. *Buddleia davidii* and other shrubs and climbers that flower on the current season's wood are best pruned in early spring, the previous year's wood being cut back to a low framework of branches.

In the case of some plants that are susceptible to particular diseases, the risk of infection can be reduced by pruning when they are least vulnerable. Silver leaf is a serious fungal disease of plums and other stone fruits and also of some ornamentals. The wind-borne spores, which gain entry to the plant through fresh wounds, including pruning cuts, are released ·by the fruiting bodies of the fungus from early autumn to late spring.

Summer pruning greatly lessens the risk of infection, especially if a wound paint is applied as soon as the cut has been made.

Another reason for adjusting the time of pruning is the tendency of some plants, mainly deciduous, to bleed if wounded or cut in late winter or early spring. The loss of sap is not necessarily a serious problem and normally ceases when the plant breaks into leaf. But if there is a heavy flow the plant may be weakened and there can be die-back. Susceptible plants, such as the grape vine and, among trees and shrubs, the birches (*Betula*) and maples (*Acer*), are best pruned in summer, autumn, or early winter rather than in late winter or early spring.

The risk of frost or cold winds damaging young growths is another reason for choosing the time to prune with care. For example, young growth stimulated by early spring pruning of evergreens may be damaged by cold weather. At the other end of the growing season, plants that are richly fed and pruned in late summer will produce soft growths that may not ripen before the onset of cold weather.

As a final point on timing, it is worth remembering that pruning can be used to delay flowering. Rose exhibitors, for example, often stage pruning over several weeks to ensure a good supply of blooms for a series of shows in the summer. The flowering time of fuchsias, geraniums (pelargoniums), and cascade chrysanthemums can also be advanced or retarded by prolonging or shortening the period in which the growing points are pinched out.

Above: The climbing and rambling roses need support and in general must be tied in. 'Pink Perpétue' is moderately vigorous and suitable for training on a pillar, tripod, or arch. The second flush of flowers, in early autumn, is encouraged by removing spent flowers in summer.

Right: Pruning and training techniques can be applied to a number of sub-shrubs and even herbaceous plants, such as spray chrysanthemums.

Left: Clematis are among the most popular flowering climbers, but they are often allowed to form tangled messes because their pruning is not understood. 'Mme Julia Correvon' is a large-flowered cultivar that blooms in the second half of summer. This and clematis like it are best pruned hard in late winter or early spring.

ORNAMENTALS

The woody plants that are the principal subject of this first part of the book are extremely important components of any garden. They include trees, shrubs, and climbers grown for their foliage, flowers, fruit, and stems, either as specimens or as constituents of mixed plantings. In addition, there are roses grown in bedding schemes and plants that respond to rigorous pruning and training as hedges and topiary.

The pruning and training of these woody plants are rarely, if ever, as mysterious as the novice often fears, but dealing with them at the right time and in the right way makes a flourishing and colorful garden, whereas inappropriate action or neglect can result in chaos or a desert inhabited by maimed survivors.

To enlarge the usefulness of the techniques described here, listings of plants – roses on pages 38-9 and other ornamentals on pages 120-28 – have been cross-referenced to them. In the selection of the entries for these listings emphasis has been given to plants grown in temperate regions, but no attempt has been made to indicate their hardiness ratings.

The final section (pp. 129-35) deals with the technique of pinch pruning. This is used in the pruning and training of sub-shrubs, such as fuchsias, and perennials, such as spray chrysanthemums, as standards and other forms.

Above: *Hydrangea paniculata* 'Grandiflora', like many shrubs that flower on the current season's wood, benefits from hard pruning in spring. It is usually grown with a low framework of branches, but can be trained as a standard.

Far left: Laburnums and many other small trees with pendant flowers, bracts or fruits, are often shown to best effect when grown with a clear stem. This method of training avoids the risk of low branches being damaged when grass is cut, but care must be taken to avoid injury to the bark of the trunk.

Left: Many fine ornamentals need little pruning and training. *Magnolia* x *soulangeana*, like most of the flowering trees and shrubs in this genus, may need gentle formative pruning, but on mature specimens it is rarely necessary to do more than remove damaged or dead wood.

Left: Where a uniform effect is important, as in most formal hedges and in avenues, such as this one of southern live oaks (*Quercus virginiana*), initial plant selection and formative pruning and training all play important roles. To ensure consistent growth rate, habit, and coloring use plants of the same clone.

Right: *Cornus stolonifera* 'Flaviramea' is one of several shrubs that are grown for their attractively colored stems. As it is the young wood that colors best, these shrubs are cut back each year in spring.

ROSES

Roses could quite properly be grouped with other shrubs and climbers, but they are such an important category of ornamentals that it is convenient to treat them separately. There is considerable variation in the growth and flowering habit of the prodigious number of roses in cultivation: there are sprawling giants and compact miniatures, some that flower once only in mid-summer and others that are in bloom for four months or more. The best results are achieved by using the pruning and training regime for the category to which a particular rose belongs.

Three broad categories stand out. The most important in terms of numbers grown are the modern bush roses, especially the Hybrid Teas (large-flowered bush roses) and Floribundas (cluster-flowered bush roses), but this group also includes Polyanthas and the increasingly popular miniatures. The species and shrub roses form a more mixed group, including wild roses, old garden roses – such as the Albas, Bourbons and Damasks – and modern shrub roses. Roses requiring support, the climbers and ramblers, are also a mixed group. They include species and near-species roses, some old garden roses, such as the climbing teas and noisettes, and many modern climbers and ramblers, some of which flower recurrently. A selection of roses listed according to these categories is given on pages 38-9.

Right: Floribundas are the most popular roses for mass planting because they flower freely over a long season. In sheltered situations they can be trained as standards combined with suitable underplanting. Here, the vivid pink of 'Dearest' floats above the blue of lavender.

Above: Most of the vigorous climbing species and their close relatives, such as 'Seagull', require little pruning and are at their best when allowed to climb freely into trees or to sprawl over a sturdy support.

Right: Many hybrid roses are of complex, often unknown, parentage, and defy tidy classification. 'Perle d'Or', introduced in 1883, is generally considered a China. Its twiggy growth needs lighter pruning than some of the other "old roses" that repeat flower.

Pruning, training and general cultivation

In the wild, roses regularly produce vigorous new growths from the base to replace old wood that has already flowered. As wood ages it declines in vigor and flowering potential, and eventually dies. The pruning and training of cultivated roses is an accelerated and tidied version of this natural process of growth and decay.

Unfortunately, many popular roses are much more susceptible to disease than their wild ancestors. Pruning and training which result in uncrowded stems, allowing light and air to get to leaves, greatly increases the chances of healthy growth. Successful pruning creates a balance between old and new wood, resulting in the optimum floral display of which a rose is capable, while maintaining the plant in good health over an extended life. Training and pruning are also

Below: Vigorous shrub roses with flexible stems as well as climbers can be trained out horizontally to stimulate the development of flowering laterals. Here, a stone balustrade provides an ideal support for the modern shrub 'Wilhelm'.

important in presenting many vigorous roses to best advantage; their managed growth on supports such as arches, trellis screens, and pergolas creating some of the most lavish effects of which roses are capable.

Although correct pruning and training are important operations, they need to be matched by good general culture, which includes feeding and pest and disease control. When choosing where to put roses, especially if they are combined with other plants, bear in mind that easy access will make general cultivation as well as pruning and training much simpler.

When to prune and train

The traditional season in cold climates for planting bare-root roses is early spring. In mild climate regions, shipping of bare-root roses usually begins in January and may continue into March.

The availability of container-grown roses, often in full leaf and well budded, has made it possible to plant at almost any time of the year, except winter, although early spring is still recommended. Proper pruning should already have been carried out on stock sold after spring. Containerized (as opposed to container-grown) or packaged roses are bare-root roses that have been potted up to extend the plants' selling life.

The period from early winter to mid-spring is the main rose-pruning season. As a general rule, in areas with a mild climate prune early; where the winters are severe, prune late. The development of growth buds is a useful guide to timing: prune when those that are about halfway up strong stems begin to swell. If there is very cold weather after pruning, and this applies especially to roses cut back in autumn or early winter, check the roses over in early spring and cut back any dead wood to a healthy bud.

In the following pages the period recommended for the major pruning operations of many categories is early winter for mild regions, early spring in cool, temperate regions, and, in the north, when the risk of serious frost damage has passed, but before roses waste energy putting on growth that will have to be cut off. However, some autumn pruning is recommended for climbers and ramblers to minimize the risk of wind damage in rough weather. Tipping back long growths on shrub and bush roses has the same purpose.

Roses that are trained against, on or over supports need their extension growths tied in at regular intervals throughout the growing season. The framework of stems should be firmly secured before the beginning of the growing season and checked in autumn to ensure that there is no risk of loose stems being damaged during winter gales.

The removal of faded flowers (deadheading) in summer is in effect a kind of pruning, and also encourages repeat flowering. It prevents the plant's energies from going into seed production and removes decaying petals, a possible seat of infection. Do not continue removing dead flowers in late summer as this may encourage the growth of shoots. Late growth is unlikely to ripen before winter and may suffer damage in cold weather. In addition, the hips of some roses can be very ornamental, and the removal of spent flowers would mean the loss of these fruits.

Pruning cuts

Making the right kind of pruning cut ensures that the wound heals quickly, reduces the chances of disease, and encourages growth in the desired direction. The basic cuts are the same for all roses.

1. Use a sharp instrument to make clean cuts. In general hand pruners are easier to use than a knife, but a sharp knife is useful in case cuts need to be tidied. For thick stems use long-handled pruners or a fine-toothed saw with a curved blade.

2. Always cut back to live healthy wood, in which the pith is white or greenish-white, not dark or discolored.

3. Cut on a slant, starting about 2½in (6.5cm) above an eye or growth bud, with the cut angled away from the bud toward the base of the stem so that moisture will drain away from the eye. A cut that is too close to the eye will damage it, but if the cut is too high the stem is likely to die back.

**THE PARTS OF
A ROSE**
A. Union
B. Leaf with usually 5 or 7 leaflets
C. Blind Shoot
D. Flower Truss
E. Hip (or hep)
F. Snag
G. Sucker

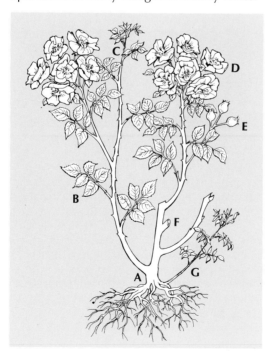

4. Prune to an eye pointing in the direction in which growth is wanted. In most cases this will mean pruning to an eye facing out from the center of a bush or shrub rose so that the new growth will leave the center itself open and uncluttered. It is mainly with roses of a spreading habit that it is useful to prune to inward-facing eyes, which will encourage more upright growth.

Pruning basics

The recommendations on the following pages deal with the specific requirements of the major categories of roses. Whatever the category, deal with the following priorities at the beginning of the major pruning carried out in winter in mild regions and early spring in the north. If you do not know the category to which a rose belongs – as might be the case if you take over a garden in autumn or winter – make sure that at least the priority pruning operations are carried out.

1. Cut out dead, diseased or damaged stems, if necessary cutting right back to the union or, in the case of a lateral, to a junction with a main stem. Dead wood is brown and brittle and diseased wood is generally discolored.

2. Cut back weak or spindly growth to the union or the junction with a strong stem.

3. Where two stems rub or cross, take one out, cutting back to a main stem or, if necessary, to the union. If the center of the plant still remains crowded, take out one or two stems to open up the plant to light and to allow air to circulate freely.

4. If two or more shoots grow from an eye after pruning, reduce to one.

5. Destroy prunings to reduce the risk of spreading disease.

SHOOT REDUCTION

Some roses, especially vigorous modern cultivars, develop more than one shoot from an eye after pruning. Limit the number of shoots to one. Young shoots are easily dislodged. Carefully rub or pinch off those that are unwanted as soon as possible.

PRUNING CUTS

1 Use a sharp tool – pruning shears and long-handled pruners are easier to use than a knife. Cut back to live healthy wood.

2 Cut to an eye that will produce growth in the direction that is wanted. Cut to an eye facing out from the center to create an open-centered, uncluttered plant.

3 Slant the cut, starting about 2½in (6.5cm) above an eye, and angle it toward the base of the stem.

Removal of suckers

Most roses bought from nurseries consist of the named cultivar budded (grafted) onto a selected rootstock. The union between rootstock and cultivar is generally at ground level, but in the case of standards the rootstock provides the leg, the cultivar being budded at the top of this stem. Any shoot growing from the rootstock below the union will compete with the cultivar and will eventually replace it if not removed.

Tracing these shoots or suckers to their point of origin is the best way of identifying them. Although their leaves and thorns look different from those of the cultivar, the commonly held view that sucker and cultivar can be reliably distinguished by the number of leaflets on each leaf is mistaken.

When a sucker rises from below ground level, remove soil from around it to expose the point at which it is growing from a root. Pull it off with a vigorous tug and then replace the soil. Cutting off suckers at ground level will simply encourage the development of more suckers. Shoots growing on the stems of standards below the union with the grafted variety can be pulled off or cut away with a sharp knife.

Blind shoots

Shoots that carry no flower buds, known as blind shoots, are produced by some cultivars of Hybrid Teas, Floribundas and climbers. To encourage the development of strong flowering shoots cut these blind shoots hard back to an eye.

Above: Most pruning cuts are made to outward-facing buds to ensure that the center of the rose remains open. Pruning shears must be sharp to give a clean cut without bruising.

MODERN BUSH ROSES

PRUNING

1 Buy plants with 3 or 4 strong shoots and a well-developed root system. Trim long, coarse or damaged roots of bare-rooted or containerized (packaged) plants, unless the plants are in full leaf, in which case avoid disturbing the roots. If planting in autumn or early winter in mild climates, cut back damaged or unripe growth at the ends of the shoots.

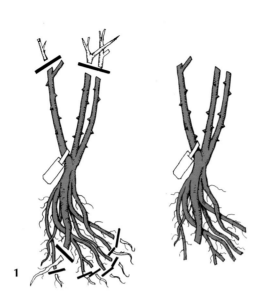

2 If planting in autumn or early winter in mild climates, weak or damaged growth will be cut out in the initial rather severe pruning. Cut stems to outward-facing buds at about 6in (15cm) above the ground, from which new shoots develop in late spring and early summer.

3 Annually, in early spring, begin basic pruning by taking out dead, diseased or damaged wood and weak stems. If stems are rubbing or crossing, cut one out. On a mature plant cut 1 or 2 main stems of the oldest wood right to the base.

4 After basic pruning, cut back remaining stems to a bud 6-10in (15-25cm) above ground level.

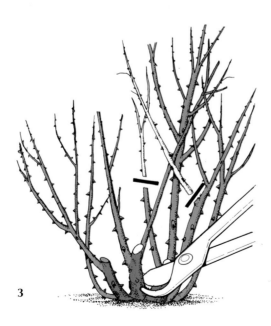

HYBRID TEAS

These roses – also known as "large-flowered bush roses" – are deciduous thorny shrubs that flower recurrently in summer and early autumn. Bushes regularly carry odd flowers between the two distinct flushes, the first in early to mid-summer, the second in late summer and early autumn. There is considerable variation in vigor among the innumerable cultivars that have been developed since the introduction in 1867 of the first officially recognized Hybrid Tea, 'La France'. 'Peace', for example, can easily reach 5ft (1.5m), but most grow to between 3-4ft (90-120cm). The growth tends to be stiff and upright, but the large, high-centered, conical flowers that are produced are admired for their elegance.

The aim of pruning is generally to encourage a good garden display, with the bushes either planted out in beds or mixed with other ornamentals. However, the Hybrid Teas are also the most important group of roses grown for exhibition purposes. A modified pruning regime (see p. 36) is necessary to produce flowers of exhibition quality. For the pruning of Hybrid Teas grown as standards see pages 34-5. For the pruning of the climbing sports of Hybrid Teas see page 32.

The moderate pruning regime recommended here will suit most reasonably vigorous Hybrid Teas growing in good

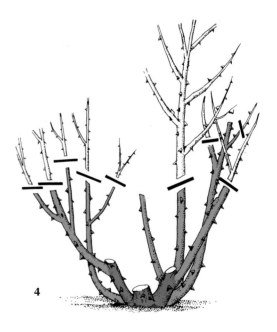

conditions. Vigorous cultivars, such as 'Peace', should be pruned more lightly, with stems cut back to about 2-3ft (60-90cm). In general, the poorer the conditions in which the rose is growing the lighter the pruning should be.

Initial pruning

Plants often suffer minor injury at the nursery or in transit. Any damaged or unripe wood and long coarse roots should be cut out at planting. Hard pruning in the late winter or early spring of the first year will encourage the development of vigorous growth. Inexperienced gardeners are often reluctant to cut back severely in the first year, but the penalty to pay for sparing the knife is a weak bush. Two to four eyes will generally be visible on stems that have been cut back to about 6in (15cm).

Main pruning

In mid- to late autumn it is good practice to cut out unripe growth and to tip back stems carrying faded flowers. In exposed gardens, shortening stems by about a third will reduce the risk of damage by winter winds.

After carrying out basic pruning in the spring, cut back the remaining stems to a bud between 6-10in (15-25cm) above ground level. Cut back weak growth more severely than strong stems, and to encourage new growth, cut out to the base one or two main stems of the oldest wood.

Summer pruning

The capacity of Hybrid Teas to repeat well is greatly reduced if their energies go into producing seed. Another reason for removing spent flowers is that decaying petals can become a seat of infection. Remove faded flowers regularly from early to mid-summer, cutting back to the first well-placed, strong eye or shoot below the flower.

HYBRID PERPETUALS

These modern bush roses, which are the immediate forerunners of the Hybrid Teas, are generally grown and pruned in the same way. However, to counteract their lankiness and tendency to produce flowers only at the ends of stems, they can be grown with the stems pegged down, which encourages much heavier flowering with a more even distribution over the plant (see p. 35).

Above: Cone-shaped buds of most Hybrid Teas open to fully double flowers. In contrast, 'Mrs Oakley Fisher' is single-flowered, blooming over a long season if regularly deadheaded.

Left: From early to mid-summer, cut back faded flowers to the first strong and well-placed eye or shoot below the inflorescence.

SUMMER PRUNING
When summer pruning, do not take off leaves unnecessarily, but always cut to a bud or shoot that will grow in the desired direction.

FLORIBUNDAS

1 Plant in winter in mild climates and in early spring in cold regions, trimming damaged and long roots. Few dormant roses are available for autumn planting in the north.

2 In early spring hard prune all newly planted Floribundas. Take out completely any weak shoots. Cut back stems to outward-facing buds at a height of 6-9in (15-23cm) above ground level. Roses hard pruned in this way will produce new shoots in the next 2 months.

3 In the late winter or early autumn of subsequent years, remove crossing, inward-growing, dead, diseased, and weak stems. Reduce young basal shoots by a third and cut back laterals to 4-6in (10-15cm). Cut out older stems to about 6-8in (15-20cm) above ground level and, if growth is crowded, remove some of the old wood.

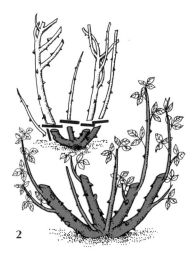

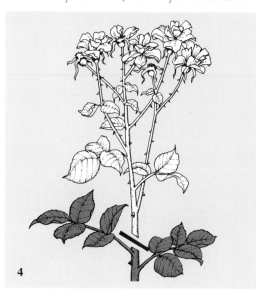

FLORIBUNDAS

These roses are also known as "cluster-flowered bush roses", and are generally considered stronger-growing, hardier and healthier than Hybrid Teas. Like the Hybrid Teas, they are usually stiff upright plants, with most of the cultivars making a bush about 3ft (90cm) in height. Individual flowers are less elegantly formed and smaller than those of Hybrid Teas, but they are borne in great profusion with good continuity over a long season. Floribundas are the most effective roses for bedding, but are also used in mixed plantings.

Grandifloras, a fairly new American class of roses, are stronger growing than the Floribundas. For pruning, treat Grandifloras as Floribundas or Hybrid Teas.

Initial pruning

When planting (in spring in the north, in January through March in mild climates), trim roots if necessary and cut back lightly the tips of stems and laterals. When heavy frosts cease and growth begins, cut stems to about 6-8in (15-20cm) above ground level. Stems hard pruned in this way will have from three to five eyes. Take out any weak shoots.

Main pruning

At the end of the growing and flowering season it is good practice to cut out any soft unripe wood and to tip back the main stems. This mid-autumn pruning is particularly beneficial in exposed gardens.

A sustained floral display is most easily achieved using a variation of the moderate pruning regime recommended for Hybrid Teas. In early spring begin with basic pruning (see p. 21), clearing out where

4 From early to mid-summer remove faded flowers promptly to encourage new growth and continuity of flowering. Cut off the whole flower truss, not just individual flowers, at the first strong well-placed eye.

Far left: Many of the taller-growing miniatures and "patio roses" such as 'Pretty Polly' can be treated as small Floribundas. However, they often require more thinning of twiggy growth.

DWARF POLYANTHAS

These roses can be treated as Floribundas, but respond better to lighter pruning. In late winter and early spring, at initial pruning and subsequently, cut out weak stems and reduce main stems by about a third. Keep the bush open-centered by taking out twiggy growth and some old wood.

necessary any wood that is not strong and healthy and any growths cluttering the center of the bush. Then shorten strong young stems by about a third, always cutting to a well-placed bud.

As bushes mature there will be older wood that will need to be cut back to between 6-9in (15-23cm) from ground level. On a bush with numerous stems, cut out one or two old growths right back to the base, and then shorten any laterals that remain to between 4-6in (10-15cm). The ideal balance between young and older wood may take a few years to establish.

The more vigorous cultivars generally perform better with lighter pruning. 'Iceberg' and 'Pink Parfait', for example, are less stiff in growth than most Floribundas and make attractive specimen roses when grown to a height of about 4ft (1.2m). The extremely vigorous Grandiflora 'Queen Elizabeth', which is capable of exceeding 6ft (1.8m) in height, is best treated as a modern shrub.

Summer pruning

The only summer pruning needed is the removal of spent flowers. To encourage new growth and continuity of flowering over the summer remove the whole flower truss, not just individual flowers.

DWARF POLYANTHAS

Forerunners of the Floribundas, these roses generally grow to a height of 2-3ft (60-90cm), with a tendency to make a lot of twiggy growth. They can be treated as Floribundas, but a slightly lighter pruning regime suits them best. At the initial pruning and in subsequent years, cut the main stems back by a third. Old wood may need to be cut out to maintain an open center.

MINIATURES

There is no sharp divide between miniatures and so-called "patio roses". At the initial pruning of the shorter-growing twiggy miniatures (generally less than 2ft (60cm) in height), cut back strong shoots to a height of 4-6in (10-15cm) above ground level and take out any weak stems. When carrying out basic pruning in the early spring of subsequent years pay particular attention to the removal of diseased wood and stems that have died back. Take out weak growth and cut strong stems back to 4-6in (10-15cm) above ground level. In summer cut out trusses of flowers as they fade. Some miniatures throw up abnormally vigorous shoots and these should be cut out at their base. The alternative is to treat these miniatures as low-growing Floribundas.

SPECIES AND SHRUB ROSES

GROUP 1: Rare species and roses and hybrids that are close to them; most flower only once.

These roses are often described as the nonclimbing roses that are unsuitable for bedding. There are in fact three broad groups of roses that make up this large and valuable category of ornamentals: the species roses and roses that are close to their species parents known as near-species; the "old roses", that is the rose cultivars grown prior to the introduction of the Hybrid Teas in the late 19th century; and the modern shrub roses, consisting of the cultivars other than bedding roses developed in the 20th century.

General pruning

Despite great variations in size, growth pattern and flowering performance, there are pruning recommendations that apply to all shrub roses: generally, a much lighter pruning regime than that recommended for Hybrid Teas and Hybrid Perpetuals or Floribundas gives the best results.

At planting, trim any long or coarse roots, but do not prune stems back severely; the only shortening necessary is to cut out damaged tips and soft unripe growth.

A light tipping back of vigorous shoots following basic pruning will remove any

unripe wood, a possible source of disease, and encourage the production of flowering laterals the following year. If roses are growing in exposed positions, tip back very long growths in autumn to minimize wind damage. In summer remove flowers once they have faded (this benefits those that will flower again), other than on roses grown for their hips.

This basic program can be adapted to the needs of specific roses. Three main variations are given here. If in doubt about the group into which a shrub rose should be placed, follow the recommendations for Group One.

Some vigorous examples are versatile and can be trained up supports in the same way as pillar roses (see p. 33).

GROUP ONE

The species and near-species roses, including the Scotch or Burnet roses derived from *Rosa pimpinellifolia* (*R. spinosissima*), require little more than minimal pruning. The aim should be to give large roses, such as *R. moyesii*, enough space to allow the full development of their naturally arching growth. On mature specimens cutting out older wood that is flowering sparsely will encourage the development of vigorous shoots from the base. In particular, the Rugosa roses benefit from occasional drastic clearing out of old wood.

The Gallicas and Hybrid Musks, which do not fit easily in any group, are perhaps best placed here. The Gallicas tend to make a lot of twiggy growth which needs to be thinned out as part of the basic pruning in late winter or early spring. To encourage a good crop of flowers on Hybrid Musks, shorten laterals in late winter or early spring and remove spent flowers. Hybrid Musks sometimes produce stems of excessive length, which can be cut right back.

Above left: *Rosa moyesii* is a large shrub species which is best allowed to develop with a minimum of pruning. Its highly ornamental hips are its main feature and therefore it should not be deadheaded during the summer.

Left: A number of species and near-species, of which 'Canary Bird' is an early-flowering example, make densely furnished, arching shrubs. Lightly prune and remove dead, damaged or weak shoots.

GROUP TWO

In the initial stages treat in the same way as all other shrub roses. Once plants are established, prune in late winter or early spring by cutting back by up to a third the vigorous shoots that developed during the preceding growing season. At the same time cut back laterals growing from older wood to about 6in (15cm). Excessive cutting back of the young wood will destroy the arching habit of these roses and also reduce their flowering potential.

The flowers of many of the "old roses" – including the Albas, Centifolias, Moss roses, and most of the Damasks, which come into this group – are produced in summer on laterals or sub-laterals growing from wood that is two or more years old. The long stems may be pulled down by the weight of the flowers they carry, and should be pruned to a moderate length. Fortunately, these roses, and also most of the modern shrub roses that do not repeat, freely produce vigorous basal shoots. As plants mature, cut out old wood which is flowering sparsely.

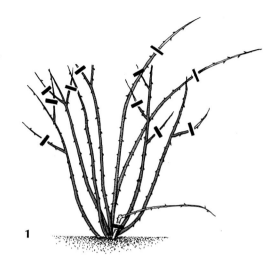

1

2

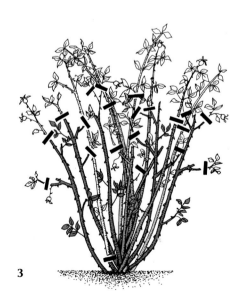

3

Above: 'Constance Spry' is a modern shrub rose that produces a glorious display in mid-summer, but does not repeat. Its vigorous growths should be moderately pruned in the dormant season. Like many of the larger shrub roses, it can also be trained as a climber.

GROUP 2: Most of the single-flowering "old roses" – including the Albas, Centifolias, Damasks, and Moss roses – and modern shrub roses that do not repeat bloom.

PRUNING

1 In early winter in mild regions and early spring in the north remove dead and diseased wood and take out weak and badly placed shoots. Shorten by up to a third long new shoots that have grown from the base, and cut back laterals on shoots that have flowered to 4-6in (10-15cm).

2 In mid- to late autumn tip back very long growths, especially if roses are growing in exposed positions.

3 When mature, prune as recommended in 1. Cut out at their base 1 or 2 old shoots that are flowering sparsely.

GROUP THREE

A variation of the pruning recommended for roses in Group Two suits a number of roses that flower recurrently in summer and autumn. They include most of the Bourbons, the Chinas, and many modern shrub roses. Vigorous Hybrid Teas and Hybrid Perpetuals, such as the Hybrid Tea 'Alexander', can be grown successfully as large informal specimens and are then best pruned according to the Group Three method. The English roses, modern cultivars but in the style of the "old roses", belong in this group. So also do many recently introduced cultivars that are described as "ground-cover" roses. This term is sometimes an optimistic description of relatively low-growing and dense shrub roses. They often need no pruning beyond an annual clearing out in winter.

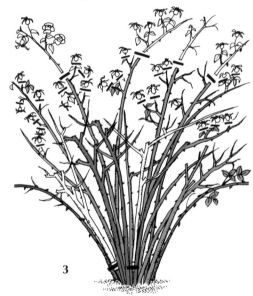

GROUP 3: "Old roses" that flower more than once, such as the Chinas and many Bourbons, and repeat-flowering modern shrub roses.

PRUNING

1 In late winter or early spring carry out basic pruning. Reduce long shoots produced during the previous growing season by up to a third. Shorten to 4-6in (10-15cm) laterals on wood that has already flowered, reducing any excessive twiggy growth that remains. On mature plants, cut out at their base 1 or 2 old stems if they are no longer bearing flowers freely.

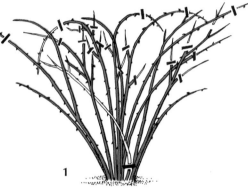

2 In early to mid-summer remove all faded flowers.

3 If roses are growing in exposed positions, tip back very long growths in mid-autumn to reduce wind damage.

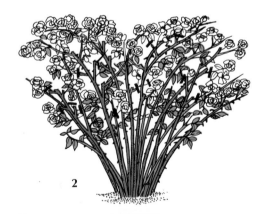

Top: Ground-cover roses such as 'Essex' are in reality dense and low-growing modern shrub roses.

Right: 'Nevada' is a modern shrub rose that needs light pruning only.

Group Three roses flower on laterals and sub-laterals growing from second-year or older wood, and also from vigorous new stems produced during the flowering season. Most tend to produce a lot of twiggy growth: this should be lightly thinned during the growing season when faded flowers are removed, and also at pruning in late winter or early spring.

As with the Group Two roses, in the main pruning season shorten very long shoots by up to a third and cut back laterals to about 6in (15cm). In general, however, relatively light pruning produces the best results.

CLIMBERS AND RAMBLERS

The climbers and ramblers include roses of very different characters. There are climbing species, some vigorous enough to clamber 50ft (15m) or more into a tree; classic ramblers which have obligingly pliant canes and a prodigal display of flowers in summer; and there is also a useful range of climbing hybrids, some of which repeat well and are relatively resistant to disease.

It has to be admitted than many of these roses flourish despite neglect; some even defy pruning and training. Many, however, respond well to a regular program of management, and this is often the only satisfactory way of controlling their vigor and accommodating them in anything but a wild garden. Training also makes it possible to arch flexible stems and hold them near the horizontal. The result of this simple maneuver is that stems produce flowers along much of their length and not merely at their tips. Five groups have been identified according to the appropriate method of pruning and training.

Below: Many climbing roses are sports of bush cultivars, which have a tendency to revert if hard pruned at planting. The bush form of 'Pompon de Paris' was widely grown as a pot plant in the 19th century, but now the climbing form is better known.

Bottom: 'Chaplin's Pink' is a vigorous rambler on which canes are cut back to replacement leaders in autumn.

Left: Climbing and rambling roses need firm support and good air circulation. Supports can include trellis or wires on walls, tripods or other free-standing supports. In a large garden a sequence of arches or a pergola can produce a lavish summer display.

GROUP 1: Ramblers derived from *Rosa wichuraiana*, flowering once in summer, mainly on canes produced in the previous year.

GROUP ONE

A number of vigorous ramblers regularly produce new canes from the base, and these carry flowers in their second year. Because old canes decline in vigor and produce fewer and fewer flowers, the ideal pruning and training regime consists of removing each year all or most of the canes that have flowered and tying in new canes as replacements. A less rigorous regime, in which some, even most, of the old canes are retained, but all laterals are cut back annually to 4-6in (10-15cm), will often give reasonably good results.

'Dorothy Perkins' and most other ramblers in this group are very susceptible to mildew and should therefore be grown where there is good air circulation. For this reason, avoid placing them against walls or fences.

Initial pruning and training

Plants received at normal planting seasons should have three to four shoots and a well-developed root system. Before planting, trim long and coarse roots and cut back shoots to 8-16in (20-41cm). Shoots are sometimes shortened before being dispatched by the nursery. If this is the case, check cuts and trim if necessary. Tie in the long, lax shoots or canes that are produced during the following growing season. There will be no flowers in the first year.

Pruning and training established plants

In second and subsequent years these ramblers will flower in early summer or, more rarely, in mid- to late summer. Train in the young shoots that develop from the base, as nearly horizontal as possible, and tie in. In late summer or early autumn, when flowering has finished, cut out right to the base the canes that have flowered. A few may need to be retained if the framework of replacement canes is inadequate. Cut back laterals on these to 4-6in (10-15cm).

GROUP 1

1 At planting in winter (in mild areas) or spring, cut back stems to 8-16in (20-41cm) and trim any long and coarse roots.

2 Throughout the growing season train in the vigorous shoots that develop from the base and below pruning cuts; keep them as near horizontal as possible. There will be no flowers in the first year.

3 In late summer or autumn cut back to their base all or most of the canes that have carried flowers in the summer, only retaining canes if there are inadequate new shoots to train in. Shorten all laterals to 4-6in (10-15cm).

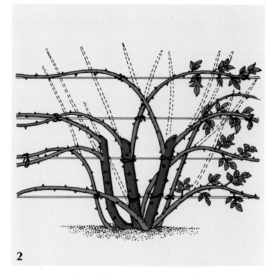

2

3

GROUP TWO

The ramblers, such as 'Albertine', that make up this group are in many ways similar to those in Group One: they do not repeat, but produce a mass of flowers in summer on the laterals of vigorous shoots produced the previous year. However, unlike Group One ramblers, they produce few new canes from the base, vigorous replacement growth originating from a framework of older stems. Ideally, most of the old wood that has produced flowers is cut back to a point where there is a vigorous new leader. Treat in the same way as roses in Group One at planting and in the training of shoots.

Pruning and training established plants

In late summer or early autumn take out all or most of the stems that have produced flowering laterals, cutting back to a point where a vigorous replacement leader is growing. If there is a shortage of replacement leaders, retain some of the old wood. Cut back laterals to about 6in (15cm). Tie in all leaders and basal shoots, keeping them as nearly horizontal as possible. On mature plants cutting back some of the oldest shoots to a height of 1-1 1/2ft (30-46cm) will encourage new growth from the base.

GROUP 2

1 At planting prune these roses in the same way as those in Group 1. Subsequently train in leaders and any canes that develop from the base; keep them as nearly horizontal as possible. Plants will begin flowering in their second year. On established plants train in fresh shoots during the growing season. After pruning train in any new shoots that have replaced wood cut out during the annual pruning.

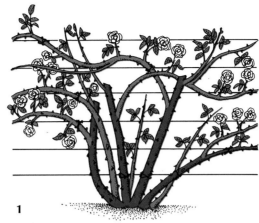

GROUP 2: Ramblers which flower once in summer, mainly on growths produced during the previous year on a framework of old stems.

1

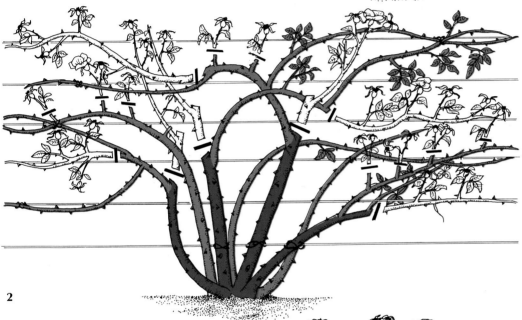

2 In late summer or early autumn cut back wood that has carried flowers to a point where a vigorous new leader is developing. On wood that is retained cut back weak leaders and laterals that have flowered to about 6in (15cm).

2

3 To encourage vigorous new growth from the base of mature plants, cut back 1 or 2 old shoots to 1-1½ft (30-46cm) as part of the late-summer or early-autumn pruning program.

3

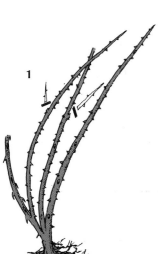

GROUP 3

1 At planting trim long and coarse roots, but do not prune shoots except to cut out damaged tips, unripe growth and weak side shoots. Train stems as near to the horizontal as possible.

2 Tie in shoots as they develop during the first, and subsequent, summers. Remove faded flowers. In summer or early spring cut back to about 6in (15cm) all laterals that flowered, and remove dead, diseased or weak wood. When mature, take out at the base stems that carry few flowers.

GROUP THREE

This is a versatile group of roses which includes the climbing sports of the Hybrid Teas and Floribundas. Many repeat well (although the climbing sports generally flower less freely than the bush forms) and show fair to good resistance to disease. The most disease-resistant are among the best climbers and ramblers to train against walls and fences.

Group Three roses flower on new wood. Vigorous new stems rarely grow from the base, new shoots growing from old wood higher on the plant. Training to establish a balanced framework is especially important in the early stages.

At planting

The stems – generally 4-5ft (1.2-1.5m) in length – should not be hard pruned: severe pruning may cause climbing sports to revert to bush form. Trim long roots and only tip back damaged ends of stems, unripe growth and any weak side shoots. Begin training as soon as the rose is planted. Do not force stiff stems, but whenever possible train them horizontally or at an angle.

Pruning and training established plants

Basic pruning (see pp. 19-20) should be carried out and flowered laterals cut back to

about 6in (15cm). Little additional pruning is necessary, but cutting back leaders to vigorous shoots and occasionally taking out old stems at near ground level will encourage the development of new growth. Train in new stems to fill in gaps and to avoid stems rubbing. In summer remove flowers once they have faded.

GROUP FOUR

In effect, this group is a variant of Group Three: the pillar roses that belong to it are short-growing, upright climbers rarely exceeding a height of 10ft (3m). Examples include 'Aloha' and 'Pink Perpétue'.

The roses are sometimes trained against "pillars" in the form of tree trunks, 8-10ft (2.4-3m) high, set firmly in the ground. Branch stubs are left on these trunks to make tying-in easier. It is worth noting that these trunks can look very gaunt in winter when not hidden by flowers or foliage. Tripods of rustic poles and metal frames are also suitable supports and Group Four roses can also be trained satisfactorily against walls. Their bareness at the base may need to be masked by other planting. Any with flexible stems should have these trained spirally around their support.

Initial pruning and training

At planting follow the recommendations for pruning climbers and ramblers in Group Three, avoiding cutting back shoots except for trimming. As most Group Four plants will have a naturally upright growth, do not attempt to train them horizontally, but instead tie the stems into their support. Begin the spiral training of those with more flexible stems.

Pruning and training of established plants

Throughout the summer train in all new growth, and remove flower trusses as blooms fade. Basic pruning in spring includes cutting back flowered laterals and dead, diseased or weak stems. Some shortening of leaders and vigorous laterals may be necessary to maintain balanced growth. Cutting back the less vigorous stems by as much as two-thirds will encourage new growth from the base. If the stems of mature plants are crowded, cut out one or two of the oldest completely. When these procedures have been completed, tie in all stems.

GROUP 4: Described as "pillar" roses, repeat-flowering climbers; the flowers are carried on laterals growing from a compact permanent framework of stems.

Left: Metal frames, wooden tripods and tree trunks with branch stumps are all suitable supports for some of the shorter-growing climbers that are also known as "pillar roses". Like many of these roses, 'Pink Perpétue' is rather stiff-stemmed and will reach a height of about 10ft (3m).

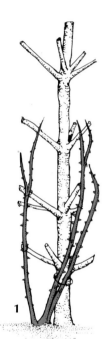

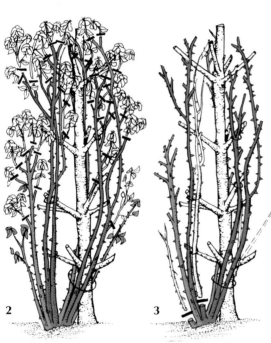

GROUP 4

1 At planting, plants should have 3 or 4 good stems which are generally between 2½-4ft (76-120cm) in length. Cut back any long roots and tip back unripe wood, damaged ends of stems, and weak growth. However, do not prune stems hard back. Tie shoots into their support. Train in a spiral any stems that are sufficiently flexible.

2 Remove faded blooms in summer to encourage repeat flowering, and tie in any new growths as they develop. In late summer or autumn cut back laterals that have flowered.

3 At the same time cut out diseased or dead wood and weak stems. It may be necessary to prune new leaders to maintain balanced growth. If stems are crowded, cut out 1 or 2 of the oldest to ground level. Check that all stems are tied in.

GROUP FIVE

Many of the climbing species and near-species are extremely vigorous. The classic example is *Rosa filipes* 'Kiftsgate' which can reach a height of more than 30ft (9.1m). They are at their best when trained into trees and then left more or less to their own devices. An old but strong fruit tree makes a suitable support. Pruning the rose often becomes quite impractical but when it is possible, cut out dead and diseased wood.

Plant about 5ft (1.5m) from the tree's base, leading the flexible stems into the tree along bamboo canes.

These roses may be too rampant for restricted suburban lots and are best left to more spacious country gardens.

GROUP 5: Exceptionally vigorous species and hybrids, capable, for example, of climbing into trees.

Left: 'Bobby James', typical of strong growing species and near-species, needs plenty of space to develop freely. It is often impracticable to prune or train established roses in Group 5, but every effort should be made to take out dead or diseased wood.

STANDARD ROSES

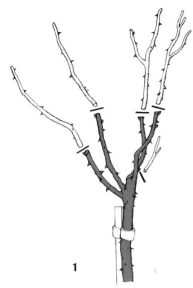

When roses are grown as standards, the rootstock, commonly *Rosa rugosa*, provides the supporting stem, and the cultivar is budded at the top, preferably two or three buds being used so that a balanced head can be created. Standard roses are not suitable for exposed positions nor for regions with extreme winters. All need permanent staking. The stake should reach to the budded union, with a tie just below the union and another half way up the stem. All shoots growing from the rootstock should be removed to avoid competition (see p. 21).

Bush and shrub standards

Hybrid Teas and Floribundas, the most commonly grown standards, are normally sold as full standards, with stems 3-3½ft (90-110cm) high, or half standards, with stems between 2½-2¾ft (76-84cm) in height. Some nurseries offer the smaller Floribundas or "patio roses" as quarter standards, with a stem height of 1¾-2ft (51-60cm). The stems of miniature standards are normally 1ft (30cm) tall.

In principle, the normal pruning used for the appropriate cultivar is followed when it is grown as a standard. The Hybrid Tea illustrated here serves as an example. In the case of Floribundas, prune the older wood to about 6in (15cm) and younger shoots to about 10in (25cm). With all standard roses it is important to keep the head reasonably symmetrical. The few shrub roses grown as tall standards are the most difficult to manage. Their character is lost if they are heavily pruned, but some cutting back is usually needed to maintain a good head.

STANDARD HYBRID TEAS

1 At planting secure the standard to a stake by ties, one just below the union and another about halfway up the stem. In spring shorten main stems to about 6in (15cm) and take out any weak growths.

2 To lessen the risk of wind damage, check ties in autumn and, in mild·climates, reduce the head by tipping back main stems. In the north, wrap the stem and head in burlap.

3 In early spring carry out basic pruning; cut out dead or diseased wood and any crossing stems. Bearing the overall shape of the head in mind, cut back vigorous shoots to about 6in (15cm) and shorten any laterals on the remaining wood to 4-6in (10-15cm). On mature standards some old shoots may need to be cut back to the union with the rootstock.

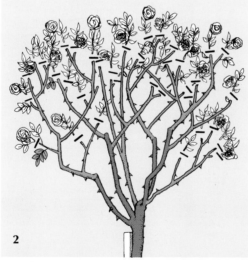

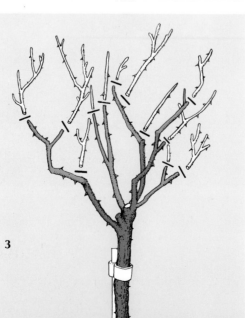

Above: A weeping standard is formed by budding a rambler on a clear stem. 'Wedding Day' is vigorous and difficult to keep well shaped.

Above right: The Hybrid Perpetual 'Ulrich Brunner' flowers all along the pegged-down stems.

Left: 'Ballerina', a Hybrid Musk, keeps its shape well when grown as a standard.

Weeping standards

When climbers or ramblers with flexible shoots, generally from Group One (see p. 30), are budded on a stem 5-6ft (1.5-1.8m) high they make attractive weeping standards. Using umbrella-shaped wire frames spreads the shoots evenly.

Weeping standards flower on two-year-old wood. In late summer or early autumn, cut right back to the union all or most of the shoots that have carried flowers. Some may need to be retained if there are insufficient or unevenly distributed replacement shoots; cut back the laterals of these older shoots to 6in (15cm). Occasionally ramblers and climbers from Group Two are also grown as weeping standards. Some old wood can be cut out in late summer or early autumn, but otherwise shorten laterals to about 6in (15cm).

Pegging down

If left to develop as bushes, some roses, the Hybrid Perpetuals in particular, tend to produce flowers only at the tips of their long stems. However, if these stems are trained near the horizontal, flowering laterals develop along much of their length. In their heyday, the Hybrid Perpetuals were often grown in this way, with the stems pegged down, tied to stakes (as illustrated here), or trained onto a framework of wires strung about 1ft (30cm) above the ground. The effect can be spectacular, but this form of training is labor intensive, and both the removal of faded flowers and weeding can be troublesome. Arching stems over will also encourage flowering laterals to break. The best way to avoid this is to tie the arched stems to low hoops of bamboo inserted around a bush.

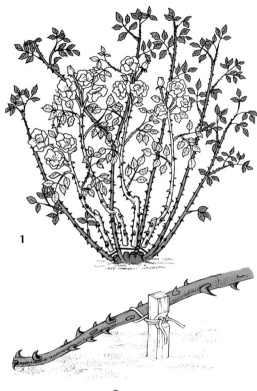

1

2

3

PEGGING DOWN

1 In the autumn, on a rose that has been grown as a bush for a year – such as a Hybrid Perpetual – cut out stems that have flowered. Tip back the remaining vigorous shoots growing from the base; remove flowers and any weak growth.

2 Carefully bend these shoots down to near ground level and tie to stakes or a framework of wires, or peg down. Cut back any laterals at 4-6in (10-15cm).

3 Subsequently, cut out at the base about half the pegged down shoots that have flowered and peg down new vigorous shoots as replacements. Eliminate any weak growths and shorten laterals to between 4-6in (10-15cm).

EXHIBITION ROSES

Many rose enthusiasts exhibit regularly at shows organized by local and national rose societies. If you are interested in showing, the first step is to join a society and to obtain the schedules that state the rules. Here, the aim is not to produce a step-by-step guide that takes into account the generally high standard of cultivation required for shows, but instead to outline the kind of planned pruning that the rose exhibitor needs to follow in order to produce blooms of exhibition quality.

Experienced exhibitors generally grow a large range of reliable and weather-resistant cultivars in the categories they are going to show. The classic exhibition rose is the Hybrid Tea, but Floribundas and miniatures are also popular and show schedules include categories of other roses. Hybrid Teas normally bloom 13-18 weeks after pruning, but local conditions and unseasonal weather can cause variations, and there are differences according to cultivar. The timing of pruning is geared to ensure that blooms are available for major shows. As an insurance, many exhibitors stagger their pruning, with up to 30 per cent of the roses in any category being pruned 10-15 days later than the rest. Roses grown for exhibition are generally hard-pruned to give fewer but larger flowers than those obtained from the moderate pruning recommended for garden display. Hybrid Teas are generally cut back to 1-2in (2.5-5cm). The older stems on Floribundas should be cut to the same length, but the previous season's growth to 8-12in (20-30cm).

On Hybrid Teas the removal of excess flower buds begins in early summer. Taking out side buds and the side shoots carrying buds allows the terminal bud the best chance of becoming a flower of exhibition quality. On Floribundas the terminal bud of the flower cluster is removed at an early stage. Sometimes other excess buds may also need to be taken out so that the remaining buds develop fully.

To ensure a good supply of blooms for exhibiting later in the season, all faded flowers must be removed promptly. Flowers that would open between shows are often removed at bud stage. This, along with the removal of faded flowers, is carried out to conserve the plant's energies.

PRUNING
As part of the pruning program to produce Hybrid Tea flowers of exhibition size and quality, only one flower is allowed to develop on each stem. Side buds and side shoots carrying buds are removed.

Above: 'Precious Platinum' is a Hybrid Tea that is sometimes grown for exhibition purposes. Not all Hybrid Teas are worth growing to exhibit: even good cultivation and rigorous pruning may not result in flowers of show quality.

Right: Shrub roses such as the Hybrid Musk 'Penelope' make effective summer screens when they are grown on a post-and-wire system.

ROSE HEDGES/RENOVATION

Hedges

Although roses are deciduous and therefore do not provide an effective screen in winter, they can make very attractive informal hedges. The most suitable roses are well clothed with foliage to the base, repeat well, and require little pruning. The Rugosas, such as 'Roseraie de l'Haÿ' and 'Scabrosa', deserve their popularity.

In choosing roses for hedging it is important to allow adequate room for spread: a hedge of the *Rugosa* 'Roseraie de l'Haÿ' can be up to 6ft (1.8m) high and as much as 5ft (1.5m) in width. When trimming hedge roses, follow the pruning appropriate to the cultivar. Do not try to impose an unnatural shape.

An alternative to the informal hedge is a screen of roses grown on a frame of posts and wires. Although more time-consuming to train, the screen has the great advantage of being narrow in width. Climbers trained and pruned in the ordinary way are an obvious choice, but many shrub roses can also be trained onto such a frame, the Hybrid Musks, such as 'Buff Beauty', 'Cornelia' and 'Penelope', being particularly effective.

Renovation of neglected roses

Although some roses will continue blooming freely despite neglect, the flowering of most will decline if they are not regularly pruned. Sometimes, if a rose has become an overgrown tangled mass of stems with no more than a token flower display, the only sensible course is to take it out altogether. Many roses, however, show remarkable powers of recovery and will often return to their free-flowering ways if severely pruned, well fed and watered.

Drastic pruning to renovate a rose can be carried out in one season or, alternatively, a program can be spread over several years. The course recommended here is to stage the hard-pruning over two years, giving the gardener a reasonably quick result while giving the rose time to improve its vigor. It is essential to mulch and feed the rose after hard-pruning, and to keep it well watered throughout the growing season. If the rose does not send up vigorous new growths from the base after the first hard pruning, it is not worth continuing the renovation program. Long-handled pruners are particularly useful for this operation.

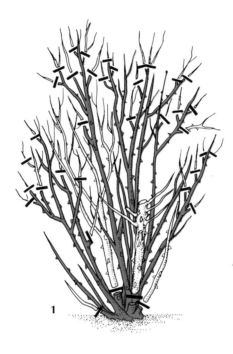

1

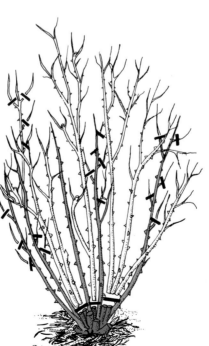

3

RENOVATION

1 In late winter or early spring of the first year take out dead or diseased wood, and any weak or twiggy growth. Cut out about half of the main stems: keep the youngest and most vigorous. Shorten remaining laterals to about 6in (15cm).

2 It is often necessary to use loppers when cutting out old stems of roses that are being renovated. If stubs are left, pare these down with a sharp knife.

2

3 In late winter (in mild areas) or early spring of the second year cut out the main stems left at the first renovation pruning. Shorten to about 6in (15cm) laterals on the new stems that have developed during the preceding growing season.

A-Z OF ROSES

MODERN BUSH ROSES

The following list includes Hybrid Teas (HT), Hybrid Perpetuals (HP), Floribundas (Fl), Dwarf Polyanthas (DP), and Miniatures (M). All the roses listed below are to some extent repeat-flowering. For pruning and training recommendations see as follows: Hybrid Teas and Hybrid Perpetuals, pp. 22-3; Floribundas, pp. 24-5; Dwarf Polyanthas and Miniatures, p. 25.

'Admiral Rodney', HT
'Alec's Red', HT
'Alexander', HT or Shrub G3
'Amber Queen', Fl
'Amazing Grace', HT
'Angela Rippon', M
'Anisley Dickson', Fl
'Anna Ford', short Fl
'Anne Harkness', Fl
'Apricot Silk', HT
'Arthur Bell', Fl
'Baby Darling', M
'Baby Gold Star', M
'Bambino', M
'Baroness Rothschild', HP
'Baronne Prévost', HP
'Bianco', short Fl
'Blessings', HT
'Bloomfield Abundance',
  Polyantha hybrid (as DP)
'Blue Moon', HT
'Bobby Charlton', HT
'Bobolink', M
'Bright Smile', short Fl
'Brown Velvet', Fl
'Cécile Brunner', DP
'Cheshire Life', HT
'Chicago Peace', HT
'Chrysler Imperial', HT
'Cinderella', M
'City of Belfast', Fl
'City of Leeds', Fl
'Colorama', HT
'Congratulations', HT
'Daily Sketch', Fl
'Dainty Dinah', short Fl
'Dame of Sark', Fl
'Dearest', Fl
'Deep Secret', HT
'Diorama', HT
'Dresden Doll', M
'Easter Morning', M
'Elizabeth Harkness', HT
'Elizabeth of Glamis', Fl
'Ena Harkness', HT
'English Miss', Fl
'Ernest H. Morse', HT
'Europeana', Fl
'Evelyn Fison', Fl
'Evening Star', Fl
'Eye Paint', Fl
'Fairy Changeling', DP
'Fragrant Cloud', HT
'Fragrant Delight', Fl
'Frau Karl Druschki', HP
'Frensham', Fl
'Général Jacqueminot', HP
'Gentle Touch', short Fl
'Georg Arends', HP
'Glad Tidings', Fl
'Glenfiddich', Fl

'Gloria Mundi', DP
'Grandpa Dickson', HT
'Gypsy Jewel', M
'Hannah Gordon', Fl
'Harry Wheatcroft', HT
'Harvest Fayre', Fl
'Hula Girl', M
'Iceberg', Fl or Shrub G3
'Iced Ginger', Fl
'John F. Kennedy, HT
'John Waterer', HT
'Josephine Bruce', HT
'Just Joey', HT
'King's Ransom', HT
'Korresia', Fl
'Lady Sylvia', HT
'Lilac Charm', Fl
'Lilli Marlene', Fl
'Lincoln Cathedral', HT
'Little Buckaroo', M
'Little Flirt', M
'Little Prince', short Fl
'Little White Pet', DP
'Lover's Meeting', HT
'Margaret Merril', Fl
'Masquerade', Fl
'Matangi', Fl
'Minijet', M
'Mischief', HT
'Monique', HT
'Mountbatten', Fl
'Mrs John Laing', HP
'My Choice', HT
'Nathalie Nypels', DP
'National Trust', HT
'New Penny', M
'News',.Fl
'Orange Sensation', Fl
'Paddy McGredy', Fl
'Papa Meilland', HT
'Paprika', Fl
'Para Ti', M
'Pascali', HT
'Paul Crampel', DP
'Paul Neyron', HP
'Paul Shirville', HT
'Peace', HT or Shrub G3
'Peaudouce', HT
'Peek-A-Boo', short Fl
'Peer Gynt', HT
'Perla de Montserrat', M
'Perle d'Or', Polyantha hybrid (as DP)
'Picasso', Fl
'Piccadilly', HT
'Pink Parfait', Fl or Shrub G3
'Petit Four', short Fl
'Plentiful', Fl
'Polar Star', HT
'Queen Elizabeth', Fl (as Shrub G3)
'Red Devil', HT
'Red Imp', M
'Red Rascal', short Fl
'Reine des Violettes', HP
'Robin Redbreast', short Fl
'Rob Roy', Fl
'Roger Lambelin', HP
'Rose Gaujard', HT
'Rosemary Harkness', HT
'Rosemary Rose', Fl
'Roulettii', M
'Royal William', HT
'Sheri Anne', M
'Silver Jubilee', HT
'Southampton', Fl

'Souvenir du Docteur Jamain', HP
'Stacey Sue', M
'Starina', M
'Sterling Silver', HT
'Sunblest', HT
'Super Star', HT
'Sweet Magic', short Fl
'Tangi', Fl
'The Fairy', DP
'Tiffany', HT
'Troika', HT
'Tropicana', HT
'Trumpeter', short Fl
'Ulrich Brunner', HP
'Vick's Caprice', HP
'Violet Carson', Fl
'Virgo', HT
'Wee Jock', short Fl
'Wendy Cussons', HT
'Whisky Mac', HT
'Wishing', short Fl
'Yellow Doll', M
'Yvonne Rabier', DP

SHRUB ROSES

The following list contains the species roses (including some hybrids close in character to species roses), the old roses of hybrid origin that were cultivated before the development of the Hybrid Teas, and Modern Shrub Roses. An "R" indicates that the rose is to some extent repeat-flowering. Some of the taller roses in this section, especially among the Bourbons and Modern Shrubs, can be satisfactorily trained as short climbers, in which case they should be treated as the pillar roses, Climbers and Ramblers, Group 4, p. 33. For pruning and training details see as follows: Group 1 (G1), p. 26; Group 2 (G2), p. 27; Group 3 (G3), p. 28.

'Adam Messerich' (Bourbon), G3, R
'Agnes' (Rugosa), G1, R
'Alba Maxima' (Alba), G2
'Alba Semiplena' (Alba), G2
'Alain Blanchard' (Gallica), G1
'Aloha' (Modern Shrub), G3, R
'Angelina' (Modern Shrub), G3, R
Austrian briar see R. foetida
Austrian copper see R. foetida 'Bicolor'
'Ballerina' (Hybrid Musk), G1, R
'Belinda' (Hybrid Musk), G1, R
'Belle Amour' (Alba), G2
'Belle de Crécy' (Gallica), G1
'Berlin' (Modern Shrub), G3, R
'Bonn' (Modern Shrub), G3, R
'Boule de Neige' (Bourbon), G3, R
'Bourbon Queen' (Bourbon), G3, R
'Buff Beauty' (Hybrid Musk), G1, R
californica 'Plena' (Species), G1
'Camaieux' (Gallica), G1
'Canary Bird' (Species), G1
canina 'Andersonii' (Species), G1
'Cantabrigiensis' (Species), G1
'Cardinal de Richelieu' (Gallica), G1
'Celestial' (Alba), G2

'Charles de Mills' (Gallica), G1
'Blanc Double de Coubert' (Rugosa), G1, R
'Blush Damask' (Damask), G2
'Butterfly Wings' (Modern Shrub), G3, R
'Captain John Ingram' (Moss), G2
'Celsiana' (Damask), G2
x centifolia (Centifolia), G2
x c. 'Bullata' (Centifolia), G2
x c. 'Cristata' see 'Chapeau de Napoléon'
x c. 'Muscosa' (Centifolia), G2
x c. 'Parvifolia' (Centifolia), G2
'Chapeau de Napoléon' (Centifolia), G2
'Chinatown' (Modern Shrub), prune as Fl, R
'Clair Matin' (Modern Shrub), G3, R
'Commandant Beaurepaire' (Bourbon), G2
'Common Moss' (Moss), G2
'Complicata' (Gallica), G1
'Comte de Chambord' (Portland), G3, R
'Comtesse du Cayla' (China), G3, R
'Comtesse de Murinais' (Moss), G2
'Conrad Ferdinand Meyer' (Rugosa), G1, R
'Constance Spry' (Modern Shrub), G2
'Cornelia' (Hybrid Musk), G1, R
'Coupe d'Hébé' (Bourbon), G2
'Danaë' (Hybrid Musk), G1, R
'De Meaux' (Centifolia), G2
'Dortmund' (Modern Shrub), G3, R
'Duc de Fitzjames' (Centifolia), G2
'Duc de Guiche' (Gallica), G1
'Du Maître d'Ecole' (Gallica), G1
'Dupontii' (Species), G1
ecae (Species), G1
'Elmshorn' (Modern Shrub), G3, R
'English Garden' (English Rose), G3, R
'Erfurt' (Modern Shrub), G3, R
'Fantin-Latour' (Centifolia), G2
farreri persetosa (Species), G1
fedtschenkoana (Species), G1, R
'Felicia' (Hybrid Musk), G1, R
'Félicité Parmentier' (Alba), G2
'Fellemberg' (China), G3, R
'Ferdinand Pichard' (Bourbon), G3, R
'Fimbriata' (Rugosa), G1
'Fisherman's Friend' (English Rose), G3, R
foetida (Species), G1
foetidia 'Bicolor' (Species), G1
'Fountain' (Modern Shrub), G2, R
'Francofurtana' (Gallica), G1
'Frau Dagmar Hartopp' see 'Fru Dagmar Hastrup'
'Fred Loads' (Modern Shrub), prune as Fl, R
'Fritz Nobis' (Modern Shrub), G3
'Fru Dagmar Hastrup' (Rugosa), G1, R
'Frühlingsanfang' (Species), G1
'Frühlingsduft' (Species), G1
'Frühlingsgold' (Species), G1
'Frühlingsmorgen' (Species), G1, R
gallica officinalis (Gallica), G1
'Général Kléber' (Moss), G2
'Gloire des Mousseux' (Moss), G2

'Golden Chersonese' (Species), G1
'Golden Wings' (Species), G1, R
'Graham Thomas' (English Rose), G3, R
'Great Maiden's Blush' (Alba), G2
'Grootendorst Supreme' (Rugosa), G1, R
'Grouse' (prostrate Modern Shrub), G3
x *harisonii* 'Harison's Yellow' (Species), G1
'Heidelberg' (Modern Shrub), G3, R
'Henri Martin' (Moss), G2
'Heritage' (English Rose), G3, R
'Hermosa' (China), G3, R
'Honorine de Brabant' (Bourbon), G3, R
hugonis (Species), G1
'Ispahan' (Damask), G2
'Jacques Cartier' (Portland), G3, R
'Jenny Duval' (Gallica), G1
'Juno' (Centifolia), G2
'Kathleen Ferrier' (Modern Shrub), prune as Fl, R
'Königin von Dänemark' (Alba), G2
'La Noblesse' (Centifolia), G2
'La Reine Victoria' (Bourbon), G3, R
'Lavender Lassie' (Modern Shrub), G3, R
'Leda' (Damask), G2
'Louise Odier' (Bourbon), G3, R
'Mme Delaroche-Lambert' (Moss), G2
'Mme Ernst Calvat' (Bourbon), G3, R
'Mme Hardy' (Damask), G2
'Mme Isaac Pereire' (Bourbon), G3, R
'Mme Legras de St Germain' (Alba), G2
'Mme Pierre Oger' (Bourbon), G3, R
'Mme Plantier' (Alba), G2
'Maiden's Blush' (Alba), G2
'Marguerite Hilling' (Modern Shrub), G3, R
'Mary Rose' (English Rose), G3, R
'Max Graf' (prostrate Modern Shrub), G3, R
'Moonlight' (Hybrid Musk), G1, R
Moss rose see *R.* x *centifolia* 'Muscosa'
'Mousseline' (Moss), G2
moyesii (Species), G1
moyesii 'Geranium' (Species), G1
'Mutabilis' (China), G3, R
'Nevada' (Modern Shrub), G3, R
'Nozomi' (prostrate Modern Shrub), G3, R
'Nova Zembla' (Rugosa), G1, R
'Nuits de Young' (Moss), G2
'Nur Mahal' (Hybrid Musk), G1, R
'Nymphenburg' (Modern Shrub), G3, R
'Old Blush' (China), G3, R
'Othello' (English Rose), G3, R
'Partridge' (prostrate Modern Shrub), G3, R
'Paul Ricault' (Centifolia), G2
'Paulii' (prostrate Species), G1
'Pax' (Hybrid Musk), G1, R
'Penelope' (Hybrid Musk), G1, R

'Petite de Hollande' (Centifolia), G2
'Petite Lisette' (Damask), G2
'Pheasant' (prostrate Modern Shrub), G3
'Pink Grootendorst' (Rugosa), G2, R
'Pink Prosperity' (Hybrid Musk), G1, R
pomifera (Species), G1
'Pompon de Paris' (China), G3
'Président de Sèze' (Gallica), G1
'Prosperity' (Hybrid Musk), G1, R
'Quatre Saisons' (Damask), G1, R
'Raubritter' (prostrate Modern Shrub), G3
'Robert le Diable' (Centifolia), G2
'Rosa Mundi' (Gallica), G1
'Roseraie de l'Haÿ' (Rugosa), G1, R
rubrifolia (Species), G1
rugosa 'Alba' (Rugosa), G1, R
r. 'Rubra' (Rugosa), G1, R
r. 'Scabrosa' (Rugosa), G1, R
'Sarah van Fleet' (Rugosa), G1, R
'Scarlet Fire' (Gallica), G1
'Schneezwerg' (Rugosa), G1, R
sericea pteracantha (Species), G1
'Serratipetala' (China), G3, R
'Slater's Crimson China' (China), G3, R
'Souvenir de la Malmaison' (Bourbon), G3, R
'Spong' (Centifolia), G2
'Stanwell Perpetual' (Species), G3, R
'Surpasse Tout' (Gallica), G1
'Surrey' (prostrate Modern Shrub), G3, R
'Swan' (English Rose), G3, R
'The Bishop' (Centifolia), G2
'The Countryman' (English Rose), G3, R
'Thisbe' (Hybrid Musk), G1, R
'Tour de Malakoff' (Centifolia), G2
Threepenny-bit rose see *R. farreri persetosa*
'Tuscany Superb' (Gallica), G1
'Uncle Walter' (Modern Shrub), as Hybrid Tea, R
'Unique Blanche' (Centifolia), G2
'Vanity' (Hybrid Musk), G1, R
'Variegata de Bologna' (Bourbon), G3, R
'Versicolor' (Damask), G2
'Viridiflora' (China), G3, R
'Wilhelm' (Hybrid Musk), G1, R
'William Lobb' (Moss), G2
'William Shakespeare' (English Rose), G3, R
'Will Scarlet' (Hybrid Musk), G1, R
'Winchester Cathedral' (English Rose), G3, R
xanthina x *spontanea* see 'Canary Bird'

CLIMBERS AND RAMBLERS
An "R" indicates that the rose is to some extent repeat-flowering. Most of the Group 4 roses can be grown as free-standing shrubs, in which case they are best treated as Shrub Roses, Group 3, p. 28. For pruning and training as Climbers and

Ramblers see as follows: Group 1 (G1), p. 30; Group 2 (G2), p. 31; Group 3 (G3), p. 32; Group 4 (G4) and Group (G5), p. 33.

'Adélaïde d'Orléans', G1
'Albéric Barbier', G2 (prune in winter), R
'Albertine', G2
'Alister Stella Gray', G3, R
'Allen Chandler', G3, R
'Allgold, Climbing', G3, R
'Aloha', G4, R
'Altissimo', G3, R
'American Pillar', G1
'Auguste Gervais', G3
banksiae banksiae, G5
banksiae 'Lutea', G5
'Bantry Bay', G3 or G4, R
'Blairii No. 2', G3, R
'Blush Noisette', G3, R
'Bobbie James', G5
'Breath of Life', G3, R
'Breeze Hill', G2
brunonii 'La Mortola', G5
'Casino', G4, R
'Brenda Colvin', G5
'Cécile Brunner, Climbing', G3, R
'Céline Forestier', G3 or G4, R
'Chaplin's Pink Climber', G2
'Compassion', G4, R
'Copenhagen', G4, R
'Coral Dawn', G4, R
'Crimson Shower', G1
'Danse du Feu', G4, R
'Débutante', G1
'Desprez à Fleur Jaune', G3, R
'Dorothy Perkins', G1
'Dortmund', G4, R
'Dr W. Van Fleet', G3
'Dublin Bay', G4, R
'Easlea's Golden Rambler', G3
'Elegance', G3
'Emily Gray', G1
'Ena Harkness, Climbing', G4, R
'Ernest H. Morse, Climbing', G3, R
'Etoile de Hollande, Climbing', G3, R
'Excelsa', G1
'Félicité et Perpétue', G1
filipes 'Kiftsgate', G5
'Fragrant Cloud, Climbing', G3, R
'François Juranville', G1
'Galway Bay', G3, R
gigantea, G5
'Gloire de Dijon', G3, R
'Golden Showers', G4, R
'Goldfinch', G1
'Grand Hotel', G3, R
'Guinée', G3, R
'Handel', G4, R
helenae, G5
'Hiawatha', G1
'Iceberg, Climbing', G3, R
'Jaune Desprez' see 'Desprez à Fleur Jaune'
'Josephine Bruce, Climbing', G3, R
'Kathleen Harrop', G4, R
'Kew Rambler', G1
'Kiftsgate' see *R. filipes* 'Kiftsgate'
'Lady Hillingdon, Climbing', G3, R
'Lady Sylvia, Climbing', G3, R
'Lady Waterloo', G3, R
laevigata, G5
'Lavinia', G4, R

'Lawrence Johnston', G3, R
'Leverkusen', G4, R
longicuspis, G5
'Mme Alfred Carrière', G3, R
'Mme Butterfly, Climbing', G3, R
'Mme Caroline Testout', Climbing, G3, R
'Mme Edouard Herriot', Climbing, G4, R
'Mme Grégoire Staechelin', G3
'Mme Sancy de Parabère', G3
'Maigold', G4, R
'Maréchal Niel', G3, R
'Masquerade, Climbing', G4, R
'Meg', G3,
'Mermaid', G3 (minimal pruning), R
'Mrs Herbert Stevens', Climbing, G3, R
'Mrs Sam McGredy, Climbing', G3, R
mulliganii, G5
'New Dawn', G3 or G4, R
'Ophelia, Climbing', G3, R
'Parade', G3, R
'Parkdirektor Riggers', G3, R
'Paul's Himalayan Musk Rambler', G5
'Paul's Lemon Pillar', G3
'Paul's Scarlet Climber', G3
'Phyllis Bide', G3, R
'Pink Perpétue', G4, R
'Rambling Rector', G5
'Ramona', G3
'Rêve d'Or', G3, R
'Ritter von Barmstede', G3, R
'Rosy Mantle', G4, R
'Royal Gold', G4, R
'Sander's White Rambler', G1
'Schoolgirl', G3, R
'Seagull', G5
'Shot Silk, Climbing', G4, R
'Souvenir de Claudius Denoyel', G3, R
'Souvenir du Docteur Jamain', G3 or G4, R
'Summer Wine', G3, R
'Swan Lake', G4, R
'Sympathie', G3, R
'The Garland', G2
'Veilchenblau', G5
'Wedding Day', G5
'White Cockade', G4, R
'William Allen Richardson', G3, R
'Zéphirine Drouhin', G3, R

TREES

Although the distinction is not clear cut, it is useful to divide woody plants into trees and shrubs. Most trees have a single main stem or trunk supporting a framework of branches, whereas shrubs, generally smaller, sometimes only 3 or 4in (7.5-10cm) high, have several stems arising at or just above ground level.

This book deals with two approaches to pruning and training ornamental trees, that is trees grown to please the eye rather than as a source of lumber. On the one hand there are the specialized regimes that impose forms on trees, creating the living architecture of hedges, topiary and pleaching. These regimes, which are covered on pages 96-119, are important to the gardener, but can only be applied to a relatively restricted range of plants.

The second approach can be used for most ornamental trees and relies on the natural growth of the tree which, along with its foliage, flowers, fruit, bark and twigs, make such trees worth growing. A tree that has been well chosen for a particular position rarely needs more than light pruning and, if this is carried out with respect for the tree's characteristic growth, it will enhance the tree's beauty and may extend its life. In contrast, harsh pruning that fights against the individual growth characteristics of a tree is likely to destroy a great part of its ornamental value.

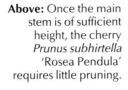

Above: Once the main stem is of sufficient height, the cherry *Prunus subhirtella* 'Rosea Pendula' requires little pruning.

Right: The holly *Ilex* x *altaclarensis* 'Camelliifolia' grows into a pyramid shape without being trimmed.

Far left: Lindens (*Tilia*) are often planted to form avenues or as specimen trees. However, they are also the classic tree for the traditional technique of pleaching (see pp.106-7), their flexible growths being trained to make airy screens and shady coverings for walks.

Left: *Magnolia soulangeana* grows into a large shrub or small tree. Like most magnolias, it will shoot readily when cut back into old wood, but large pruning cuts should be avoided because the heartwood rots quickly once the tree's own defenses have been breached.

Left: Many trees are planted with no account being taken of their ultimate height and spread. The cedar of Lebanon (*Cedrus libani*) makes a majestic tree in a large setting, but looks sadly mutilated when pruned to fit a restricted space.

Despite great variations in detail, two broad patterns of growth can be distinguished. Many trees, especially large forest trees, have a central leader that is strongly dominant. This dominance may persist throughout the life of the tree, but in maturity and old age some trees develop a spreading crown. Such trees can be grown as branched trees, with limbs almost to the ground, or as standards on a clear stem. A number of other trees have a pattern of branching in which there is no dominant leader and they form bushy-headed standards.

When the natural growth of trees is respected, pruning and training is relatively simple. In the first five to ten years the emphasis is on establishing a strong, durable, and balanced framework. This may involve little more than an initial short period of staking, the removal of badly placed shoots and, in the case of some trees, the maintenance of a strong leader. As the well-formed tree develops, there is less and less need for regular pruning, but broken, dead or diseased wood needs to be removed and sometimes there may be suckers and epicormic growths to deal with.

Sadly, many trees are planted where there is not enough space to allow them to reach their ultimate size, or changes in land use make it necessary to prune or remove established trees. The radical pruning that is frequently used in such situations is often grotesquely mutilating. Sometimes there are more sympathetic solutions and these are mentioned on pages 52-5.

It must be stressed that some pruning and all felling are major operations that should not be carried out by the amateur. Most work that requires the pruner to work above ground level and all felling and work in which a chainsaw is to be used should be carried out by professional tree surgeons for safety reasons. Unfortunately there are many people laying claim to skills they do not have and who may well leave a tree in a worse state than they found it. If employing someone to do work on trees, choose from contractors approved by a national arboricultural association or similar body.

Staking

A well-established root system and tough resilient wood are the tree's best defenses against strong winds. It may take a year or

two for the roots of a transplanted tree to take a good hold and during this interim stage some trees, especially those planted in exposed positions, benefit from being braced or staked. However, some movement is needed to stimulate the toughening of the wood. Prolonged bracing or staking that keeps the whole main stem rigid prevents this natural toughening process.

When stakes are used, they should be short, their height above ground being no more than one-third the height of the plant being staked, with a tie just below the top. When using two- or three-way bracing systems, the guys should be attached low down on the tree.

Ties are often the cause of serious damage to trees, making wounds that can provide a point of entry for pests and diseases, or constricting growth. Choose wide, well-cushioned straps, for example of rubber, that are easily loosened or tightened. When fastened they should be reasonably firm, but loose enough to allow the circumference of the stem to increase. Check all ties in spring to ensure that they are loose enough to allow for the next season's growth. This also applies to ties fixing labels to trees, which are easily overlooked as the tree grows.

STAKING

Transplanted trees may need staking for a year or two, until the root system is well established. As some movement is necessary to stimulate the toughening of wood, use a low stake, not more than a third of the height of the tree, and tie the tree to it with a broad strap just below the top of the stake.

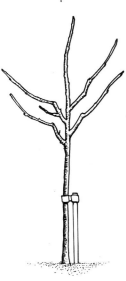

Even some long whippy stems will straighten and stiffen when left on their own. In some cases, however, for example when training in a replacement leader, it is useful to tie a long growth to an upright bamboo cane for the first year.

Pruning cuts

Any wound suffered by a tree, whether it is a pruning cut or a break caused by a storm or vandalism, may be a point of entry for disease. The tree responds to injury by compartmentalizing the damaged area, forming a protective barrier that is very resistant to penetration by pathogens. When pruning a tree or shrub it is important to make cuts that give the plant the optimum chance of making an effective response. Small cuts, especially when these are made on young trees, are much less likely to be a problem than large wounds made on mature and old trees.

The angle of the cut is of crucial importance. In flush cutting, until recently widely recommended and still commonly practiced, the branch is cut back as close as possible to the trunk or limb from which it arises. It has been normal practice to enlarge the wound by paring or scribing the bark at the margin and to apply a wound dressing on the assumption that the corky callus tissue that often develops rapidly after this treatment indicates healing. However, decay often continues beneath a large flush cut because the cut has breached the natural defenses of the tree.

The best guide to the position of a cut is provided by the bark branch ridge, which is visible on a trunk, for example, sloping back as a line of raised and generally rough bark from the junction of the trunk and branch. Its precise position varies from genus to genus and species to species. The pruning cut should leave intact the strong internal boundary that this marks and also the swollen base or collar of the branch. It should be angled to begin just outside the branch bark ridge and should slope down and slightly outwards but without leaving a stub or snag that will die back.

The angle of the cut is essentially the same whatever the size of the branch or limb to be removed. All cuts must be made cleanly, sharp hand and long-handled pruners being suitable for removing small

Below, top and bottom: To train a whippy replacement leader vertically, tie to a bamboo cane.

Left: When transplanting a large tree, it is often preferable to support the trunk with a three-way bracing system rather than a stake. Once the supports are in place, use broad straps as the guys and attach them low down on the tree.

Below: The Judas tree (*Cercis siliquastrum*) is a deciduous small tree grown mainly for its highly ornamental pea-like flowers.

ANGLE OF CUT
To remove a branch with the minimum risk of decay make the cut close to the trunk, but angled so that it is outside the branch bark ridge (a) and the branch collar (b).

branches. Use a sharp saw (see pp. 214-15) to take off branches larger than an inch (2.5cm) in diameter.

The removal of heavy and awkwardly placed limbs is potentially very dangerous and should only be carried out by a trained and experienced tree surgeon. Sometimes, however, a low limb of reasonable size can be safely removed by the home gardener. Any branch much larger than 2in (5cm) in diameter is best cut in several sections so that the removal of the final stub is easily managed. For example, make a cut on the underside of a branch about 1-1½ft (30-46cm) from its junction with the trunk, cutting about a quarter of the way through. Complete this cut from above, starting about 2in (5cm) farther from the trunk than the cut on the underside. Then remove the remaining stub in two stages, using an angled cut as previously described, first undercutting the stub and then completing the cut from the top.

When to prune
As a general rule, prune deciduous trees in the dormant season and broad-leaved evergreens just as they are coming into growth in spring. Prune cherries (*Prunus*) in mid-summer to minimize the risk of silver leaf infection. Maples (*Acer*) and birches (*Betula*) are typical of some trees, mainly deciduous, that exude a heavy flow of sap from cuts made in late winter or early spring. This bleeding is very difficult to staunch and generally continues until the tree breaks into leaf. Excessive loss of sap is likely to be harmful. Those that are prone to bleeding (see pp. 120-28) should be pruned in late autumn or early winter, as should conifers.

Suckers
The grafting or budding of trees on to compatible rootstocks is widely practiced, largely as a means of speeding up nursery production. Sometimes, however, the intention is to modify the vigor of the tree or to create a particular form, such as a weeping standard. The union between the stock and the tree (the scion) is normally clearly visible as a swelling just above ground level or sometimes, in the case of standards, between the stem and the branched head. Where the union is high on a stem, trees are described as "top-worked".

Suckers — shoots that develop from the stock — will weaken the tree and will eventually become dominant. Some rootstocks are particularly prone to suckering, but another cause is injury to roots. Suckers should be removed promptly, preferably when they are in full leaf. On small shrubs they can be ripped off. On large shrubs and trees expose the junction of the sucker and root and cut off the former where it emerges.

Removing small branches
A folding pruning saw is an extremely useful tool for removing small branches. Like large limbs, small branches are often best taken off in sections. Begin with an undercut (right, top) about 1ft (30cm) from

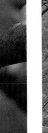

the trunk, cutting a quarter to a third of the way through and then again from above, about an inch (2.5cm) farther from the trunk (right, middle top). The undercut prevents the bark tearing when the branch is severed (above). Also undercut when making the final cut (right, middle bottom), ensuring that the cut is close to the trunk and sloping so that it runs from just outside the branch bark ridge to leave the branch collar intact (right, bottom).

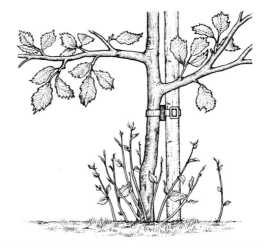

SUCKERS (Left) AND EPICORMIC SHOOTS (Far left)

Suckers sometimes develop at the base of trees that are grafted or budded on to a rootstock. If the tree has been top-worked, suckers may develop on the main stem below the union. To prevent suckers weakening the tree, pull them away as soon as possible. If they are simply cut off, more suckers are likely to grow. In contrast, epicormic shoots, which develop in clusters from dormant or adventitious buds on the trunks and main branches of trees, are generally caused by wounding or some other form of stress. These shoots should be cut back each year in late autumn and early spring.

Epicormic shoots

Trees that have been wounded or are otherwise stressed often produce strong shoots, known as epicormic shoots, from dormant and adventitious buds on the trunk or main branches. It is very common, for example, to find clusters of shoots round large flush cuts or growing from the stubs of trees that have been topped. They are less likely to develop on a tree that is in a good state of health and where major surgery has not been necessary because of good formative pruning.

Epicormic growths are generally considered unsightly and draw on food supplies that should go to other parts of the tree. They are best cut back when in full leaf but, because they grow again year after year, it is necessary to prune them annually.

It should be noted, too, that epicormic shoots are weakly attached and if allowed to develop into large branches, for example on a linden (*Tilia*) or poplar (*Populus*), they are potentially dangerous (see Lopping, p. 54).

Trees and the law

Most gardeners never have cause to think about the legal dimension of tree ownership, but it is as well to be aware that it exists. Most potential problems are avoided by maintaining trees in a good state and adopting a neighborly approach to any difficulties that result from trees extending beyond boundaries.

Lopping or felling of trees should never be undertaken lightly and before any action is decided upon a check should be made on any regulations governing the removal of all or part of the tree.

Removing large Branches

When a branch can be removed safely by a home gardener, cut it in manageable sections (top left). Begin each stage with an undercut about a quarter of the way through the branch followed by a top cut about an inch (2.5cm) further from the trunk. When removing the final section (bottom left and top right), angle the cut so that both the branch bark ridge and branch collar are left intact (bottom right) (see p. 43).

BRANCHED TREES

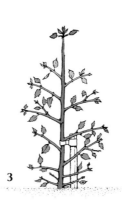
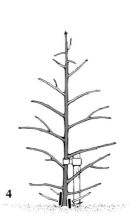

BRANCHED TREE
1 Plant young trees in the dormant season with a short stake, attaching with an adjustable tie.

2 In mid- to late autumn of the first year cut out basal shoots and badly placed or damaged laterals. Leave other laterals unpruned.

3 As growth is made in the second spring and summer check the tie and loosen if necessary.

4 In mid- to late autumn of the second year remove any weak laterals at the base. Cut out any dead, damaged or diseased wood.

5 By the third year the tree should no longer need staking. If during the growing season any lateral competes with the leader, cut it out.

Many deciduous trees naturally form a strong central leader furnished more or less symmetrically with laterals over most of its length. Typical species that readily form a branched tree, as this form is called, are the silver birch (*Betula pendula*), sweet gum (*Liquidambar styraciflua*) and the tulip tree (*Liriodendron tulipifera*).

Branched trees are easily trained and generally require very little pruning. There is no cutting back of the central leader at planting and staking should be for a maximum of two to three years.

The main points to watch for on the developing tree are vigorous shoots that threaten the typical growth pattern. Young plants sometimes throw up strong growths from the base. Normally these should be removed in mid- to late autumn. In some circumstances, however, it may be desirable to allow the basal shoot to develop, resulting in a multi-stemmed tree.

The development of a forked or double leader should be dealt with promptly because a narrow-angled crotch will be a serious weakness in the mature tree. Included bark, indicated by the branch bark ridge turning inwards, is frequently an additional weakness in a narrow "V" crotch.

Right: Most of the birches will naturally make branched trees with a single main stem. *Betula ermanii* 'Grayswood Form' is an example of the many birches that have attractive bark, which is seen to best effect when grown as a standard. Because birches often bleed badly when cut in spring, pruning should be carried out in late summer or autumn.

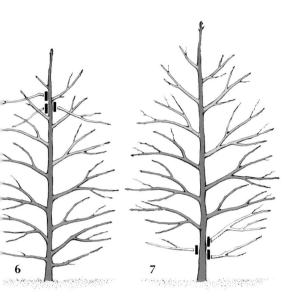

6 In mid- to late autumn of the third year cut out weak and badly placed growths that spoil the tree's balanced shape.

7 In the fourth and subsequent years prune as needed in mid- to late autumn. To make a clear stem, remove the lowest laterals to the desired height.

To rectify the situation, retain the most vigorous leader and cut out its rival completely. Sometimes a cluster of small shoots form at the tip of the main stem. In this case the best course is to cut back to a bud or lateral below the cluster, subsequently training in the replacement leader. The central leader often loses its dominance when the tree reaches maturity or old age, the branching growth then begins to form a spreading crown.

Normally the laterals on a branched tree do not need pruning to maintain reasonable spacing and a balanced overall shape. However, if laterals are too close or too vigorous and compete with the leader, thin them selectively in mid- to late autumn. The desirable spacing between the main framework branches on a mature tree will depend on the species or cultivar, but in general branches should not be less than 1 ft (30cm) apart and one branch should not directly overshadow another. Where there is a choice of laterals to prune, retain those with wide angles in preference to those that form a sharp angle with the trunk. However, in the case of many fastigiate trees that have numerous erect branches of small diameter, such as the Lombardy poplar (*Populus nigra* 'Italica'), the density of growth and the narrowness of the angle between branch and trunk is not normally a source of weakness. Weak laterals near the base of the tree can be removed in the third or fourth year, leaving a short clear stem.

Above: Many species of *Sorbus*, including *S. commixta* shown here, require little training to form a strong central lead.

Broad-leaved evergreens

A number of evergreens, including holly (*Ilex*) and holm oak (*Quercus ilex*), tolerate clipping and are used for hedging and topiary. When they are grown as free-standing specimens they are best treated as branched trees. The hollies, for example, show considerable variation in their pattern of growth, some, such as *I.* x *altaclerensis*, retaining the central leader more strongly than others. With all of them aim to keep the central leader going for as long as possible and, if it is damaged, train in a replacement.

Above: Many pines, including *Pinus sylvestris*, eventually make very large trees and pruning may need to be carried out by a tree surgeon.

Top right: There are several glaucous forms of the Colorado spruce (*Picea pungens*), most with strong central leaders and whorls of branches making a regular cone shape.

Conifers

In maturity and old age some conifers, such as cedars (*Cedrus*), develop broad heads, but as young trees most have a single central leader. The branches radiate from the trunk randomly or in whorls, their even development commonly resulting in a conical shape.

The formative training of conifers is much the same as that of a branched deciduous tree, with the emphasis on maintaining a single central leader. It is important that young conifers should have good all-round exposure to light, because crowding and overshadowing are likely to cause die-back.

If the terminal bud is damaged on a young vigorous tree, a shoot from the topmost whorl will usually take over as a replacement leader. This new leader can be helped by training it to a bamboo cane and removing completely any competing shoots.

With yew (*Taxus*) as a notable exception, conifers usually do not produce new growth when cut back into older wood, there being very few dormant buds where there is no foliage. In general the pruning of mature trees should be limited to the removal of dead wood. If it is necessary to cut back into living wood, prune in the dormant season.

STANDARD TREES

Standards are more commonly used in ornamental planting than branched trees. They are especially valuable in the smaller garden, trees with a clear stem of 5ft (1.5m) or more creating a much lighter effect than those clothed to the ground. In general, standards make for much freer movement in the garden and are less likely than branched trees to be damaged by lawn-mowers when they are grown as lawn specimens, although there is the risk of careless mowing causing bark damage. Combined with an underplanting of shrubs and herbaceous plants, they can create some of the most rewarding planting schemes for the garden.

The central-leader standard

This is simply a branched tree that has had the lower laterals removed to a height of approximately 5-7ft (1.5-2.1m). Among the most splendid specimens are mature landscape trees that have been browsed to a uniform height by cattle.

The lower laterals should not be removed in a single operation for their presence helps to protect and strengthen the main stem. The normal practice is to shorten them by about half in the first year, when they have made about 9-12in (23-30cm) of growth, and to cut them back to the main stem, generally in late autumn or early winter. However, there is room for flexibility in the pruning of these laterals and when starting with a maiden that is a weak grower it is worth retaining the shortened laterals for three or four years.

Right: Many branched-head standards have a spreading crown. In the case of *Sorbus* x *thuringiaca* 'Fastigiata' numerous upright branches form a head of tightly ovoid shape.

STEM HEIGHT
The central-leader standard is simply a branched tree that has a clear stem to a height of about 6ft (1.8m).

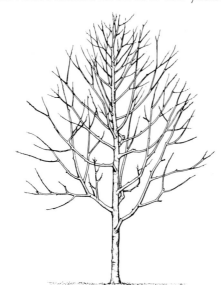

Branched-head standard

This form is suitable for many small trees, including ornamental cherries (*Prunus*) and crab-apples (*Malus*). Oaks (*Quercus*) and many other forest trees commonly develop branched crowns when mature, but these large trees should not be trained as branched-head standards. Instead, the formative pruning should maintain the dominance of the central leader.

The aim in training a branched-head standard is to establish a clear stem to a height of about 4-6ft (1.3-1.8m). If the tree is growing on its own roots or is grafted near ground level, the main stem will have to be trained up for two or three years to gain sufficient height before cutting it back to stimulate the growth of laterals that will form the branches of the head.

BRANCHED-HEAD STANDARD

For the first few years the training is the same as for a central-leader tree (see pp. 46-7)

1 In mid- to late autumn of the third year cut back the leader to a strong bud or lateral about 1-1½ft (30-46cm) above the length of clear stem required.

2 From the fourth summer staking should not be necessary. Laterals and sub-laterals develop as a result of pruning.

3 In mid- to late autumn of the fourth year simplify the head. Aim to retain a framework of 3-5 laterals. Remove any strong upright growth that might develop as a new leader.

4 In mid- to late autumn of the fifth and subsequent years prune to maintain an open-centered symmetrical head. Remove any shoots on the main stem.

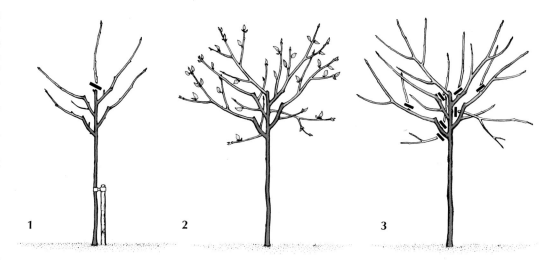

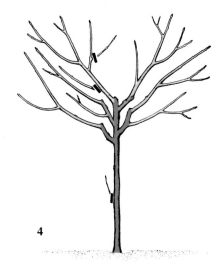

Established branched-head trees sometimes require thinning of congested growth to maintain a reasonably open center. Any growths, such as vigorous upright shoots, that distort the symmetry of the head should be cut back to a well placed lateral. If necessary, a whole branch can be cut back to the main stem.

The initial training is similar to that for a central-leader standard, with the cut-back laterals retained on the main stem for the first two or three years for strength and protection. The leader needs to be cut back to a strong bud or shoot about 1½-2ft (46-60cm) above the height at which the lowest branch is wanted. Usually three to five well-spaced laterals are allowed to develop and form the framework of the head.

The formative pruning of branched-head standards is often done at the nursery. In some cases the tree is top-worked, that is to say a selected cultivar is grafted on a clear stem of a compatible stock, the union being clearly visible just below the lowest branch. With these trees all growths on the clear stem should be rubbed out as soon as they appear.

Weeping trees

Many weeping trees are top-worked branched-head standards. The weeping form of the purple osier (*Salix purpurea* 'Pendula'), for example, is commonly grafted on to a stock of the ordinary *S. purpurea*. As with all top-worked trees, it is essential to remove any growths that develop on the main stem.

The head of a weeping tree often forms a very close overlay of pendulous branches just above the union. To create a more open head, train the topmost lateral 1-1 1/2 ft (30-46cm) up a cane as a continuation of the main stem, and allow the laterals growing from it to form an upper tier of branches.

The weeping silver pear (*Pyrus salicifolia* 'Pendula') is typical of many trees of pendulous habit that benefit from occasional drastic clearing out of the inner tangle that has been overlaid by subsequent growths.

The weeping willows (*Salix babylonica* and *S.* x. *sepulcralis*) and a few other large weeping trees are normally grown on their own roots. With these the central leader should be maintained for as long as possible.

Above: Most weeping trees grown on their own roots, as is the case with the weeping ash (*Fraxinus excelsior* 'Pendula'), need the central leader taken up to a suitable height to allow the full extension of the pendulous branches.

Far left: Most of the ornamental and fruiting cherries, including the double form of the wild cherry (*Prunus avium* 'Plena'), naturally form a branched head.

Left: Many of the flowering crabs, including the Japanese crab (*Malus floribunda*), lose their leads quickly. They make attractive branched-head trees that are suitable for gardens of modest size.

THE CARE OF ESTABLISHED TREES

Established trees often require very little pruning over many years. Sometimes the average gardener can deal safely with the removal of dead, damaged or diseased branches, which is the principal operation that needs to be carried out. However, the scale and mechanics of much tree pruning makes it potentially hazardous. Felling, the cutting back to sound wood of large limbs damaged by storm or snow that cannot be dealt with from ground level, and all tree work close to power lines should only be tackled by experienced tree surgeons.

The following information is given so that the home gardener can make intelligent decisions about the best way of caring for established trees.

Crown lifting
In the formative pruning of standards, branches below a certain height are removed to leave a clear stem (see pp. 49-51). The creation of a clear zone beneath the crown is certainly best carried out when the tree is young, but on older trees the weight of their lower branches tends to bring them down and may result in a number of problems, including shading, obstruction of access, and the blocking of view.

Lifting the crown by removing some of the lower branches or their laterals is sometimes relatively straightforward, although excessive removal of foliage from the lower part of a tree can be harmful to it. Furthermore, crown lifting may require the removal of sizeable limbs, resulting in large wounds, and on a mature tree it is often advisable to spread the pruning over two or three years.

The gardener may be able to carry out this work, removing limbs in sections (see p. 45). However, large-scale work should be done by an experienced professional tree surgeon, especially if it is carried out at a roadside or elsewhere where there is a risk to the public.

The extent of the work required is best reviewed in the second half of summer, when foliage is at its fullest. The work itself can even be carried out at this time or alternatively in the dormant season. Provided it does not mean stripping a tree, aim to maintain a balanced shape, even if it is only on one side of the tree that branches are causing shading or obstruction.

Top and above: Crown lifting, the removal of lower branches to leave a clear trunk to a given height, is best carried out when trees are young.

Crown reduction
The most sympathetic way of reducing the overall height and spread of a crown is by cutting back selected branches to lower limbs or laterals, while retaining the natural lines of the tree. After pruning, the tree will make fresh extension growth and so to maintain the crown at its new height this operation needs to be repeated on a regular basis, in some cases as frequently as every four years. A professional tree surgeon should carry out this work, for considerable experience is required in judging where it is best to make cuts and most of the work is well above ground level.

Not all trees respond equally well to this treatment. On birches (*Betula*) and poplars (*Populus*), for example, wounded tissues are prone to rotting. Some trees are intolerant of heavy cutting back; common beech (*Fagus sylvatica*) is just such a tree and should not be reduced by more than ten per cent. As a general rule, fairly young trees with relatively light branches respond better than more mature specimens. Heavy pruning can be avoided by initiating crown reduction before the tree has reached the intended height.

CROWN REDUCTION Considerable skill is needed to cut back branches to lower limbs or laterals in a way that retains the natural lines of a tree.

Crown reduction must be repeated periodically to maintain a tree at a fixed height.

Left and far left: A young *Sorbus* with a cluttered head of secondary and small branches (far left) has been crown thinned (left) to allow greater light penetration and freer circulation of air.

Left: As part of the operation of crown thinning, secondary and small branches, especially those that are crossing, are removed.

Crown thinning

This is a highly skilled technique of pruning established broad-leaved trees, mainly deciduous, by removing a proportion of secondary and small branches. It does not reduce the overall height or spread of a tree and is not used in the general course of pruning and training, but can be very beneficial in individual cases. Usually this pruning needs to be carried out by a trained tree surgeon for, quite apart from the knowledge and experience required to create a balanced head, it generally means work at some height.

The most common reason for crown thinning is to allow greater light penetration and freer circulation of air, resulting in healthier and stronger growth on trees that have produced a surplus of slender branches with few laterals. Trees with a weak branch or root system are also less vulnerable to wind damage once the head has been lightened by this type of pruning. Crown thinning is sometimes carried out when it is desirable to reduce the amount of shade cast on buildings or on other plants, and can be used to good aesthetic effect when a tree has an interesting branch structure that is obscured by heavy foliage.

Crown thinning can be carried out in the dormant season and in mid-summer. Pruning when the branches are bare is easier, but with summer pruning the increase in light penetration can be assessed immediately.

The experienced tree surgeon generally starts at the top and carries out the whole operation as one exercise. If an amateur is to prune a manageable tree, it may be necessary to carry out the work in two or more stages. Begin by taking out all dead, diseased or damaged wood. Then take out rubbing and crossing branches, shoots that are growing in to the center of the tree, and growths that form narrow angles. Further thinning may still be necessary and it is at this point that a judgment has to be made on the best branches to retain. As a general guide, retain at least two-thirds of the branches, depending on the vigor of the plant and the growing conditions.

Lopping and topping
The lopping of side branches and the topping of the main trunk are crude methods of reducing the height of trees that have become too large for the positions in which they were planted. Typically, they are used by unqualified people claiming to be experienced tree surgeons.

Lopping and topping cannot be recommended as methods of pruning: they destroy the natural shape of trees and are frequently the source of major problems. The large wounds that they create often lead to serious decay, which is not always easily detected. Furthermore, the epicormic growths that result from using these methods are normally only weakly attached and are therefore vulnerable to wind damage,

especially in towns and cities where wind speeds can be increased by the funnelling effect of buildings.

When a lopped or topped tree is part of a newly acquired garden a decision has to be made as to the best course of action. If inspection reveals that the tree is unsound, one option is to replace it with a tree or shrub that can be allowed to reach its mature size in the space available. This is generally preferable to cutting back further to sound wood. Trees that are sound will almost certainly benefit from crown reduction to reduce the risk of wind damage, or crown thinning to give the tree a more balanced and natural head.

Above: In crown thinning the *Sorbus* illustrated on the previous page, the tree surgeon has cut out branches forming narrow angles.

LARGE CUTS
The removal of large limbs frequently stimulates the growth of strong shoots from dormant or adventitious buds on the trunk of a tree. Cut these right out, preferably in the dormant season.

Above: Lindens and London planes planted in cities are often permanently maintained at a fixed height, being cut back to stumps at regular intervals. It is difficult to abandon such a regime once it has been started for, if left, trees develop long branches that are only weakly attached to the main trunk.

Pollarding and coppicing

These are traditional Old World methods of management for lumber in which trees are cut back regularly at or near ground level (coppicing) or at a suitable height (pollarding), normally above the browsing level of cattle. They are sometimes used as methods of pruning ornamentals, for example, to ensure the regular production of young colorful stems on some willows (*Salix*) or to maintain a large tree at shrub-like proportions (see also p. 72).

Pollarding is commonly used as a method of holding town trees at a fixed height, with new growth being cut back to a stump or stumps at intervals of two or three years. The

typical trees used in towns are the London plane (*Platanus* x *acerifolia*) and linden (*Tilia*). The result with planes, which are more tolerant of this type of treatment than most trees, is swollen and distorted branch stubs.

Pollarding is not a recommended method of pruning planes and lindens, but where a newly acquired garden contains trees that have been treated in this way the best course may be to continue cutting back in the dormant season. It is difficult to give a more natural shape to pollarded trees, but the best chance is by thinning and shortening long thin branches over a period of several years.

Above: The scarlet willow (*Salix alba* 'Chermesina') has colorful stems in winter. The regular cutting back of these pollarded trees maintains a supply of young stems, which color better than older wood.

Left: Regular cutting back of lindens and London planes produces characteristically swollen stubs.

SHRUBS

Provided that they are growing in suitable conditions, a great many shrubs require only minimal pruning from one year to the next. In some cases all that is needed is the cutting out of dead, diseased or damaged wood as soon as it is noticed, and the removal of the odd stray shoot that could spoil the plant's overall shape. However, with some shrubs regular pruning geared to the plant's pattern of growth and flowering can enhance the size and number of flowers and the decorative effect of foliage and stems.

On the following pages, the shrubs have been divided into six groups – four containing mainly deciduous shrubs and two for evergreens – depending on the pruning regime that is most suitable. Further examples of pruning methods are included in "Climbers and Wall Shrubs" (see pp. 80-95).

Pruning and training on their own do not guarantee optimum results. Like all plants, shrubs benefit from sound garden management and need an adequate supply of water and nutrients, especially when heavily and frequently pruned. Routine cultivation should include feeding with a general fertilizer in early spring and the application of a thick mulch of organic material.

Right: Apart from formative pruning of weak specimens, many broad-leaved evergreens, including camellias, remain shapely and bushy with a minimum of pruning.

Top right: Many deciduous shrubs flower most freely on young wood. In the case of the cultivars of French hydrangea (*Hydrangea* x *macrophylla*) new growth is stimulated by cutting out a proportion of the old wood each spring.

Center right: Although mixed plantings of shrubs require little maintenance, some annual pruning is generally needed.

Left: A number of shrubs do not respond well to pruning and some of these are relatively short-lived. *Cytisus* species and hybrids (brooms) are best replaced when they become straggly or overgrown.

Below: Regular pruning enhances the ornamental value of some shrubs. Young stems of several *Cornus* species, such as *C. stolonifera* 'Flaviramea', are brightly colored, the best results being achieved with plants that are hard-pruned each year.

CORRECTING UNEVEN GROWTH
1-4 Cut vigorous growths back lightly and weak growths hard (1). Hard pruning promotes vigorous growth and light pruning only moderate growth (2). Cutting vigorous shoots back hard and weak shoots lightly (3) exaggerates unbalanced growth (4).

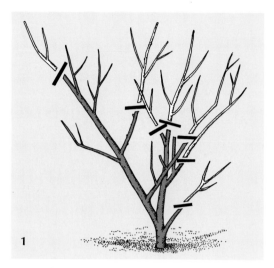

1

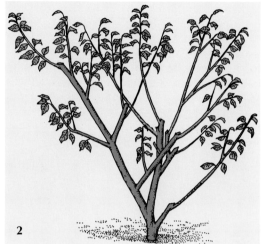

2

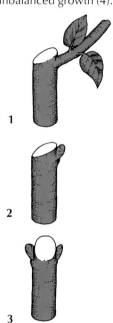

1

2

3

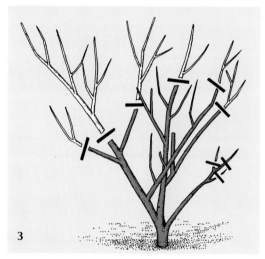

3

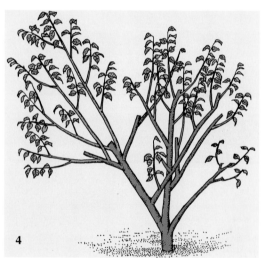

4

PRUNING CUTS
1-3 Make cuts just above and sloping back from a shoot (1), bud (2) or, in the case of plants with opposite leaves, a strong pair of buds (3). Cut to shoots or buds that are pointing in the direction that growth is desired, which is normally away from the center.

Choosing and buying plants

Many of the problems that gardeners attempt to solve by savage pruning are the consequence of bad planting and often of overplanting. In some cases bad planting is a matter of starting with poor stock that subsequently needs corrective pruning. So when buying shrubs look for plants that are bushy and well-shaped. Good nursery stock should have strong root systems, but a plant that has been left in a container too long will be root bound and will not establish well. However, making a few slashes around a tight root ball with a sharp knife or loosening and untangling the roots should help. The general management of a nursery is worth noting, for good stock is often spoiled by poor attention to detail. Plants that have suffered stress through inadequate watering and competition from weeds are generally slow to become established, show poor resistance to pests and diseases, and may never make strong plants.

Bad planting is sometimes simply a matter of placing a good plant in a position where it does not have the space to develop or where conditions, such as the degree of exposure to light, are unsuitable. Pruning is rarely a satisfactory solution to the plant that is out of scale with its setting, nor can it deal effectively with a plant that is developing in an uncharacteristic way — for example, a sun-lover making untypical elongated growths having been planted in shade. Some positions in the garden are more difficult to plant than others, but there is such a wide range of shrubs that something of appropriate size and habit can usually be found.

Close spacing of shrubs is a legitimate method of creating an early impression of maturity, but it must be combined with a program of thinning when the "fillers" are no longer needed. In an overplanted garden in which no thinning has been carried out, vigorous bullying shrubs generally win out over choicer plants. When taking over an established garden in which the planting is so dense that shrubs need cutting back, begin by culling.

Early pruning and training
With most shrubs the main effort in pruning and training is concentrated in the first few years. To establish a well-balanced framework some cutting out of surplus and badly placed shoots is often necessary. It is particularly important that this is done at an early stage with shrubs such as magnolias and witch hazels (*Hamamelis*) that rarely produce new growth from the base.

Whatever the age of the plant, a badly made cut can result in die-back or provide an entry for disease. When pruning back to main stems, cut close so that no snag is left. When removing large branches, follow the advice given for trees (see pp. 40-55). All other cuts should be made just above a single bud or shoot (or above a pair when the arrangement is opposite), facing in the direction that growth is wanted.

Very few shrubs need staking at planting, even in exposed positions. Other methods of protection are much more effective at the start. A mesh screen can cut considerably the force of the wind and reduce its dehydrating capacity. An anti-dessicant spray can give additional protection to vulnerable conifers.

Pruning established shrubs
The most usual pruning requirement of mature shrubs is to correct an unbalanced shape. The first impulse is often to reduce drastically the length of the longest branches, but cutting back hard stimulates vigorous growth. The only effective way to restore a more balanced shape is by pruning weak growths hard and cutting vigorous growths back only lightly.

On some shrubs suckers may present a problem. Although many shrubs are grown on their own roots, some are budded or grafted on to stocks. When shrubs have a naturally suckering habit and specimens on

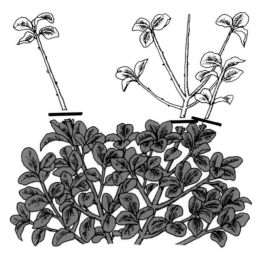

MAINTAINING THE SHAPE
Many shrubs have a naturally neat shape which is easily maintained by removing the occasional shoot that spoils the outline.

Left: *Elaeagnus pungens* 'Maculata', like a number of variegated plants, may develop shoots with pure green leaves. Shoots that have reverted should be cut out as soon as they appear for, if left, they will become dominant, growing more quickly and vigorously than the rest of the plant.

their own roots produce suckers, it is often desirable to keep these. The sarcococcas, for example, make useful groundcover when allowed to build up clumps. However, suckers that develop from the rootstock of a budded or grafted plant should be removed promptly, for if they are left they will develop at the expense of the grafted plant.

Many shrubs that are grown for their variegated foliage will sometimes throw up shoots that are a reversion to the green-leaved form of the plant. If left, these shoots generally become dominant, being more vigorous than variegated growths, and eventually almost none of the variegation will remain visible. Cut out completely growths that revert, and subsequently keep a close eye on the plant, removing any further growths that show reversion.

DECIDUOUS SHRUBS

Group 1: Deciduous shrubs requiring little pruning when mature, making most of their extension growth on the perimeter of a permanent framework of branches.

GROUP ONE

Some deciduous species and hybrids of magnolia are among a large number of shrubs that require little pruning when fully grown. However, they and the other shrubs in this group sometimes need gentle guidance when young to produce a well-balanced framework of branches.

Formative pruning and training

At planting, between late autumn and mid-spring, many specimens in this group will require no pruning at all, but any weak growths and crossing shoots should be taken out. In the spring of the second year some additional corrective pruning may be necessary if laterals or extension growths are too closely spaced.

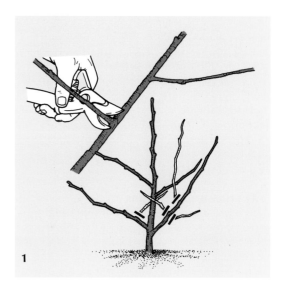

Pruning and training the mature shrub

In the third and subsequent years little more than routine pruning will be required to remove dead or diseased wood and weak shoots. Shrubs in Group One occasionally produce vigorous new shoots from the base or low on framework branches. These can sometimes be trained in as replacement growths, but when this is not possible they should be cut out at their base in order to prevent the framework of branches becoming congested.

MAGNOLIA STELLATA (STAR MAGNOLIA)

1 At planting, in late autumn or (in the north) mid-spring, cut out any badly placed growths and weak shoots.

2 In mid- to late spring of the second year little pruning is necessary unless growths are badly spaced.

3 In general, pruning is not needed in the third and subsequent years other than to remove dead, diseased or damaged wood.

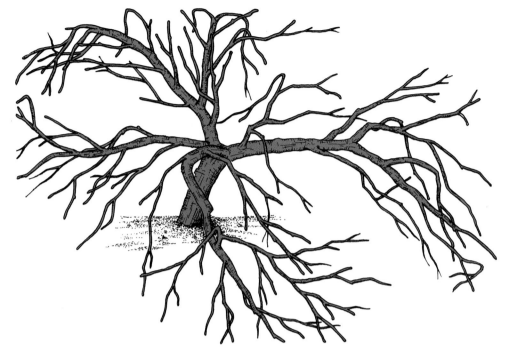

ACER PALMATUM
The growth pattern of the Japanese maples (*Acer palmatum*) is naturally intricate, and the character of these plants is spoiled by pruning to correct crossing branches.

Above left: *Acer palmatum* 'Dissectum Atropurpureum' is one of the many cultivars of the Japanese maple. Although some light pruning may be needed in the early stages, subsequent pruning is minimal.

Left: The tiered growth of *Viburnum plicatum* 'Mariesii' is a distinctive feature of the shrub and must be respected when pruning cuts are made. Occasionally it may be desirable to cut out old branches so that they can be replaced by young growths.

Above: *Magnolia stellata*, among the most useful in this genus for the small garden, requires little pruning once the framework has been established. However, like most magnolias, this species will generally make strong new growth when cut back into old wood.

GROUP 2: Shrubs that flower on shoots produced in the previous growing season and which are pruned annually after flowering.

GROUP TWO

Many deciduous shrubs that flower in the spring or early summer produce the flower-bearing shoots in the previous growing season. If left unpruned, these shrubs tend to make excessive twiggy growth and on neglected plants there is often no more than a sparse scattering of poor-quality flowers at the top of an ungainly specimen. The annual cutting out of wood that has carried flowers encourages the development of replacement shoots low down on the shrub and, everything else being equal, these vigorous shoots will flower freely the following year. This annual pruning keeps the shrub compact and shapely, but it is imperative that it is carried out immediately after flowering to give new wood time to develop and ripen before winter.

DEUTZIA

1 At planting, cut out damaged or weak growths and tip back all main shoots to a strong pair of buds. On shrubs that have alternate leaves, cut to an outward-facing bud.

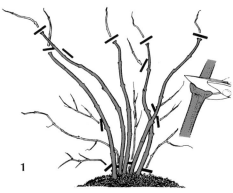

1

Right: *Forsythia* x *intermedia* and other forsythias are vivid flowering shrubs of early spring. To maintain their profuse display take out a proportion of flowered wood in late spring or early summer.

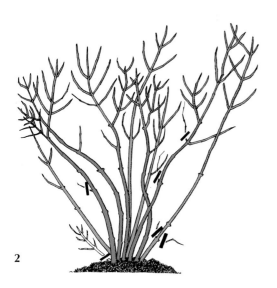

2

3

2 In the first autumn lightly prune, cutting out weak shoots and growths that create an unbalanced framework.

3 In mid-summer of the second year, as soon as blooms fade, cut back stems that have flowered to new vigorous growths low down on the main stems. Cut out any weak growths and shoots that unbalance the shape. Repeat annually and, if main stems are crowded, cut out the oldest.

Formative pruning

The aim of formative pruning, for the first year or two in the nursery and the first year in the garden, is to establish a strong and balanced framework of branches. After planting a nursery-raised specimen, any damaged or weak growth should be cut out. To encourage vigorous growth, main shoots should be cut back, normally by less than 6in (15cm), to a strong bud or pair of buds. If any flowers appear in the first season after planting, the pruning regime for the established plant should be followed, and the wood that has carried flowers cut back to strong shoots immediately after flowering. In the following autumn weak growth and badly placed shoots are removed, and the plant's shape is corrected where necessary.

Pruning the established plant

Most Group Two shrubs will get into their stride the second year after planting. As they come into flower, new growths begin to develop below the flowering wood. The strongest shoots are usually those lowest on the stem, and these are generally the best to select as replacement shoots when pruning immediately after flowering. However, this is not a guideline to follow slavishly, for pruning must also maintain a good shape.

Renewal pruning may be insufficient and a more radical cutting out of stems required if growth on the mature plant becomes crowded. Up to a quarter of old stems can be cut out when flowered wood is removed.

Above: The beauty bush (*Kolkwitzia amabilis*) can make a tall arching shrub with a height and spread of about 10ft (3m). The delicately shaded flowers are carried in great profusion in late spring and early summer. Take out whole lengths of older wood when flowering has finished.

Above: The scented flowers of *Deutzia* x *elegantissima* are carried on short laterals growing on wood produced in the previous season. When pruning after flowering aim to maintain a well-balanced shrub.

KERRIA JAPONICA

1 At planting, in autumn or early spring, retain vigorous stems and their laterals, but cut out weak shoots.

2 During the growing season new shoots and suckers grow from the base. Once flowering has finished, cut wood that has flowered back to ground level or to vigorous new shoots growing from low down on strong stems.

GROUP TWO VARIANTS

There are a number of shrubs which require variations on the basic Group Two pruning regime. Kerrias, mophead hydrangeas, and brooms are among the most widely grown of the shrubs that fall into this category.

Kerria

The shrubs in this small sub-group, the most widely grown of which is *Kerria japonica*, differ from other shrubs in Group Two by making most of their new growth from ground level. Wood that has flowered generally dies back before or during winter, but to keep these shrubs looking attractive and to encourage new shoots it is best removed immediately after flowering.

Hydrangea

The popular mophead and lacecap hydrangeas (cultivars of *H.* x *macrophylla*) will often flower quite satisfactorily with little or no pruning other than light trimming. A policy of benign neglect is better than a program of drastic pruning every spring in the hope that the new growth produced will flower at the end of the growing season. Although these hydrangeas are late flowering, the buds that produce the flowering shoots are formed in the previous growing season, so that a plant that is drastically pruned in spring is likely to produce few if any flowers in the same summer. However, established plants often make a lot of twiggy growth and cutting out a

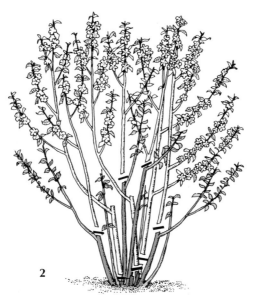

1

2

Right: 'Générale Vicomtesse de Vibraye', a mophead cultivar of *Hydrangea* x *macrophylla*, is best pruned in spring. Removing some of the older wood aids the growth of vigorous replacement shoots.

Far right: *Kerria japonica* 'Pleniflora' blooms profusely in spring but, if left unpruned, most of the flower-bearing wood will die back by winter. Cut out all stems that have flowers in early to mid-summer.

proportion of the older wood is beneficial. Vigorous replacement shoots will flower the following growing season, and the exposure of wood to light and air aids flowering.

Broom

Although brooms (*Cytisus scoparius* and its hybrids) are often left unpruned, they tend to become top-heavy, and it is rarely possible to correct their legginess by cutting back into old wood. Start renewal pruning the first year that brooms flower, cutting back to vigorous young growths low down on the shrub.

Above: The old flower heads of the mophead hydrangeas should be left on the plant throughout winter as they can be quite attractive and give some protection to young shoots.

Top right: A mophead hydrangea in early spring before (top right) and after (top far right) pruning to take out some of the old growths.

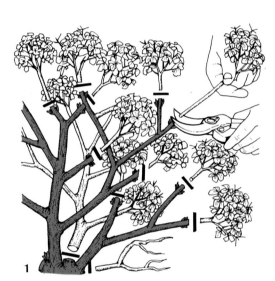

HYDRANGEA x MACROPHYLLA

1 On established plants cut out a third to a quarter of old stems, and on remaining stems cut old flower heads back to a strong pair of buds. Also remove any weak shoots.

2 Plants flower in summer and early autumn. Most flowers are carried on shoots that are at least a year old, but some of the strongest shoots resulting from pruning in spring will flower in the same year.

BROOMS

Prune brooms in early to mid-summer, immediately after flowering, cutting back the wood that has flowered to young growths at its base.

Group 3: Deciduous shrubs bearing flowers on the current season's wood, that are pruned in early spring.

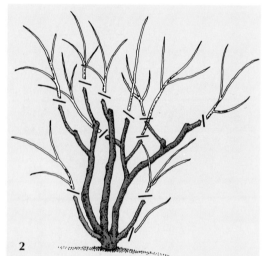

DECIDUOUS CEANOTHUS

1 At planting cut out weak or damaged growths and any badly placed shoots. Tip back main shoots, making the cuts at outward-facing buds.

2 Between early and mid-spring of the second year, cut back by about half all growth made in the previous growing season, making the cuts at strong outward-facing buds. Take out any weak shoots.

3 In early to mid-spring of subsequent years cut back shoots, leaving no more than 1 or 2 buds of the previous season's growth.

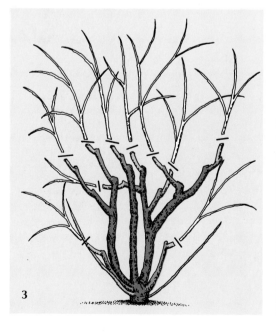

GROUP THREE

This group contains a number of valuable shrubs that flower in summer or autumn on the current season's wood and are hard pruned in early spring to promote vigorous growth. If left unpruned, these plants tend to put on new growth over a tangled twiggy core and although the flowers may be reasonably numerous, they grow at the ends of the topmost stems and steadily diminish in size as the shrub ages. Hard pruning alone will not produce vigorous growth and well-sized flowers: plants require adequate moisture and nutrients for optimum results. A good mulch applied at pruning time will help provide the right conditions for growth.

Group Three includes vigorous plants such as *Buddleia davidii*, but also some more lightly framed, including hardy fuchsias and the Russian sage, *Perovskia*. Three examples are illustrated, to show how best to prune Group Three shrubs of differing vigor.

Formative pruning

At planting, between late autumn and early spring, weak, damaged and badly placed shoots are removed. In early spring of the first year, pruning should be limited to cutting back stems; the more vigorous the

plant, the more severe the pruning. The shoots of buddleias can be cut back by up to three-quarters of their length, but in the case of *Perovskia* it is only necessary to tip back the shoots to a pair of strong buds. Most of these shrubs will flower in their first summer.

Pruning the established plant

The annual pruning should be carried out in early to mid-spring to allow maximum time for plants to make growth in spring and summer. In the case of vigorous and moderately vigorous shrubs, the annual pruning cuts back the previous season's growth close to a more or less permanent framework of branches. In the case of sub-shrubs such as *Perovskia*, all growths can be cut to near ground level. However, even some sub-shrubs can be grown with a short woody base that can give the plant useful additional height in a border.

If the framework branches become congested, as generally happens on mature buddleias, some old wood can be cut out during the annual pruning. In general, no other pruning is necessary. However, in exposed gardens it may be advisable to trim back shoots that have flowered in late autumn to avoid the risk of wind damage.

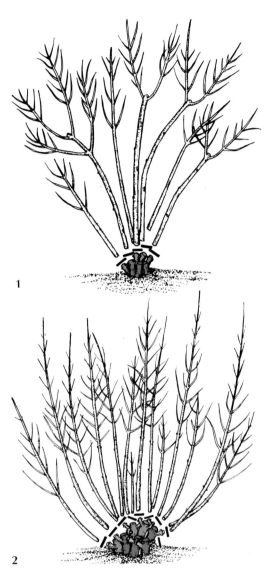

1

2

Left: *Hydrangea paniculata* carries handsome heads of flowers at the ends of growths made in the current season. Growths are cut back annually in autumn, leaving a low framework of branches.

PEROVSKIA (RUSSIAN SAGE)
At planting tip back shoots to a pair of strong buds.

1 In early to mid-spring of the second year cut stems back to strong pairs of buds, just above the ground.

2 In the third and subsequent years repeat the pruning carried out in the second year. Do not leave snags, which are likely to die back in the following year.

Right, top and bottom: In the standard method of pruning *Perovskia* all growths are cut down, just above ground level, in early to mid-spring. The plant can also be grown with a short permanent woody base to give it additional height.

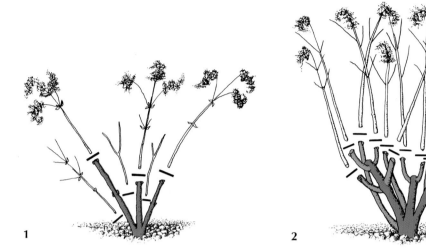

1

2

Above: *Ceratostigma willmottianum* (Chinese plumbago) is pruned in a similar way to *Perovskia*, all growths being cut back to near ground level in mid-spring.

Right: *Buddleia davidii, B. fallowiana* and their hybrids, such as 'West Hill', illustrated here, are vigorous shrubs that are cut back to a framework of permanent branches each spring.

3

BUDDLEIA DAVIDII

1 In early to mid-spring of the first year cut out weak growth completely and shorten main shoots by half to three-quarters, cutting at strong buds or where vigorous shoots are developing. The long growths that develop during the growing season will carry flowers in late summer.

2 In early to mid-spring of the second and subsequent years cut back the growths made in the previous summer, those from the base to match the height of the framework and those that have flowered to within 1 or 2 pairs of buds of the framework.

3 If plants are growing in exposed positions, cut back main shoots by about a third in mid-autumn to minimize wind damage.

Left: *Buddleia davidii nanhoensis*, a more slender shrub than most of the butterfly bushes, is shown being pruned in mid-spring, the previous season's growth being taken back to strong buds and shoots.

4

5

4/5 On mature specimens, prune in the standard way in early to mid-spring, but if the framework has become congested cut out some old branches completely and train in new basal growths as needed.

GROUP FOUR

The combination of hard spring pruning and generous feeding improves the leaf size of several shrubs grown principally for the appearance and interest of their foliage. Cultivars of the European elder (*Sambucus nigra*) that have golden, variegated or finely cut leaves respond well to this treatment, as does the purple-leaved smokebush (*Cotinus coggygria* 'Foliis Purpureis'). Increased leaf size can also enhance the effect produced by the autumn foliage color, as in the case of *Rhus typhina*.

The drastic pruning each spring of shrubs that have attractively colored stems produces an annual crop of vigorous new growths which color more vividly in winter than wood of greater age. Among those shrubs typically treated in this way are the red- and green-stemmed dogwoods (*Cornus alba* and *Cornus stolonifera* 'Flaviramea'). Drastic annual pruning is also the best way to get maximum decorative effect from white-stemmed brambles such as *Rubus cockburnianus*. After their first winter the stems lose their ghostly whiteness.

However, as most of the shrubs in Group Four flower on wood produced in the previous year, flowering will be sacrificed when drastic spring pruning is carried out. In most cases the quality of the foliage is more than ample compensation for the lack of flowering, and this pruning allows a number of desirable plants to be grown in relatively small gardens which could not accommodate them if they were left to develop fully.

Formative pruning

Some shrubs in this group, for example the white-stemmed brambles, have a suckering habit and do not form a woody base. In the spring of their first year, all stems are cut back to ground level. Dogwoods and willows are generally cut back 3-4in (7.5-10cm) from ground level to form a low, woody framework or stool. The more vigorous shrubs, such as *Cotinus coggygria*, are cut back to form a framework of three or four main stems about 1-1½ft (30-46cm) long. In the case of all shrubs that form a woody framework, the height can be varied to suit the planting position. For example, willows are often grown as a pollard, a single stem being allowed to develop to the required height over two or three years before being cut back.

Pruning the established shrub

Shrubs that do not form a woody framework are simply cut back close to ground level in

COTINUS COGGYGRIA (SMOKEBUSH)
Cultivars grown mainly for their foliage, such as *C. c.* 'Foliis Purpureis', are best pruned hard annually, but this will result in the loss of flowers.

1 At planting, in early to mid-spring, cut out all weak growths from the base and shorten remaining strong stems to 1-1½ft (30-46cm). Vigorous shoots will carry large, well-colored foliage in the growing season.

2 In early spring of subsequent years cut the previous season's growth hard back to buds 1-2in (2.5-5cm) beyond the framework.

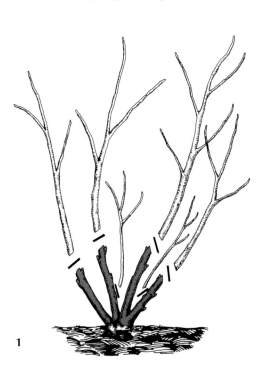

1

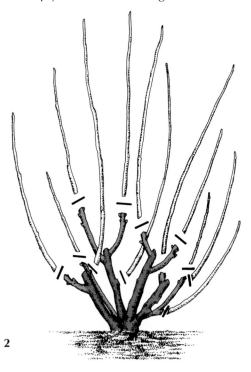

2

early to mid-spring. In general, other shrubs have all the previous season's growth cut back close to the woody framework, just as they are coming into leaf. However, less drastic pruning can often produce a fuller and more satisfactory display, particularly of plants grown primarily for their foliage. On elders, for example, in any one year only half the growths need be cut back close to the framework, the other half being shortened by about half. In the following spring all of these less heavily pruned growths should be cut back close to the framework.

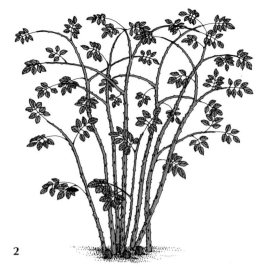

2

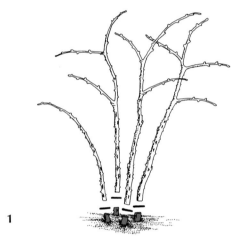

1

3

RUBUS COCKBURNIANUS

1 At planting, in early to mid-spring, cut down all stems at ground level.

2 In the first and subsequent years plants produce new stems during the growing season and these remain attractive even after their leaves have fallen.

3 In early to mid-spring of the second and subsequent years cut down all stems at ground level.

Far left: The white bloom over purple makes the stems of *Rubus cockburnianus* (grown in Europe) highly ornamental, especially in winter. New canes are produced annually, the old ones being cut down in the first half of spring.

Left: The foliage of *Cotinus coggygria* 'Flame' is brilliantly colored in autumn. Annual spring pruning enhances the effect, but at the expense of the pink flowers. Specimens that are pruned in this way should be well mulched and fed.

Right: Annual cutting back of *Cornus alba* 'Sibirica' results in brilliant crimson stems that remain attractive throughout winter.

CORNUS ALBA (TARTARIAN DOGWOOD)

1 At planting, between early and mid-spring, cut all growths hard back, leaving a short base 2-4in (5-10cm) high. The whippy shoots that develop in the growing season color well in autumn and winter.

2 In early to mid-spring of the second and subsequent years cut out all weak growths and cut back main stems to within 2-3in (5-7.5cm) of the base.

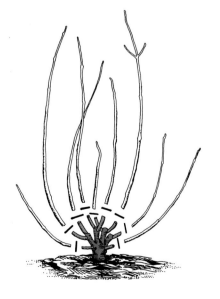

Coppiced and pollarded trees

The method of pruning used to enhance the ornamental effects of foliage and bark involves two traditional methods of woodland management, coppicing and pollarding, in which trees such as chestnut (*Castanea sativa*) are cut back regularly to produce recurrent crops of firewood and lumber. It can be used for ornamental purposes on trees that have well-colored shoots and would normally grow to a considerable height, such as cultivars of *Salix alba*, and for the tree of heaven (*Ailanthus altissima*), which produces luxuriant foliage. The eucalypts (gum trees) are included here even though, unlike other trees in this group, they are evergreens. When kept to a shrub-like scale they retain the attractive juvenile form of their foliage.

Above, top right and top left: In moist or wet soils, *Cornus stolonifera* 'Flaviramea' suckers freely, forming dense thickets of bright greenish-yellow stems (above). The color is more pronounced on young stems, so cut all shoots back to near ground level in spring (top, left and right).

Left: Many willows have colored stems that are highly ornamental in winter, such as this coppiced specimen of *Salix irrorata*, which has a white bloom over purplish brown stems.

Left: As the coloring is most striking on the young stems of *Salix irrorata* (above left), the aim of pruning is to maintain a supply of young wood. Prune annually in spring, cutting out some of the oldest wood right to the base.

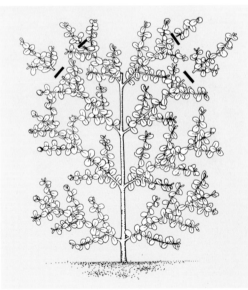

Left: At the same time as removing the older wood (above left), cut back some new basal growths as replacement framework branches. Some of the older stems should be cut back to the framework branches.

EUCALYPTUS (top and above) One method of growing *Eucalyptus*, especially applicable to those with attractive juvenile foliage such as *E. gunnii*, is to coppice or pollard specimens in mid-spring (top). When coppicing, cut all growths to near ground level. On a pollarded specimen the main stem is cut back at the desired height and the shoots cut back to this point each year. Another method is to maintain a bush form (above) by cutting back the leader just below the desired height and subsequently keeping the plant at this size by pruning back upright growths in early to mid-spring. If the plant outgrows its position, cut it back hard in mid-spring.

EVERGREEN SHRUBS

**GROUP 1: Evergreen
shrubs that require
only minimal pruning.**

CAMELLIAS
1 To encourage bushy
growth, cut back the
leader of a leggy
specimen in mid- to
late spring, making the
cut above a strong bud.

2 In early to mid-
summer train in the
topmost lateral as the
replacement leader.

Above: Although
growth patterns vary,
most established
camellias need little
pruning. Early pruning
aims to produce well-
furnished specimens.

Right: Unless seed is
needed for
propagation,
rhododendrons should
be deadheaded
immediately after
flowering. This will
produce vigorous
new growth as on this
specimen.

GROUP ONE

Most broad-leaved evergreen shrubs require very little pruning and training. Provided they are grown in appropriate conditions and given adequate space, most develop naturally bushy growth and a reasonably balanced shape.

If young evergreens, such as camellias, have weak leading shoots, corrective pruning and training will create a well-balanced shrub. Cutting back the leader by 2-3in (5-7.5cm) stimulates the development of laterals and the topmost of these can be trained in as a replacement leader.

As with all shrubs, it may be necessary from time to time to take out dead, diseased or damaged wood and to deal with crossing branches or the occasional growths that mar the plant's shape. Although most of these operations can be carried out at any time of the year, pruning that will encourage growth should only be carried out in the second half of spring. Earlier pruning will lead to precocious growth, which risks being damaged by frost and wind, and, if pruning is carried out later in the growing season, shoots are unlikely to ripen before winter and may be killed or damaged in cold weather.

The production of seed diverts energy that would otherwise go into new growth and flower buds. Whenever feasible, evergreens that produce an abundance of seed, such as rhododendrons, should be deadheaded after the flowers have faded.

Dwarf conifers

Some of the so-called "dwarf conifers" will ultimately exceed a height of 6ft (1.8m), but even these are compact slow-growing shrubs, planted as much for their distinctive forms as for the attractive color and texture of their foliage. Healthy specimens do not need pruning and any cutting away of growth is likely to spoil the character of the plant. It is rarely necessary, but the growth of species and cultivars of pine (*Pinus*) can be made more compact by pinching out the top half of the candle-like buds in spring, just as the needles begin to elongate. The tips of the needles will turn brown if damaged by cutting.

Die-back, especially of branches at the base, is commonly caused by neighboring plants cutting out light. New growth is unlikely to develop from old wood that has been cut back.

Above: Whatever pruning conifers need must take into account the characteristic growth pattern of species or cultivar.

Left: Most conifers, and especially dwarf or slow-growing species and cultivars, require very little pruning. *Picea glauca albertiana* 'Conica' has a naturally neat pyramidal habit.

GROUP 2: Broad-leaved evergreen shrubs or sub-shrubs that are hard pruned to keep them compact or to increase their flowering potential.

GROUP TWO

If left to their own devices, a number of small evergreen shrubs tend to deteriorate rather quickly, producing fewer and fewer flowers and becoming bare at the base. Some will tolerate rather brutal treatment. Cotton lavender (*Santolina*), for example, can be cut almost to ground level in spring, preferably every year, although a regime of light trimming for one or two years with drastic pruning in the second or third year is an alternative. Some shrubs grown as ground cover, such as rose of Sharon (*Hypericum calycinum*) and *Mahonia aquifolium*, are most easily dealt with by shearing off the old growths in spring.

Lavender

New shoots do not break readily from the old wood of lavenders, so these shrubs need to be kept compact from an early stage. Young plants should be cut back hard in their first year and in subsequent years trimmed in mid-spring, just as new growth is starting. Although dead flowers can be removed in autumn, in cold areas it is worth retaining them through the winter until the spring pruning for they give the foliage some protection from severe cold.

LAVENDER

1 In mid-spring of the first year, hard prune newly planted lavenders to encourage strong bushy growth.

2 To keep established plants compact and vigorous, annually in mid-spring trim off old flower spikes and 1-2in (2.5-5cm) of the growth made in the previous season.

1

2

Right: Dead lavender flower spikes protect the shoots from winter frosts. They should be retained, other than in mild temperate areas, until mid-spring.

Far right: Trim lavenders in mid-spring. Avoid cutting back into old wood and retain the bushy rounded shape.

Above: The many cultivars of *Calluna vulgaris*, such as 'H.E. Beale', are among the summer- and autumn-flowering heathers which become leggy if not trimmed in spring.

DEADHEADING
The dead flower heads on many summer- and autumn-flowering heathers remain attractive throughout the winter. Trim these off in mid-spring: cut just below the old flower spikes.

Above: Without annual pruning most lavenders, including the relatively compact *Lavandula angustifolia* 'Hidcote', will become bare at the base; once in this condition they cannot be rejuvenated by cutting back into the old wood.

Heaths and heathers
These are a mixed group, some of which require little or no pruning other than a light trim to remove old flower heads. However, the summer- and autumn-flowering plants (*Calluna vulgaris, Daboecia cantabrica, Erica ciliaris, E. vagans* and their cultivars) become leggy and flowering deteriorates if they are not trimmed regularly in spring. Some of these heaths and heathers have attractive foliage in winter.

RENOVATION

Right: Usually lilacs (*Syringa vulgaris*) will flower well for years, especially if regularly deadheaded.

RENOVATING A LILAC

1 When a lilac has become bare at the base, renovate by drastic cutting back between late autumn and late winter. Cut all main stems to within 2ft (60cm) of the ground, taking out completely any that will unbalance the plant's shape. Remove any weak growths.

2 In mid-autumn of the same year reduce the shoots on each main stem to 2 or 3, leaving the best placed and most vigorous.

Drastic pruning is often an effective way of rejuvenating a neglected shrub or one that has outgrown its space. However, this harsh remedy is not foolproof and with less common plants, for example a mature specimen of a choice rhododendron, it would be worth considering other options. It might be possible, for instance, to sacrifice a neighboring plant. It is certainly advisable to propagate any unusual plants before major surgery. The likelihood of a shrub making a good recovery after being cut back is greatly increased if it is well fed and watered; in particular the first growing season after pruning is critically important.

Deciduous shrubs

Lilacs and many other deciduous shrubs can be cut back hard in a single operation carried out in the dormant season. The aim is to cut out all but 1-2ft (30-60cm) of the main stems, retaining only the wood that is sound and well placed to form the base of the rejuvenated plant. During the subsequent growing season the stumps will produce numerous shoots. In the second winter, these need to be thinned, leaving two or three per stump that are strong and evenly spaced.

With some deciduous shrubs that have a light framework of branches, such as *Deutzia* and *Philadelphus*, heavy pruning can be staged over two years. In the first winter, only about half of the old stems should be cut out, the remainder being removed in the following dormant season. By this time there should already be vigorous new basal shoots. Flowering, reduced for two years, will return to normal in the third summer.

Evergreen shrubs

Rhododendrons and cherry laurel (*Prunus laurocerasus*), which normally require very little pruning, are typical of vigorous evergreens that may eventually outgrow their space. Most of these evergreens respond well when cut back to within about 2ft (60cm) of ground level. In order to ensure the even development of the shrub, the hard pruning is best carried out in one stage, in late spring or early summer. Rhododendrons can be dealt with as soon as they have finished flowering, but the pruning of laurel should be delayed until early summer because, like all *Prunus*, this shrub is susceptible to silver leaf and bacterial canker.

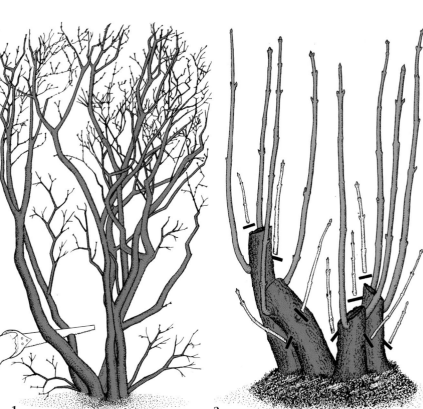

1   2

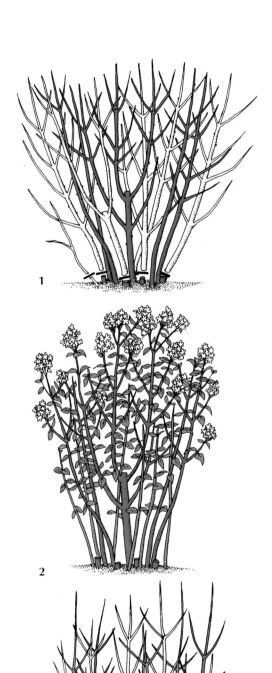

RENOVATING A DEUTZIA (Left)

1 When a *Deutzia* has become old and twiggy, renovate by drastic pruning between late autumn and late winter. In the first winter cut all twiggy growth to the base. Leave strong basal growths, but cut back to near ground level about half of the old stems.

2 In the next summer plants flower sparsely on the wood that is left. New growths develop from below ground level or near the base.

3 Between late autumn and late winter of the second year cut out the remaining old stems. In the following summer plants will flower sparsely on the growths made the previous year.

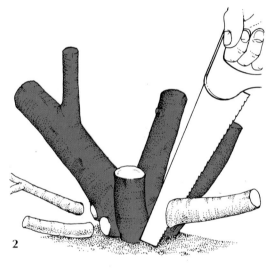

RENOVATING A CHERRY-LAUREL (Right)

1 When a cherry-laurel (*Prunus laurocerasus*) has become straggly or too large, hard prune in mid- to late spring. Cut all main stems to within 1-2ft (30-60cm) of ground level and remove any weak growths that remain.

2 At the same time cut out completely any stump that is badly placed and will lead to unbalanced growth.

3 In mid- to late spring of the second year reduce the number of shoots per stump to 2 or 3, retaining the strongest and best placed.

CLIMBERS AND WALL SHRUBS

The climbers are a versatile group of plants, often equipped with specially adapted leaves, stems or tendrils that allow them to work their way up through other plants or to climb rocks and tree trunks. It is general practice to group with the true climbers a number of shrubs that are suitable for wall training. In some cases these are shrubs that are not reliably hardy in the open garden, but which stand a much better chance of thriving when backed by a sunny wall. Others, which may be fairly lax in their growing habits, are readily trained provided that there is an adequate means of support.

Together, the climbers and wall shrubs constitute a valuable yet relatively underused group of ornamentals. Many are fast-growing, quickly masking and screening whatever is dreary or unsightly and giving an established feeling to a garden. On pergolas and arches in the open garden climbers give height and an impression of maturity that would take many years to achieve using trees. Some of these plants are of exceptional beauty and fully justify the effort needed to show them at their best. A lingering prejudice against them is based on a fear that they may damage buildings and other supports. However, provided that plants and supports are well matched there is negligible risk.

Above right: Vigorous self-clinging climbers, such as *Parthenocissus tricuspidata*, can easily swamp a small building. Even on a large building it is necessary to cut growth back from windows, doors and gutters.

Right: Wisteria and ivy (*Hedera*) can be trained in several ways. Here, wisteria grows out horizontally from the top level of a terrace, tied in to beams that span a recess in the supporting wall, and a variegated ivy has been used to highlight the arched niches in the recess.

Left: The cultivars of flowering quince (*Chaenomeles*) are among the most popular spring-flowering wall shrubs. Regular pruning after flowering forms short flower-bearing spurs.

Left: Young plants of climbing hydrangea (*Hydrangea anomala petiolaris*) may take a year or two before they cling well to their support, but once the aerial roots take hold the plant grows vigorously and is capable of climbing into a large tree.

Above: Ivy is a valuable climber that tolerates a wide range of growing conditions. It can be trained to fill almost any shape and tolerates trimming.

Types of climbers and wall shrubs

The true climbers include the natural clingers, such as English ivy (*Hedera*) and Virginia creeper (*Parthenocissus quinquefolia*). These are equipped with aerial roots or sucker pads that make it possible for them to climb most surfaces without the aid of additional supports. Another important group of climbers, including clematis and wisteria, have twining stems, leaf-stalks or tendrils. In the wild they work their way up to the light by catching hold of the stems of other plants. Some climbers use rougher scrambling methods. Roses, for example, use their hooked thorns to grip other plants or rocks. Some plants of rather floppy growth, such as *Jasminum nudiflorum*, rely on supple shoots.

Below: Twiners, such as the climbing honeysuckles (*Lonicera*), need wires, trellis or netting as a support. *Lonicera* x *americana* can be pruned immediately after flowering. Like most honeysuckles, if left unpruned it will develop unattractive, tangled growth above bare stems.

The range of shrubs that is grown against walls includes many that can be grown satisfactorily in the open garden, but which respond well to pruning and training. A wall-trained *Chaenomeles*, for example, is comparable to a restricted form of fruit tree: the spur pruning used to ensure a good display of flowers is essentially the same as the method used to get good crops from cordon- and espalier-grown apples.

In cool, temperate areas the protection offered by a wall or fence allows a number of plants of borderline hardiness to be grown outdoors. In the open garden these might stand very little chance of surviving a cold winter or spring, but can often flourish for years at the base of a sunny wall.

Methods of support

The self-clinging climbers need no more than a surface to which they can attach themselves. Whether the support is a tree or some architectural element, it should be checked for soundness.

One of the most attractive ways of growing twiners in the garden is to allow them to grow through shrubs or up into trees. The support must be sturdy enough: yew (*Taxus baccata*) topiary or hedging can take a draping of the flame creeper (*Tropaeolum speciosum*), but would be overwhelmed by *Clematis montana*, and a substantial tree is needed to support a climber as vigorous as *Hydrangea anomala petiolaris*.

It has to be admitted that the beauty of climbers and wall shrubs is often sadly marred by the inferior man-made supports against which they are trained. The range includes trellis, netting, and wires firmly fixed to walls or fences.

Free circulation of air reduces the risk of disease, so all supports need to be set slightly away from the wall. Wires should be held 6-9in (15-23cm) from the vertical surface by vine-eyes. For a mixed planting of climbers and wall shrubs, wires are normally run horizontally along the wall, but most twiners are happier with wires running vertically. Netting is often useful around old stumps, and sometimes even around living trees, as a support for the shorter climbers, such as some of the clematis.

Some of the most effective displays of climbers are those achieved on arches or pergolas. The long racemes of some wisterias – those of *Wisteria floribunda* 'Macrobotrys' can be more than 3ft (90cm) long – are seen at their elegant best when allowed to hang uncluttered. Arches and pergolas need to be solidly built and capable of supporting the considerable weight of mature plants.

General pruning and training

Climbers and wall shrubs present two extremes of pruning and training. Where there is sufficient space, climbers can be allowed to follow an unrestricted course, as much of their appeal lies in the exuberance of their growth. At the other extreme there are a number of climbers and shrubs that unless pruned and trained regularly make flopping, untidy messes, consuming space without giving an adequate return.

It must be stressed that for all climbers and wall shrubs correct planting and early training is of great importance. The soil near walls is generally poor and dry and should be improved by the addition of compost. Plant about 1 ½ ft (46cm) away from the wall with the roots fanned outward. Climbers that are intended to grow up trees are often slow starting and are best planted in well-prepared ground away from the trunk and initially trained up a cane against the tree.

Plants that have developed long, thin shoots will need cutting back at planting to encourage vigorous growth from the base. Wall shrubs and scrambling or flopping climbers need the growths to be tied in regularly, but the availability of simple twists, rings, and ties simplifies this operation.

Left: Although creepers can create a picturesque effect, the vigor of some plants, especially species of *Parthenocissus*, may cause problems if allowed to take over a building.

With wall shrubs, the early pruning of breastwood will encourage compact growth. Shrubs on which the breastwood has been allowed to grow unchecked are vulnerable to storm and snow damage.

As a general rule, the advice given for shrubs on the timing of pruning applies also to the plants in this category. Prune climbers and wall shrubs that flower in spring and early summer on growths made the previous season, as soon as they have finished flowering. Climbers and wall shrubs that flower in late summer on the current season's wood should be pruned in late winter or early spring. Some plants benefit from specific pruning regimes and examples of these are given on pages 60–77.

Above left: The self-clinging *Parthenocissus tricuspidata* 'Veitchii' needs light trimming.

Above: The shorter-growing wisterias, such as *Wisteria venusta*, are vigorous twining climbers: a pergola provides ideal support.

HEDERA

Above: The aerial roots of ivies take time to establish a firm hold. The process is speeded up if shoots can be held in position with light sticks or a wire.

Above right: Ivy lends itself to many kinds of training. Here it has been trained to form a crisscross pattern on a low wall, the design being maintained by regular trimming.

The ivies (species and cultivars of *Hedera*) are the most widely grown of the self-clinging climbers. They are outstanding for their foliage and also for their tolerance of a wide range of growing conditions, in sun or shade. In their juvenile stage they form naturally dense cover, with the overlapping leaves all arranged in the same plane and the stems clinging to their support by aerial roots. In the adult stage, which may take many years to reach, the plants form bushy, non-climbing stems with leaves that are normally unlobed. It is these stems that carry the clusters of greenish-yellow flowers and later the berries.

Very often no pruning or training is needed during the long period that plants remain in the juvenile stage. Left to themselves, ivies form a densely covered center with questing shoots creating an attractively irregular outline. However, they are easily cut back to form a specific shape, most effectively when they highlight an architectural feature, such as a niche.

Provided it has adequate support, ivy can be grown to cover almost any shape and will take regular clipping. It can be used to form low hedges on a framework of netting or more fanciful shapes on wire frames. The small-leaved cultivars of *Hedera helix* are suitable for giving a close finish to shapes that can be even freer in form than topiary in box (*Buxus*) or yew (*Taxus*).

Initial pruning and training

Ivies can be slow to start climbing, especially in exposed positions. It helps to plant with the roots fanned out from the support, and to have the shoots leaning into it and held in position (they can be tucked under a wire or tied to short lengths of light cane). Plants will often send out long shoots along the base of a wall, from which side shoots with aerial roots will grow vertically. When growing on a framework to create a specific shape, regularly pinch out shoots to encourage bushy growth and tie in.

Pruning and training established plants

While it remains in its juvenile stage, an ivy trained to a sound wall or growing up a healthy tree is unlikely to cause serious damage. Eventually, however, the aerial roots may penetrate and damage mortar, and tree growth may be depressed if ivy is allowed to spread over young branches.

The branching growth of the mature flowering wood that develops high up on an ivy can pose a more serious problem, making a wall or tree top-heavy. This is a strong reason for maintaining plants at the juvenile stage by cutting out the non-clinging shoots. Ivies may contribute to damage by hiding problems, such as cavities in trees, or by cluttering pipes and gutters. Because of this, they should be cut well back from the vulnerable parts of a building.

CLEMATIS

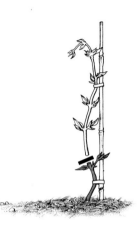

INITIAL PRUNING
In late winter of the first year cut back newly planted clematis (all groups) to the lowest pair of strong buds.

Right: Clematis can be integrated with border plants when they are grown as standards. A pole sheathed with netting provides a simple support.

In temperate gardens, the climbing species and hybrids of clematis rank after roses as the most important flowering ornamentals for covering walls and fences. In the wild, clematis hoist themselves up to the light by twisting their specially adapted leaf-stalks around the stems and branches of shrubs, trees and other climbers. Some of the most beautiful effects they can produce in the garden are achieved by allowing them to clamber through other plants. However, wire, trellis and netting are all adequate substitutes for living supports, and make it easy to train clematis over arches and pergolas as well as up walls and fences. They can also be used to disguise old tree stumps and other eyesores.

Clematis rarely need tying but if, as is sometimes recommended, they are trained up poles to add height to a border, tying will be needed if the pole is not sheathed in netting. Even when grown without support, they can be attractive, for example when planted to spill trailing stems from a tall container (chimney pots are ideal). When other plants are used as supports it is important to match the clematis to a shrub or tree of suitable vigor. Sturdy shrubs such as Japanese quince (*Chaenomeles*) and viburnums are ideal for moderately vigorous clematis, but would be swamped by *Clematis montana*. If vigorous clematis are to be trained into trees, plant in well-prepared, clear ground near the outer limit of branches and lead growths into the tree by a cane.

At planting, all clematis should be cut back to the lowest pair of strong buds to encourage the development of growths from the base. This applies even to clematis vines planted in spring or early summer that are in leaf at the time.

Although many clematis will continue to flower year after year without regular pruning, most tend to become bare at the base, carrying their flowers high up over a tangled mass of old stems. Provided they are well fed and watered, some plants will respond well to occasional and drastic pruning that involves cutting back into old wood. However, the response is far from predictable, as brutal surgery can result in sudden death or weakened growth.

With regular pruning a plant can be kept manageable and free-flowering. However, no single method satisfactorily meets the

needs of all clematis, some of which flower on wood produced in the previous year, some on the current season's growth, and yet others that flower on both old and new wood. In the recommendations that follow, clematis have been treated as three groups depending on the way in which they flower.

GROUP 1: Species and hybrids that flower in summer and autumn on growths produced in the current season.

Below: The large-flowered hybrid 'Perle d'Azur' should be cut back hard annually in late winter.

GROUP ONE

This group includes species such as *Clematis orientalis* and *C. tangutica*; *C. texensis*, *C. viticella*, and the cultivars that are closely related to them; along with a number of large-flowered hybrids, such as *C.* x *jackmanii* and 'Perle d'Azur'. If not pruned back regularly, the new growths – and therefore the flowers – are produced at a progressively greater height over bare stems. The standard advice is to cut these clematis back to the lowest pair of strong buds on each stem in the second half of winter. In areas with a mild climate, this winter pruning can be carried out as soon as the plants become dormant.

1

GROUP 1
Cut back at planting (see p.85). Train in all growths during the following growing season. Plants may carry a few flowers.

1 In mid- to late winter of the second year cut back each stem to the lowest pair of strong buds.

2 Train in spring and summer growth to the wires. Flowers will be carried on the current season's growth.

3 In the third and subsequent years, repeat the second-year pruning: cut back all stems to the lowest pair of strong buds.

2

3

GROUP TWO

These are best pruned just after flowering to give ample growing time for the wood that will carry flowers the following year. On moderate growers such as *Clematis alpina*, *C. macropetala* and their cultivars, it is a simple operation to cut back laterals that have flowered to one or two buds from the framework branches; it is more difficult to carry out on such vigorous clematis as *C. montana* and its cultivars, as they can make 40ft (12.2m) of growth. Fortunately these will tolerate being sheared over in early summer, and where practicable this is a better option than leaving the plant unpruned.

Most of the clematis in this group will tolerate drastic cutting back. Plants that are hard-pruned in early summer and well-watered and fed during the growing season should flower again the following spring, whereas if the pruning is done in winter a whole flowering season will be lost.

GROUP 2: Spring-flowering species and cultivars, some very vigorous, which flower early on short shoots produced from growths formed the previous summer.

Right: *Clematis montana* and its cultivars are vigorous climbers that flower in spring. They tend to build up tangled growth if left unpruned, and the simplest method of dealing with them is to shear them over once they have flowered.

GROUP 2
At planting cut back stems (see p. 85). Train in the growth that is made during the following spring and summer.

1 In mid- to late winter of the second year shorten the growths made the previous year by about half: cut each stem at a pair of strong buds to encourage vigorous growth low down on the plant. Train in growths made during the following spring and summer.

2 In early summer prune established plants wherever this is possible by cutting back growths that have flowered to within 1 or 2 buds of the framework branches.

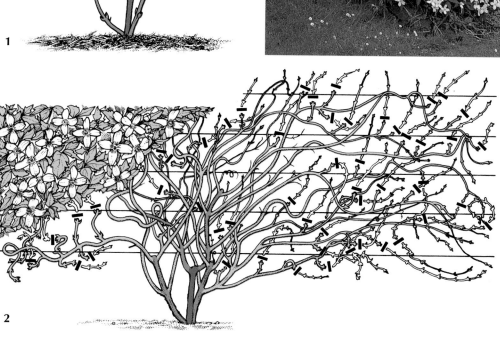

Group 3: Clematis that flower on old wood and subsequently, in the same season, on new wood.

GROUP THREE

Clematis in this group include 'Mrs N. Thompson', 'Nelly Moser', 'The President' and 'Vyvyan Pennell'. The last example, like several others, has double blooms in its first flowering and single blooms later in the season. The advice sometimes given for large-flowered hybrids is to leave them entirely unpruned or only very lightly pruned. In situations where it is difficult to disentangle the stems, for example when they are grown among shrubs, this may be the only sensible course to follow. However, the tangled growth will eventually need to be cleared by cutting right back to old wood. If this is done in late winter, there will be no flowers in early summer.

A course often followed, sometimes in ignorance but also sometimes intentionally, is to prune these clematis regularly in the same way as those in Group One. The result of cutting away the previous season's wood is the loss of the first crop of flowers, but as compensation the plants bear a good second crop in late summer or autumn.

A renewal system of pruning offers the best chance of keeping plants manageable and producing flowers in early summer and again later in the season. The aim is to cut back a proportion of the stems – about a quarter to a third – as soon as the first flush of blooms has faded. The flowers of the second flush will be carried on young shoots produced during the growing season. The renewal pruning can be carried out in late winter, but the first and main flowering will be reduced greatly.

GROUP 3:
Cut back at planting (see p. 85), and train in growths made in the following spring and summer.

1 In mid-to late winter of the second year cut back by about half all main stems that developed in the previous growing season. This will stimulate growth from low down on the plant.

2 If necessary, train in wayward growths during the second summer. There will probably be some flowers on the current season's wood in late summer or autumn.

3 Begin renewal pruning in the third year. In mid-summer, immediately after the first flowering has finished, cut a quarter to a third of old stems to within 1ft (30cm) of the ground.

Left: Wherever possible a renewal system of pruning is best suited to the large-flowered hybrids such as 'Nelly Moser' that bloom in early summer and often again in late summer or autumn. If this is not practicable, the best course is to leave these hybrids unpruned.

Right and far right: The flowers produced on the old wood of 'Vyvyan Pennell' are large and double (right), but those produced later in the year (far right) on the current season's growth are single and smaller. Some old wood can be cut out after the first flowering.

WISTERIAS

Wisterias are vigorous twining climbers that deserve to be well trained in order to display their beautiful pendulous racemes of pea flowers to the best advantage. They can make a spectacular sight when allowed to grow freely, for example scaling a robust tree, but eventually can kill the tree. Even the exceptionally vigorous Chinese wisteria (*Wisteria sinensis*), which if left to its own devices can extend for 100ft (30m), can be controlled by pruning and training to create a permanent framework of branches draped over a pergola, or espaliered against a sunny wall. Wisterias can also be grown successfully as standards, the branched head being supported on a clear stem 4-5ft (1.2-1.5m) high, and even in bush form, with the branches grown to a height of about 6ft (1.8m) and tied to stakes for support.

The formative pruning of an espalier is described below. The technique does not differ greatly for other forms, except that the main stem must be cut back at the right point to stimulate the growth of laterals where they are needed to form the permanent branches. For a specimen that is being grown on a pergola, this means training a main stem up to the horizontal level of the pergola before making the cut; for a bush specimen, the cut must be made near ground level.

In all methods of training, plants need initial support and ruthless thinning of surplus growth. Annual cutting back of the vigorous laterals that are produced in summer, and subsequent shortening in winter, form flower-bearing spurs, so that by controlling growth in this way ("spur pruning") the flowering potential is increased considerably. Wisterias have a reputation for being slow to come to flowering, but if spur pruning is started early plants should begin flowering in their fourth or fifth year.

Forming an espalier
The aim in forming an espalier is to create a framework of well-spaced, horizontal branches trained to left and right of a main stem. The method described can be adapted for training a wisteria against a house wall, where allowance must be made for doors and windows. On an uninterrupted wall the branches should be spaced about 1.5ft (46cm) apart so that the flowers from one tier do not hang down over those of the tier below. The supporting wires should be in place before planting. They need to be 9-12in (23-30cm) apart to allow for the alternate arrangement of branches; the lowest wire should be 2-3ft (60-90cm) above ground level. From the second year, formative pruning of the framework should go hand in hand with spur pruning.

At planting, in autumn or early spring, select a strong shoot as the main stem and cut it back to 2.5-3ft (76-90cm) above ground level. Remove all other shoots and tie the stem to a cane. This tipping back will stimulate the development of laterals. Tie in the topmost as an extension of the main stem, and select two that are well placed to train in left and right as the first pair of arms. As horizontal training of laterals in the first year might severely check their growth, train them in at an angle of approximately 45 degrees. When these are lowered to the horizontal in the following winter, shorten them by about a third. The laterals that

Below: The long racemes of *Wisteria floribunda* 'Macrobotrys' need to hang freely from a support such as a pergola if they are to be seen to best effect.

FORMING AN ESPALIER

1 In winter or early spring cut back the main stem of a newly planted wisteria at a bud 2.5-3ft (76-90cm) above ground level. Remove all other shoots and tie the stem to a cane.

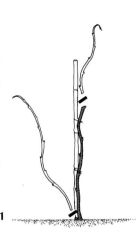

1

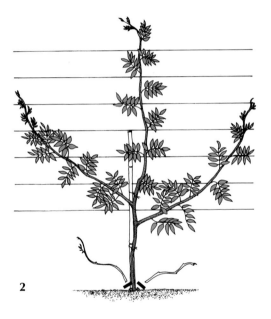

2

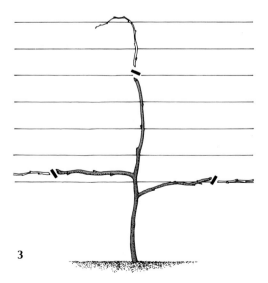

3

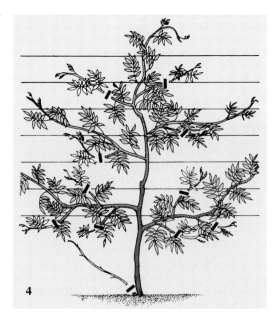
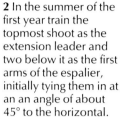
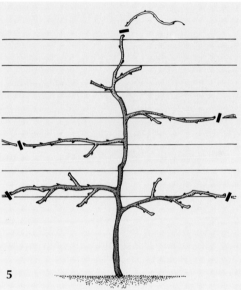

4

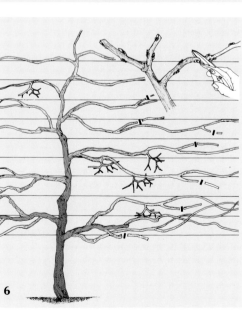

5

6

2 In the summer of the first year train the topmost shoot as the extension leader and two below it as the first arms of the espalier, initially tying them in at an angle of about 45° to the horizontal.

3 In winter of the second year lower the arms to the horizontal and shorten them by about a third. Cut back the vertical leader to within 30-36in (75-90cm) of the bottom pair of arms.

4 In early to mid-summer train the topmost lateral as a new vertical leader and two laterals below it, initially at an angle of 45°, as a further pair of arms. Remove any basal shoots and cut back surplus laterals and sub-laterals to 6-9in (15-23cm).

5 In the third winter lower the arms to the horizontal and shorten them by about a third. Cut back the vertical leader to within 2.5-3ft (76-90cm) of the topmost pair of arms. Shorten horizontal arms by a third. Continue this pruning and training to form the required number of arms.

6 Spur prune 2-3 weeks after mid-summer by cutting back growths not wanted for the framework branches to leave about 6in (15cm). In winter shorten these growths again leaving 3-4in (7.5-10cm).

Right and far right, top and bottom: Although wisterias are most commonly trained on pergolas (far right, top) or walls, they can also be grown as standards (right) or as shrubs (far right, bottom). Whatever the support, the pruning method used to promote the growth of flowering spurs is the same.

Above: To encourage the formation of flowering spurs, prune extension growths of wisterias in summer and shorten the same growths again in winter.

develop as a result of this pruning are subsequently shortened to form the flowering spurs.

The method of building up the next and subsequent tiers is essentially the same. The vertical leader is cut back in winter about 2.5-3ft (76-90cm) above the topmost of the last pair of arms to have been formed. Of the laterals that develop, the topmost is trained vertically, and two that are well spaced are trained out to left and right, initially at an angle of about 45 degrees. In winter they are brought down to the horizontal and shortened by about a third. Any growths from the base or surplus shoots on the main stem should be cut out completely. For the last tier simply train a pair of laterals horizontally.

Spur pruning an established plant
The simplest method of spur pruning is to shorten extension growth and laterals in two stages. In the first stage, two or three weeks after mid-summer, cut back these growths to within 6in (15cm) of the framework branches. This is followed in early to mid-winter by shortening them further to 3-4in (7.5-10cm), so that each spur carries two or three buds. An even heavier furnishing of

spurs can be achieved by more rigorous summer pruning. Cutting back the extension growth to 6in (15cm) every two weeks throughout the summer stimulates the production of further laterals, which are also cut back when they have made 6in (15cm).

CEANOTHUS

In many cool temperate gardens the evergreen species and hybrids of *Ceanothus* are of borderline hardiness and need the protection of a sunny wall. Most of these shrubs are too tender for much of the United States and thrive only on the Pacific Coast. Unless planted close to the wall and trained in, they tend to flop forward and are then prone to wind and snow damage. Neglected and damaged specimens are difficult to deal with as *Ceanothus* does not produce new growth readily when cut back into old wood. It is best to prune regularly to maintain compact growth close to the support.

The deciduous species and hybrids are hardier and are normally grown in the open garden. They flower in late summer and autumn on the current season's wood and are pruned lightly in mid-spring.

Formative pruning and training

After spring planting, which is advisable for all evergreen *Ceanothus*, tie in the main shoot vertically and the laterals spaced out evenly on either side. Badly placed shoots, such as those facing into the wall, may need to be cut back to the main stem, but breastwood can be trimmed back to 2-3in (5-7.5cm). Unless it is tied in regularly, the rapid growth made in spring and summer will lean out from the wall, and it is difficult to redirect shoots once the wood has ripened. In mid-summer trim back breastwood to 3-4in (7.5-10cm).

Train the extension growth in subsequent growing seasons until the available space is filled.

Training and pruning the established plant

Most evergreen *Ceanothus* flower in late spring or early summer on growths made the previous year, and are best pruned immediately after flowering. Trim over the growth made in the previous season to within 4-6in (10-15cm) of the permanent framework. Any excessively vigorous breastwood should be cut back in late summer.

A few evergreen hybrids, including 'Autumnal Blue' and 'Burkwoodii', flower in summer and autumn on growth made the previous growing season and on wood of the current season. These are best pruned in mid-spring, although this may result in the loss of early flowers.

Left: Where they are of borderline hardiness, the evergreen species, cultivars and hybrids of *Ceanothus* benefit from being grown against a sunny wall. This mature plant of *C. impressus* shows the plant's tendency to produce abundant breastwood, which should be checked by early pruning.

EVERGREEN CEANOTHUS

1 At planting, tie in the vertical leader and well-spaced laterals. Cut out misplaced shoots. Cut back breastwood, leaving 2-3in (5-7.5cm). During the growing season tie in extension growth, but in mid-summer cut back breastwood that is longer than 4in (10cm).

2 Annually cut breastwood to 4in (10cm) in early summer; tie in the leader and laterals in the growing season.

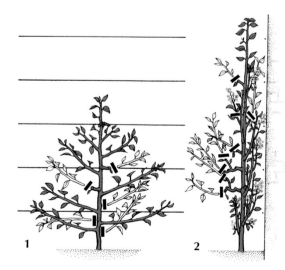

CHAENOMELES AND PYRACANTHA

The common names "japonica" and "flowering quince" cover several species of *Chaenomeles* and their numerous cultivars and hybrids, all of which are grown for their early spring flowers. They are versatile shrubs which can be grown in the open garden, either as bushes or as hedges, or trained against walls and fences. The evergreen firethorns (*Pyracantha*) are equally versatile, but their main appeal lies less in their flowers than in the clusters of conspicuous scarlet, orange or yellow berries that are carried in autumn and sometimes well into winter. Most *Pyracantha* are armed with fierce spines, as are some *Chaenomeles*, and it is therefore advisable to wear gloves when working with these plants.

There are two basic methods of training *Chaenomeles* and *Pyracantha* against walls, both methods requiring a system of horizontal wires, which should be spaced 9-12in (23-30cm) apart. They can be grown informally, with leaders spaced out evenly and trained in to the wires, summer pruning keeping growths close to the support and encouraging the formation of flowering spurs. More rigorous training in the early stages can create fans, cordons or espaliers. Both *Chaenomeles* and *Pyracantha* are most

Below, top and bottom: The japonicas or flowering quinces (*Chaenomeles*) can be grown as shrubs in the open garden or trained against walls and fences. Although formal training as a fan can produce an attractive plant (top), this is less common than a freer approach (bottom). Whatever the framework of the plant, summer pruning is necessary to control the growth of breastwood and to encourage the formation of flowering spurs.

CHAENOMELES

1 In mid-autumn or early spring, train a clearly defined central leader vertically and laterals close to the horizontal. Plants with several leaders can be trained to form an irregular or more formal fan. Cut out laterals that are badly spaced and cannot be trained to make a well-spaced framework.

2 During the summer, train in all well-placed extension growths until the plant fills the space. In mid-summer, cut back all breastwood to 4-6 leaves. If possible, treat other badly placed shoots, such as those that are crossing, in the same way, or cut back to the framework.

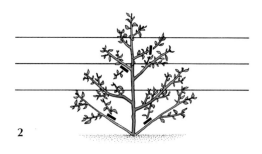

3 Starting in the first year, prune in late summer or early autumn; cut back breastwood, surplus laterals and sub-laterals to 2-3 leaves. Maintain the plant at the desired size by stopping leaders and main laterals in early to mid-spring.

commonly trained informally, and this is the best method for all but the most vigorous hybrids and cultivars of *Chaenomeles*. *Pyracantha*, however, respond well to espalier training.

Informal training

Young plants of *Chaenomeles* usually have several shoots growing from near the base and these should be spaced out and tied in to the wires. It is generally not necessary to cut back leaders to stimulate growth. Young specimens of *Pyracantha* are more likely to have a strong central leader. Train this vertically, tying in laterals as near the horizontal as possible. If lateral growths are weak, cut back the leader by 6-12in (15-30in) in mid-spring.

On either plant, laterals that are growing into the wall and which cannot be trained into a suitable position should be cut back to the main stem. During the first growing season train in shoots that are needed to extend the framework. Two or three weeks before mid-summer cut back other shoots, including those that are outward-growing or which are crossing, at four to six leaves. This summer pruning initiates the formation of short spurs that will carry flowers in subsequent years. Pruned shoots may make further growth later in the season, and this should be cut back to two or three leaves in late summer or early autumn.

In subsequent years, vigorous growths can be trained in to fill out the framework. The main emphasis, however, is on summer pruning to control the growth of breastwood; the effect being the formation of flowering spurs. Summer pruning of *Pyracantha* also exposes the ornamental berries. Secondary growths made after the summer pruning should be cut back to two or three leaves in late summer or early autumn.

Training restricted forms

To form an espalier *Pyracantha*, for example, train the central leader vertically and select pairs of branches to tie in left and right on horizontal wires. Cut off all surplus shoots close to the main stem. If laterals are lacking in vigor, cut back the main stem in mid-spring at the topmost of three shoots or buds so that, as they develop, the two lowest can form arms of the espalier, while the topmost becomes a new leader. This process can be repeated for subsequent tiers. Spur pruning in summer is essential to control growth and encourage flowering.

Left and above: The firethorns (*Pyracantha*) will grow on shady and sunny walls and, although best handled with gloves because of their spines, are easily trained in a formal way, for example as an espalier (left) or in a freer form (above).

Summer pruning of young growth, followed if necessary by pruning of secondary growth in autumn, encourages the development of flowering spurs.

HEDGES

The typical hedge consists of trees or shrubs of a particular kind planted in line and maintained by trimming to a uniform height and width. There are, however, many variations on the typical hedge, not least in scale. In the sixteenth and seventeenth centuries, dwarf box (*Buxus sempervirens* 'Suffruticosa') and other low shrubs were used for making the florid patterns of parterres or the more severe geometric divisions of knot gardens.

At the other extreme, hedges of English yew (*Taxus baccata*), the hardier Japanese yew (*T. cuspidata*) and Italian cypress (*Cupressus sempervirens*) can create massive architectural effects or, like the lighter but often taller hedges of hornbeam (*Carpinus betulus*) and avenues of pleached linden (*Tilia*), define the axes of large formal gardens.

There are also considerable variations in texture and density. Among the most valuable hedging plants are several small-leaved evergreens, including conifers, that with regular trimming form a close-textured surface. Although most deciduous trees give a coarser finish than the classic evergreens such as yew, regular clipping will create a dense leafy wall, and among them are some, like beech (*Fagus sylvatica*), that retain their leaves in winter.

The conventional hedge is rigorously shaped, but many trees and shrubs, including a number that do not respond well to regular trimming, can make attractive and useful informal hedges which can be maintained with a very light pruning regime. Such hedges need more space than comparable hedges trimmed formally, but the looser shape often sits more comfortably in areas with relaxed planting and there is sometimes the bonus of an attractive display of flowers.

Right: The side shoots of a young beech hedge, such as this, need cutting back to encourage bushy growth. Although beech is deciduous, a mature hedge remains well clothed with tawny leaves throughout the winter.

Left: In formal gardens hedges are often used to create a patterned structure. In the splendid recreation of a garden in the style of the 17th century at Villandry, France, box compartments are filled with a variety of spring flowers.

Top: Linden is the tree most commonly used for pleaching. The branches are trained in a single plane above a clear stem, eventually interlacing with those of neighboring trees so that they form a continuous surface.

Above: Yew is one of the finest evergreens for making a close-textured hedge and once established generally needs only one cut a year. As this tunnel demonstrates, it can be trimmed with architectural precision.

FORMAL HEDGES

The formative pruning of three groups of formal hedge is covered on pages 100-3. There are, however, some general points that are relevant to the cutting of most hedges, particularly those which rely for their ornamental and practical value on being maintained as regular shapes.

Choice of plant

In choosing hedging plants a major point to consider, after suitability for the growing conditions, is rate of growth. The speed with which fast growers such as Leyland cypress (x *Cupressocyparis leylandii*) create shelter and privacy is in some situations a deciding factor in their favor. However, the fast growers generally continue to grow vigorously even when mature and therefore require cutting several times each summer. Architectural hedges, for example of yew (*Taxus baccata* and *T. cuspidata*), may take half as long again to reach the same height, but even with only one cut a year will keep their shape and retain a dense surface. The fast growers are generally an unsuitable choice for hedges that are ornamented with architectural detail (see pp. 104-5).

Where the aim is to create a surface of uniform color and texture it is important to obtain plants of the same clone.

Hedge shape

Whatever the scale of a formal hedge, its sides should be shaped and maintained to form an angle of between 15 and 25 degrees to the vertical. The purpose of the batter, as the slope is called, is to allow reasonably even exposure to light over the whole surface of the hedge. Insufficient light reaching the bottom of a hedge is the most common cause of die-back and gaps at the base of a hedge. This is often a problem with hedges that have perpendicular faces and is even more acute when hedges are poorly maintained and the face develops an outward-curving bow.

A number of variations on the shape of formal hedges are mentioned on pages 104-5. The top of a conventional hedge can be cut flat, with all angles sharply defined. This architectural effect is most easily achieved with dense small-leaved hedging plants such as box (*Buxus sempervirens*) and yew.

Conventional hedges are also often finished with a rounded top, either broadly curved or softening the triangular cross-section of a narrow-topped hedge.

The weight of snow can cause serious damage to all hedges, especially evergreen hedges with broad tops. Wherever it is practicable, heavy accumulations of snow should be carefully dislodged.

Below: The common holly (*Ilex aquifolium*), of which there are many cultivars, responds well to regular clipping and can make an excellent formal hedge. Annual trimming, which is best carried out in mid-summer, will result in the loss of most or all of the red berries on female plants.

Above: When flowering shrubs are given the close clipping needed to shape a formal hedge much of the flower will be lost. With some of the hawthorns, including *Crataegus* *oxycantha* 'Paul's Scarlet' which is a showy plant when flowering in late spring, it is probably worth tolerating a rough finish in order to retain a display of spring blossom.

Frequency and timing of cutting

As a general point it may be said that many of the most valuable hedging plants, including yew and box, need only one annual cut if this is carried out in the second half of summer. If they are cut too early they may make sufficient growth before the end of summer to require a second trim. Fast-growing plants such as common privet (*Ligustrum ovalifolium*) and Leyland cypress may need several cuts in summer, the number depending on the growing conditions.

Most deciduous hedging plants are best cut in late summer, but this can be continued into autumn and even winter in mild climates, although no pruning should be carried out when there is frost.

The frequency and timing of cutting for specific plants is indicated in the A-Z section on pages 120-28.

Cutting established hedges

Provided that a hedge is properly maintained, the growth that needs to be removed is relatively light and easily cut with a sharp pair of long-bladed shears. These should be used with the blades lying flat against the surface, not pointing into it.

Mechanically powered shears are well worth considering where there is a lot of hedge to cut, especially if it will need more than one trim in a year. Petrol-driven models tend to be heavy, produce unpleasant fumes, and are noisy enough to make it necessary for the user to wear earmuffs. Electric hedge-trimmers are lighter and generally quieter, and there is a choice between cordless battery-or generator-driven models, and those that are powered by cable from house outlets.

Among safety features that reduce the risk of accidental injury are two-handed switches that make it impossible for the machine to operate unless it is correctly held, and a short blade-stopping time (under half a second). Machines should also have blade extensions that project beyond the tips of the blades and help to prevent hands or fingers touching them. Beware of the risk of the power cable being cut accidentally.

Whatever tools are being used, particular care must be taken when working above ground level. Ladders are often difficult to fix securely and involve a lot of up and down

work. A simple and convenient platform can be made by running planks between trestles or pairs of steps.

When trimming an established hedge, the top is first cut to make it level, if possible, by cutting half the width from one side and completing from the other side. As work advances, clippings are lightly swept off. It may well be possible to maintain an accurate level by eye, especially if it is simply a matter of removing short new growth from a shape that is already well defined. However, this is often difficult to do when working close to the hedge, especially if the hedge is

particularly low or high. In these cases it is useful to fix guidelines on each side of the hedge. This can be achieved by inserting stakes at either end of the hedge, with intermediate stakes if necessary, and tying a taut line between them.

Some form of guide may be useful to obtain an even batter although, once a face has been established, the old surface beneath the new growth is often adequate. A string running between the top guideline and another fixed along the base is the simplest to improvise. It needs to be taut enough to give a straight line and free-running so that it can be slipped along the face as clipping proceeds. For a low hedge an alternative is a simple A-frame made to the size of the hedge's cross-section. A more elaborate device consists of an upright and an arm swinging from the base that can be held in position at the desired angle by a crosspiece at the top. A plumb-line attached to the vertical makes it possible to ensure that this is held perpendicular, so giving a true angle.

Below: Box is among the most widely used evergreens for low formal hedges. Here it makes a vertical extension to a brick wall against a background of a beech (*Fagus sylvatica*) hedge.

Above: An impressive finish can be given to a formal hedge by shaping part of the hedging material as a piece of topiary. Trimming these shapes is best done using manually operated hedging tools.

GROUP 1: Deciduous and evergreen shrubs and trees that require severe initial pruning to make dense growth.

Right: Of the many cultivars of the common box, one of the best for forming a dense hedge of moderate height is 'Handsworthensis', which in the initial stages makes strong upright growth.

GROUP ONE

A good formal hedge must be densely furnished from top to ground level. A number of shrubs will only make bushy growth at the base if hard pruned in the early stages. Deciduous and semi-evergreen examples include hawthorn (*Crataegus*), privet (*Ligustrum*), myrobalan plum (*Prunus cerasifera*), and blackthorn (*P. spinosa*). Evergreens requiring similar, though less severe, initial pruning include box (*Buxus sempervirens*) and *Lonicera nitida*.

Initial pruning
After planting deciduous shrubs in the dormant season, in mid-autumn or early spring, all growth should be cut back to 6in (15cm) from ground level. Evergreens are best planted in early to mid-spring and cut back by a third. The semi-evergreen privets should be planted at the same time, but pruned in the same way as deciduous forms.

Further hard pruning is necessary in the second year to establish a bushy framework that is clothed to the base. In late winter or early spring the main growths of deciduous shrubs should be cut back by about half. Any remaining laterals can be cut back to within 2-3in (5-7.5cm) of the framework stems. This severe pruning may need to be repeated in late winter or early spring of the following year if there is only thin growth at the base.

In their second year, evergreens in this group should be pruned in early to mid-spring, cutting all growth back by a third.

Trimming to form a batter should begin early in the growing season of the second year. In the first few years it should take place several times in the summer to create a dense surface. Until the hedge reaches the required height, the top should be trimmed only lightly in late summer.

Cutting established hedges
Once their shape has been established, some hedges in this group, such as box, need only one cut a year. Others, such as privet and *Lonicera nitida*, need to be trimmed two or, in mild climates, four times each summer.

FORMATIVE PRUNING
1 Plant Group 1 deciduous hedges in the dormant season, evergreens and semi-evergreens between early and mid-spring. After planting cut hard back, evergreens by a third, deciduous and semi-evergreen kinds to 6in (15cm) from ground level.

2 In early to mid-summer of the first year trim sides lightly to encourage denser growth of side shoots.

1

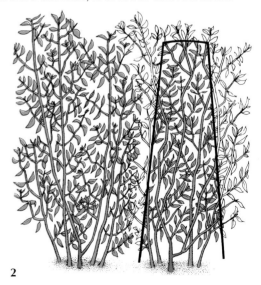

2

Far left: The overall appearance of this well-trimmed hawthorn hedge is marred by the weeds at its base.

Left: To make a satisfactory formal hedge hawthorns need close trimming.

Left: The oval-leaf privet, including its golden form (*Ligustrum ovalifolium* 'Aureum'), needs to be pruned hard during the first 2 or 3 years. It will not remain dense and compact unless clipped frequently throughout the growing season.

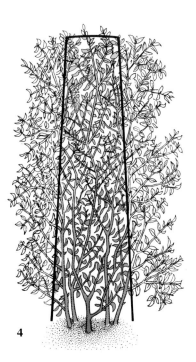

3 In the second year cut back the previous season's growth on deciduous and semi-evergreen kinds by a half, the former in late winter or, in the north, early spring, the latter between early and mid-spring. Reduce the previous season's growth of evergreens by a third in spring.

4 Throughout the growing season of the second and subsequent years trim side growths every 4-6 weeks.

3

4

GROUP 2: Deciduous shrubs and trees that are naturally bushy at the base.

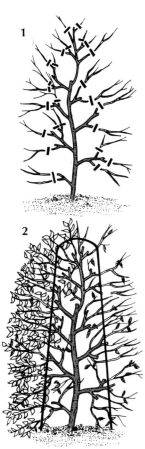

Below: Hornbeam is one of the most versatile deciduous hedging plants. It retains its brown leaves throughout the winter, and when mature normally requires only one cut a year, in late summer.

FORMATIVE PRUNING

1 Plant Group 2 hedges in mid-autumn or early spring. After planting cut back the leader and strong laterals by about a third.

2 In mid-autumn or early spring of the second year cut back the leading shoot and strong laterals, yet again by a third. Shaping of the sides can begin in the summer of the third year.

GROUP TWO

Deciduous shrubs and trees that are naturally bushy at the base require less severe initial pruning than those in Group One. The most important examples are beech (*Fagus sylvatica*) and hornbeam (*Carpinus betulus*), but several flowering shrubs are grouped with them.

Initial pruning

After planting in the dormant season, mid-autumn or early spring, cut back the main stem and all strong laterals by about a third. No further pruning need be carried out in the first year, but in the second winter the previous year's growth on main stems should be reduced and strong laterals cut by a third again. This cutting back should ensure a firm framework for the hedge that is well furnished to ground level. Routine clipping of the sides should begin in the third summer, the hedge being shaped so that the two faces slope inwards from a broad base. The top should be lightly trimmed until the desired height has been reached.

Cutting established hedges

Beech and hornbeam, which have the advantage of retaining their attractive russet leaves throughout the winter, are best trimmed in the latter half of summer. These very easily develop into hedges that are thick through unless they are cut hard each year.

There is some loss of flowering potential when shrubs such as forsythia are shaped as formal hedges. The best time to cut is immediately after flowering, although some shrubs may need a few trims in a summer.

GROUP THREE

Classic evergreen hedging plants such as yew (*Taxus baccata*) and holly (*Ilex*), and also fast-growing conifers such as Leyland cypress (x *Cupressocyparis leylandii*) require only light pruning in the initial stages.

Initial pruning

After planting, in autumn or spring, leading shoots are left unpruned but any straggling laterals are trimmed. In the first year or two plants are sometimes staked with bamboo canes. However, it is more useful in exposed positions to erect a barrier of a fine-mesh plastic or nylon to reduce the dehydrating effect of the prevailing wind.

In subsequent years the leading shoot is allowed to grow unchecked until it reaches the required height, when it can be stopped during the summer pruning. Trimming of the sides should begin in the summer of the second year to encourage dense growth. If enough growth is made in the early stages, two or three cuts can be made each summer.

Cutting established hedges

When they have made mature hedges, the fast-growing conifers such as Leyland cypress generally require two cuts a year, the first just before mid-summer and the second in late summer. One cut, in late summer, is generally sufficient for mature hedges of slower-growing plants such as holly and yew. Pyracanthas and other plants in this group which have flowers and berries that are worth retaining should have the young growth removed each year in the second half of summer.

GROUP 3: Conifers and broad-leaved evergreens of naturally bushy growth.

Left: When conifers are grown as hedging plants the leading shoots should be allowed to extend until they have reached the height required for the hedge. Clipping in late summer will maintain a close-textured surface on this western hemlock (*Tsuga heterophylla*).

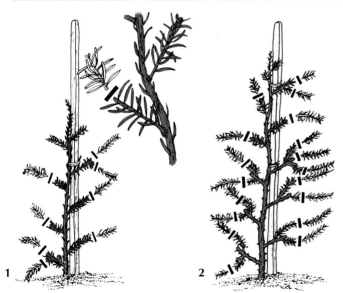
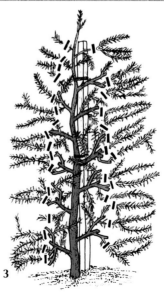

FORMATIVE PRUNING

1 Group 3 hedges can be planted in autumn or spring. After planting, lightly trim any straggly growth, but leave the leader unpruned.

2/3 In summer of the second and subsequent years trim laterals to the required shape, only stopping the leader when it has finally reached the desired height.

VARIATIONS ON FORMAL HEDGES

Simplicity of outline and uniform density, color, and texture are often prime virtues of a hedge. However, differences in color and texture and the introduction of more complex outlines and profiles can add to a hedge's ornamental value.

Mixed hedges

For true uniformity a length of hedge should be planted with shrubs or trees of the same clone. When a hedge is planted with seedlings the degree of variation may be

Below: Yew is one of the most suitable materials to use when integrating topiary shapes with the clean lines of a well cut formal hedge.

Right: Two forms of the same plant can sometimes be combined to introduce an attractive color variation in a hedge. Here the oval-leaf privet (*Ligustrum ovalifolium*) is alternated with its golden form (*L. o.* 'Aureum').

slight but nonetheless visible once it has been closely trimmed. More pronounced contrasts result from mixed planting in what is sometimes called a mosaic or tapestry hedge. Hollies (*Ilex*) and other evergreens can be combined with deciduous trees, such as hornbeam (*Carpinus betulus*), or color contrasts can be made by mixing different forms of the same plant. For example, the common beech (*Fagus sylvatica*), which has green leaves, can be mixed with the purple-leaved (*F.s.* 'Purpurea').

The principal difficulty such a hedge presents is in the early stages, when differences in growth rate can result in vigorous plants swamping those that are slower to get started. This is often a problem when combining green plants with their golden or variegated forms, which are generally much less vigorous. Until the hedge reaches the required height cutting back of more vigorous plants may be needed to allow others to become established.

Architectural details and embellishments

Architectural details are not difficult to add to a hedge, but the more complex they are the longer a hedge takes to reach the finished state. Inevitably, the maintenance of a hedge is more time consuming when there are angles, different levels, and curves that need to be kept clean cut. It is normally only worth elaborating upon the standard shape of a hedge when it is made up of plants such as holly and English yew (*Taxus baccata*) that retain a close finish with one trim a year. Ideally, the details should be planned from the outset, but it is often possible to cut such features as battlements out of an existing hedge.

Buttresses, niches, and stepped outlines are among the easiest architectural features to create, by simply cutting parts of the hedge to different thicknesses or levels. However, when heavy buttresses are wanted there should be additional planting from the outset. Refinements of level and profile are soon lost if the batters and levels are not scrupulously checked when the hedge is cut.

To form an arch connecting two sections of hedge either side of a path is a long-term project when the planting material is relatively slow-growing, such as yew. A simple framework is needed to train branches out from either side. Bamboo canes may be sufficient for a short span, but for a

Left: A hedging plant such as yew that produces a dense growth is needed to complete the architectural effect of a surface pierced by windows or doorways.

wider arch it is helpful to have wires supported by uprights fixed in the line of the hedge on either side of the path.

Windows, either circular or rectangular in shape, spaced at regular intervals or situated to give a specific view, can be formed in much the same way as a small-scale arch. The work of training is much simplified if the windows are located so that they are not immediately above the planting positions of the trees or shrubs that constitute the hedge.

Topiary shapes emerging above the outline of a hedge can be highly elaborate embellishments. The topiary is normally formed by allowing a branch or branches of a hedge of uniform planting to develop above the finished level, the subsequent pruning and training following the lines described on pages 112-19. A striking effect can be created when one kind of plant is used for the hedge proper and another for the topiary. A hawthorn (*Crataegus monogyna*) hedge, for example, might be topped by evenly-spaced balls of clipped holly.

Above: In a conventional hedge uniformity of color, texture, and density are merits, but attractive effects can be created using intentional contrasts. The bold pattern of this beech hedge has been created using a mixture of copper and plain forms.

Left: A frame is useful for training the surround of apertures in hedges, such as this window in a yew hedge, that are intended to have a sharp outline.

PLEACHING

An alternative to the formal hedge well furnished to ground level is a line of trees grown on clear stems and then shaped from a uniform height to present a flat surface. Pleaching is the technique used to create this effect. Deciduous trees that produce flexible growths are planted at a regular distance apart and all branches above a clear stem are trained horizontally in the same plane, eventually the branches of one tree being interwoven with the branches of those on either side. The terms "pleaching" and "plashing" are both used to describe the technique of weaving plants together, but the latter term is now generally used to describe the interweaving of branches in a laid hedge.

The decision to create a linked avenue by pleaching trees is generally taken for a combination of aesthetic and practical reasons. Pleaching was a typical feature of many sixteenth- and seventeenth-century gardens and is now often used in creating gardens of a historical character. A pleached

Right: Pleached hornbeam makes a dense cube, creating the effect of a hedge on stilts.

Above and above right: In the early stages of training some form of support is needed on which the branches of pleached lindens can be trained out horizontally (above). When mature, the continuous surface makes a light screen (above right).

walk provides welcome shade in summer, and can be underplanted with winter- and spring-flowering bulbs. It is less likely to cause wind turbulence than a hedge that is clothed to ground level, and it allows cold air to drain away that might otherwise create a frost pocket.

The main practical problem presented by pleaching is the overhead work involved. A tall face of pleached trees may prove difficult to maintain and in general it is advisable to keep to a modest height. Maintaining pleached trees is much easier when carried out from a platform of planks supported by trestles or steps rather than from ladders.

Lindens (*Tilia*) are the favorite trees for pleaching on account of their flexible growths and tolerance of shaping. *T.* x *euchlora* is now often favored over other lindens: it is not prone to aphid attack, as most others are, and, unlike the common linden (*T.* x *europaea*), does not produce large numbers of suckers from the base. However, its flowers are narcotic to bees and it is not a good choice for planting where children are likely to play, because of the risk of stunned bees stinging.

Hornbeam (*Carpinus betulus*) is also sometimes used for pleaching, but it makes more twiggy growth than linden, forming a conventional hedge-like shape on stilts.

Initial stages in pleaching lindens

A framework of wires is the most convenient support in the early stages of training. Braced end posts should be erected to a height of 10ft (3m), with intermediate posts at intervals of 30ft (9m). If it is intended that the pleaching be taken higher than 10ft (3m), the height of the framework must be adjusted accordingly. The bottom wire should be run at the intended height of the lowest horizontal, normally 5-6ft (1.5-1.8m) above ground level, with wires above this spaced 1-1½ft (30-46cm) apart. An alternative is to use bamboo canes tied between the trunks.

Well-matched young specimens are planted in mid-autumn or (in the north) early spring, spaced at regular intervals, with the distance between being in the range of 8-12ft (2.4-3.6m). Each should be supported with a tall cane. To encourage thickening of the trunk, it is advisable to retain side shoots below the bottom wire for the first year or two, but shorten these to about 1ft (30cm) in early to mid-summer.

The horizontal training of laterals should begin when the leader has passed the bottom wire. The aim is to restrict growth to one plane. Shoots that cannot be trained to left or right must be cut back to the main stem.

In subsequent years the central leader should be maintained and tiers of horizontally trained branches built up. In order to maintain a vertical face, shoots that cannot be trained in should be cut out during mid- to late summer. At the same time, when branches of adjoining trees meet, they should be plaited together and tied lightly.

Initial stages in pleaching hornbeam

The aim in pleaching hornbeam is to create a conventional hedge shape supported by bare trunks. A useful framework for the initial training consists of end posts and intermediate supports carrying crosspieces at 6, 9 and 12ft (1.8, 2.7 and 3.6m). These crosspieces should be 4½ft (1.4m) in length, with evenly-spaced wires running between them, but allowing for the trunks of the trees to grow up the center.

Trees should be planted about 8ft (2.4m) apart, centered on this framework. As with lindens, side shoots below the bottom wire should be retained for the first year or two to encourage thickening of the trunk. The aim is to retain a central leader until it is about 6in (15cm) below the required height of the hedge, but to encourage dense growth by cutting back laterals and, where necessary, tying shoots in to the wires of the framework.

Maintaining pleached trees

The ideal is to remove the framework once pleaching to the desired height has been achieved, but if it is inconspicuous it may be left. In maintaining the vertical face of pleached lindens, the horizontal training of growths should continue, with flexible young stems being woven into the existing framework and any shoots that stand out from the face being cut back. Much of this work can be done in the second half of summer, but some additional pruning and training may need to be carried out once the leaves have fallen. On well-established pleached lindens periodic thinning of horizontals will help to maintain the light airy effect that is such an attractive feature of pleached trees. If the common linden has been used in the planting, the suckers that develop at the base should be removed promptly.

A hornbeam hedge on stilts requires the same management as an ordinary hornbeam hedge and should be clipped in summer.

Below and bottom: Mature avenues of pleached hornbeam (below) are maintained by annual clipping in late summer. Although a framework is sometimes kept as a guide for clipping (bottom), this can be unsightly and a better solution is to set up levels when the work needs to be done.

ARBORS AND TUNNELS

The use of trees trained over frames to form arbors and tunnels has a long history in the making of gardens. Fruit trees, flowering plants such as laburnum, and classic hedging plants such as hornbeam (*Carpinus betulus*) have been among the most widely used to make covered walks. The method of training most ornamentals is essentially a variation of pleaching, with growths tied in to a permanent frame. In the past, renewable wooden frames were the standard supports. Although wood has a natural appearance, metal frames are more durable.

Hornbeam

A common mistake is to conceive an arbor on too small a scale. For a hornbeam arbor, arching supports spanning a walk that is about 8ft (2.4m) wide should rise to about 12ft (3.6m) at the center. A dense cover is achieved relatively quickly by rather close planting, about 1½ft (46cm) apart, with the central leader arched to the center and dense growth encouraged through the cutting back of laterals. More generous spacing can be used, especially if a canopy of foliage is to be supported on clear stems to a given height. More care must then be taken in training growth laterally to form a uniformly dense cover. An established hornbeam arbor should be trimmed in summer in the same way as a hornbeam hedge.

Laburnum

The most suitable laburnum for covered walks is *Laburnum* x *watereri* 'Vossii', which produces long racemes of yellow flowers very freely. A framework of well-spaced branches can be built up quickly as this is a fast-growing plant. The initial pruning should be carried out in summer, as cuts that are made in spring are likely to bleed. To create a spectacular display in early summer, established plants should be spur pruned.

Below: The Judas tree (*Cercis siliquastrum*) is generally grown as a low-branching large shrub or small tree. Here it has been trained on a framework to make a covered walk.

Right: When the hanging flowers of laburnum are at their peak this plant shows itself as one of the most spectacular subjects for training on a pergola. Plants are spur pruned, with the preceding summer's growth of young wood being cut back to two or three buds in early winter.

RENOVATING FORMAL HEDGES

With good ground preparation before planting, subsequent feeding, adequate pruning in the early stages, and then regular trimming in the growing season, many hedges will remain in a good state for many years. Gappiness in a hedge is commonly the result of neglect in the first few years and is very difficult to put right. Often the best course is to abandon all hope of renovation and to grub the hedge out. If there is space to run a new hedge parallel to the old, it may be worth retaining even a gappy hedge until its replacement is well established.

Renovation is more successful with hedges that through neglect have increased in bulk and lost their batter. Some of the best hedging plants – including box (*Buxus sempervirens*), hollies (*Ilex*), hornbeam (*Carpinus betulus*), and English yew (*Taxus baccata*) – respond remarkably well to drastic pruning in which the sides are cut back to the main stem or stems. With all of these the operation is best staged over several years.

Initial cutting back
Severe pruning to renovate deciduous hedges should be carried out in late winter, when the plants are dormant, while evergreens should be pruned in mid- to late spring. Never risk carrying out drastic pruning when the weather is frosty.

In the first year, only one side of the hedge should be pruned. After cutting the top back to the required height, cut all the branches on one side back to the main stem or stems. Plants should be fed with a balanced general fertilizer and the ground kept well watered during dry weather. A mulch of well-rotted compost or manure will help to conserve moisture and supply additional nutrients.

Completing severe pruning
The cut face needs to be making good growth before the second side is pruned back as severely as the first. With an old yew hedge, for example, there may need to be a pause of two years before further pruning, full regeneration taking six to eight years.

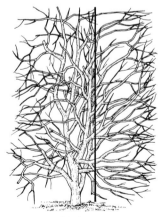

Above: An ancient hedge, such as this one of box, can sometimes take on such an individual character that any attempt to impose a rigorous geometry on it would be absurd.

Above and left: Many overgrown hedges, including those of hornbeam (left), tolerate hard cutting back (above).

INFORMAL AND RUSTIC HEDGES

Right: In many parts of Europe blackthorn (*Prunus spinosa*) is a common hedgerow plant. It can be planted and roughly trimmed to make an attractive rustic hedge.

Below: *Berberis* x *stenophylla* is an evergreen shrub that is often grown as a flowering informal hedge. It is pruned immediately after flowering.

Shrubs that are grown in a line close enough together to form a visual and physical barrier, but maintained on a light pruning regime, can make useful and ornamental informal hedges. The traditional rustic hedge, although primarily a stock-proof barrier that is periodically renovated by the technique of laying, can be very pleasing to look at and can be adapted to form a garden boundary. This type of hedge, along with more open rustic hedges, can be particularly useful in gardens that are managed in a way that is sympathetic to wildlife.

INFORMAL HEDGES

The most suitable shrubs for informal hedges are those that make naturally bushy growth, such as deutzias, osage orange (*Maclura pomifera*) and the rugosa roses. Many have attractive flowers or fruit. The aim in pruning is to retain a natural shape as far as this is consistent with the shrubs being planted in a row. The most common fault is over-zealous cutting, resulting in a hedge that looks like a failed attempt at a formal shape.

Shrubs should be pruned in much the same way as when they are grown as specimens, with the emphasis on removing old wood, taking it right back to the framework. Shrubs that flower on the current season's wood, such as *Fuchsia magellanica*, should be pruned in spring, while those that flower on old wood, for example *Berberis* x *stenophylla*, should be pruned immediately after flowering. Shrubs such as *Cotoneaster* x *simonsii*, that flower on old wood and produce ornamental berries that persist for several weeks or months, are best pruned after the berries have gone. However, on an established hedge of this kind it may be necessary to take out a proportion of the old wood after flowering.

RUSTIC HEDGES

Traditional country hedges are maintained by regular trimming, but when they become gappy, weed-ridden, and encumbered with a lot of dead wood they are renovated by the technique of laying. Hedges are first cleared of unwanted material and then the stems that are being retained are partly cut through, bent down so that they are nearly horizontal, and woven between regularly spaced uprights. Hedge laying is a craft and is best learned from an experienced practitioner.

Formative pruning and training

An authentic country hedge for large properties should consist of native species, not garden cultivars or introduced plants. In England, for example, the most frequently used hedging plant is the English hawthorn (*Crataegus monogyna*), planted bare-rooted about 9in (23cm) apart. The plants should be

cut back hard at planting, to encourage dense growth (see Group One, pp. 100-101). If there is a risk of the hedge being browsed by cattle it should be fenced off for the first four or five years. Beginning in the second winter, the hedge should be roughly shaped annually, which stimulates dense growth and helps to maintain the line.

Laying a hedge

Laying is carried out between mid-autumn and late winter and some hedges may need re-laying every ten to twenty years. To begin, the line of the hedge, which may be obscured by the development of suckers or the growth of colonizing plants, must be re-established. Then any dead wood should be taken out and the living wood thinned, leaving vigorous upright growths. A proportion of these, spaced 2-3ft (60-90cm) apart, can be used as the uprights that give the laid hedge its stability, but stakes can be used to fill gaps or, alternatively, throughout. Any growths on the bottom half to two-thirds of all stems should be removed.

The operation requiring the greatest skill is cutting the stems that are to be bent down. The experienced hedger uses a deft downward stroke with a billhook to make a sloping cut, always in the same direction and just above ground level, that leaves a hinge of living tissue. An alternative method is to use a pruning saw, making an angled cut through about three-quarters of each stem. The stems are then bent back from the cut so that they all lie in the same direction, angled slightly above the horizontal and, wherever possible, worked between the upright stems or stakes. The stubs left at the base of each bent stem must be trimmed off to prevent the accumulation of rainwater in the cleft. Traditionally, a binding of pliable hazel is then braided along the top to hold the uprights and interwoven stems in place.

Below: The renovation of a country hedge by laying is a skilled craft. Today, however, many hedges are laid without the traditional attention to detail. A well maintained hedge makes an effective stock-proof barrier.

TOPIARY

Topiary is the traditional craft of training and trimming trees and shrubs into geometric or representational shapes. This technique, which is known to have been practiced in Roman times, was much used in Italian, French, and Dutch gardens of the sixteenth and seventeenth centuries. Despite fluctuations in popularity, through the influence of these models topiary has remained an important component of the formal garden, marking focal points, changes of level, and transitions from one area to another. Cubes, balls, domes, and pyramids or combinations of these are the characteristic forms of this predominantly geometric topiary, but bird and animal shapes sometimes add a fanciful touch. Another rich vein is represented by the topiary of many modest, informal country gardens. The technique used is the same as that employed in grander formal gardens, but the extravagance or whimsicality of some of these examples is often highly original.

Gardeners are sometimes discouraged from experimenting with topiary in the belief that it is difficult and that it will take many years to create a worthwhile specimen. In fact, the technique is no more than an elaboration of the pruning and training of hedges that is applied to individual or, more rarely, small groups of shrubs or trees. Initial pruning is aimed at encouraging dense growth from the base, and subsequent trimming, normally once or twice in the growing season, maintains a clean outline. Although the most suitable plants are relatively slow growing, interesting topiary can be shaped in five to ten years, and even in their formative stages many specimens are ornamental.

Left: The aromatic sweet bay (*Laurus nobilis*) is often trained as a standard or mophead, but can also be shaped as an obelisk or drum. Pruning should be done with hand pruners to avoid finishing with a surface of partly cut leaves.

Right: In the past the holm oak (*Quercus ilex*) was often clipped into formal shapes. Nowadays it is rare to see it used for large-scale topiary, as it is in this impressive avenue of mopheads.

Far left: English yew (*Taxus baccata*) is remarkably tolerant of hard cutting back, so much so that topiary can sometimes be shaped from old free-growing specimens or reshaped from an existing form, as is probably the case in this picture.

Bottom left: Box (*Buxus sempervirens*) deserves its popularity as a subject for small scale topiary. Cutting back hard in the first few years promotes compact growth and regular trimming will maintain a closely textured surface.

Below: To form this mophead finial of box, (*Buxus sempervirens*) a leader has been kept growing when the rest of the hedge has been cut back.

Bottom: Here, leaders trained up from a hedge of English holly (*Ilex aquifolium*) have been formed into umbrella shapes.

Choice of plants

In the past, many different plants have been used for topiary work, but only a small number give really satisfactory results. It is even more desirable than with hedging to use a dense small-leaved evergreen that tolerates cutting and holds its shape well, preferably with only one trim a year. Among the plants most commonly used today are species and cultivars of box (*Buxus*) and yew (*Taxus*) and, in milder climates, the Italian or Mediterranean cypress (*Cupressus sempervirens*). Box is only suitable for small-scale pieces, up to about 4ft (1.2m) high, and has a relatively soft texture.

These classic topiary plants are comparatively slow-growing and yet it is often possible to create a respectable simple shape in five to six years. The time it takes to complete more ambitious pieces depends on scale, complexity, and growing conditions. Impatient gardeners sometimes use faster-growing plants, such as the common privet (*Ligustrum ovalifolium*), but the satisfaction of seeing a shape form quickly has to be set against the coarseness of the finish, the need for frequent trimming, and the winter bareness of a semi-evergreen plant.

A few larger-leaved plants are suitable for balls, domes, and other very simple shapes. The most commonly used are holly (*Ilex*), Portugal laurel (*Prunus lusitanica*), bay laurel (*Laurus nobilis*), and holm oak (*Quercus ilex*). It is rare for deciduous trees and shrubs

to be used for topiary, but hawthorn (*Crataegus*), which makes dense growth when trimmed, can be clipped to a simple dome shape.

Initial training

Many specimens of topiary consist of a single plant of a suitable kind that is encouraged to make bushy growth from an early age and which is gradually shaped, either by simple clipping or by a combination of clipping and training to a frame. For a large specimen, especially one of considerable girth, it may be advisable to use more than one plant, the plants soon growing together to form a single coherent shape. If, as is generally the case, the intention is for the finished specimen to look all of a piece, it is important that the constituent plants should all be of the same clone. However, another possibility is to create a shape that includes, for example, a contrast of foliage color. In a simple shape such as a sphere the golden privet (*Ligustrum ovalifolium* 'Aureum') can make an attractive combination with the common privet.

When starting from scratch it is as well to bear in mind how the specimen is going to be maintained in the long term. Even representational shapes should be bold and simple for maximum effect and because fine detail, even if it can be incorporated, is unlikely to survive repeated cutting.

With plants such as yew, it is possible to carve topiary out of already well-developed specimens. Reducing the size of a plant that is then maintained in a given shape can solve the problem of a specimen that has outgrown a position and is casting deep shade where it is not wanted or blocking a view. As with the renovation of a hedge, it may be necessary to stage the cutting back, dealing first with one half of the tree and then the second half a year or two later. Although eventually it may be possible to include a finishing detail such as a finial, the initial aim should be to create a simple shape such as a drum or cone.

Care of mature specimens

Regular feeding with a well-balanced fertilizer, applied in late winter, is important in maintaining topiary specimens in a healthy condition. It is also important to control competition from other plants, including ornamentals, when topiary is incorporated in beds or borders. As well as taking nutrients, crowding plants can cause uneven growth by shading parts of the topiary. Ivy and other climbing plants can distort the growth of topiary specimens and should be removed. More drastic damage can be caused by heavy accumulations of snow and these should be dislodged.

Topiary shaped from relatively slow-growing plants such as box and yew should be cut in the second half of summer, but the exact timing can be varied to fit in with other work in the garden. Fast-growing plants such as privet will need three or four trims during the summer. As with hedges, no clipping should be done in frosty weather.

On large specimens of simple shape the work can be done with hand shears or electric hedge-trimmers. One-handed shears are useful for more detailed work. With larger-leaved plants, such as bay laurel, it is worth cutting out whole leaves or clusters of leaves using hand pruners, so avoiding the mutilated appearance which results when remnants of leaves begin to brown.

The use of a template can simplify cutting, especially if there are a number of plants of matching shape, as in an avenue of cones. It is very difficult to maintain severely geometric forms, for example pyramids or obelisks, without using a guide for the angles and edges. One solution is a permanent or semi-permanent former, as illustrated for the obelisk on page 117. Another is the kind of adjustable guide that is sometimes used for hedges and which is described on page 99. However, much topiary is simply cut freehand, the established shape beneath the current growth providing the guide.

It is always advisable to cut lightly, examining a specimen frequently in the course of trimming to see that the shape is being maintained. Additional cuts can be made if more trimming is necessary, but when a bite is taken out of a shape it may take several years for the gap to be filled.

Renovation

Topiary may need renovation because it has been left untrimmed or badly trimmed for several years, or because the shape has suffered as a result of branches being broken, attacked by pests or disease. It is often possible with good topiary plants such as box, holly, and yew to re-establish a neglected shape, or an approximation of it,

by cutting back excess growth, even pruning back to old wood. The renovation process may need to be staged over two or three years.

Holes and larger gaps are more difficult to deal with. With drastic surgery, in which damaged branches are cut back to live and healthy wood, yew, for example, will shoot again, but the necessary enlargement of the damaged area will destroy even more of the original shape. This may be the only option, but another possibility is to establish a revised shape using a combination of pruning and training. Even when this option is followed, it make take several years to recreate a satisfactory specimen.

When topiary is being renovated it is particularly important to feed it with a balanced fertilizer and to ensure that it is well watered.

Above: A tiered piece of topiary can sometimes be carved out of an existing cone or similar shape, but a more satisfactory result is generally achieved by forming the tiers as the plant grows, a central leader being maintained until the final height is reached.

GEOMETRIC SHAPES

The easiest and among the most widely used forms of topiary are simple geometric shapes, especially those such as cones that are close to the natural shape of plants, broader at the base than at the top. There are several variants of these shapes and some of the most elaborate topiary consists of combinations of geometric shapes.

Formative pruning and training
The simplest method of forming many geometric shapes is to encourage dense growth by trimming from an early stage,

Below: This row of pot-grown topiary specimens includes a standard sweet bay (*Laurus nobilis*) with a twisted stem.

Right: In Britain, fine old topiary survives at Levens Hall. Here, a pyramid in golden yew (*Taxus baccata* 'Aurea') contrasts with fantastic shapes.

eventually imposing the desired shape on the specimen as it reaches a suitable size. The trimming can often be carried out freehand, but shapes such as cubes and drums should be checked for verticals and horizontals using a spirit level and a straight-edged board. The radius of a drum can be checked using a length of string attached to a bamboo cane insterted at its visual center.

Obelisks and pyramids
These are simple shapes, often formed in box (*Buxus*) and yew (*Taxus*), but the angles and faces need to be cut accurately and this is difficult without a guide. Alternatively, it is possible to train plants inside a former – a permanent shape made of wire mesh – clipping them back when they protrude through the mesh. Formers are sometimes put in position immediately after planting, their own shapes adding a formal touch to a garden long before the plants have grown to hide them. However, by setting formers in place at this stage they get in the way of early trimming. It is generally worth delaying for a year or two, when care should be taken to ensure that they are square and upright.

Mopheads and domes
Bay laurel (*Laurus nobilis*), Portugal laurel (*Prunus lusitanica*), and other large-leaved plants are most effective cut to these simple shapes. It is possible to buy standards, but it is easy to train young plants, which may need staking for the first few years. Allow the development of the main stem for several years, shortening side shoots to about 3in (7.5cm) in early summer, cutting them back to the main stem a year later when the next crop of side shoots should be shortened. For a mophead, cut the main stem back to a bud when it is just above the intended center of the head, and for a dome when it is just below the top of the intended head. The aim of subsequent pruning is to encourage the formation of a balanced head, cutting with pruners to take off leaves in their entirety.

Tiers and spirals
The tiered cone supported by a single stem is one of the most common variants of a simple geometric shape. The best way to create this is to form the tiers as the bush grows. A young yew, for example, can be kept lightly trimmed to a cone shape until it has reached a height of 4-5ft (1.2-1.5m). At this stage a base can be cut out, making a dense pedestal, say about 3½ft (1.1m) deep. All branches on the main stem for about 1ft (30cm) above the base are removed completely, while those farther up are retained as they will form the first tier. When carving out the base it is advisable to cut a larger shape than is wanted. It can then be trimmed so that it is circular at its top level.

To encourage the formation of the first and subsequent tiers, it is often necessary to tie branches down to the horizontal. Use tarred string, tying to branches within the base. The first tier, with a smaller radius and shallower

Left: Here, cones of yew have been used to create a mysterious grouping.

FORMING AN OBELISK

A former of wire mesh panels is placed over a plant that has been cut back for a year or two to make it bushy.

1 Growth that protrudes through the former is trimmed back in summer.

2 When the obelisk is complete the former is no longer visible.

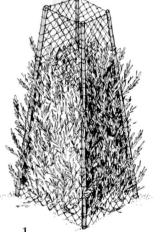

1

than the pedestal, can be carved out when the bush has made sufficient growth to leave enough bare stem and the beginnings of the second tier above it.

The dimensions suggested here can be varied to suit the vigor of the plant and personal taste. It is normal for the underside of tiers to be bare because of shading, but if not enough space is left between tiers shading may also cause bareness on the topsides as well.

Although it is sometimes suggested that spirals can be created by training a young flexible tree around a central stake, this is rarely a practical proposition. Most spirals are formed by carving into a cone-shaped bush and the best results are achieved by cutting the revolutions as the tree grows.

Topknots

Various details can be used to finish a geometric shape, such as a ball or crown, by allowing a tuft of shoots to extend at the apex and clipping them as desired. A ball is the simplest to execute. A circle can be formed using two shoots tied to a wire frame that is firmly fastened within the main shape. The wire frame can be left in place, or the two shoots can be grafted together at the top of the circle and the ring removed.

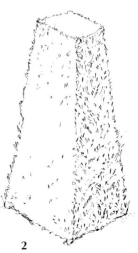

2

REPRESENTATIONAL SHAPES

Above: The topiary garden at Great Dixter, East Sussex, England, was planted early this century. A high standard of maintenance has preserved shapes such as this squirrel and pedestal in yew.

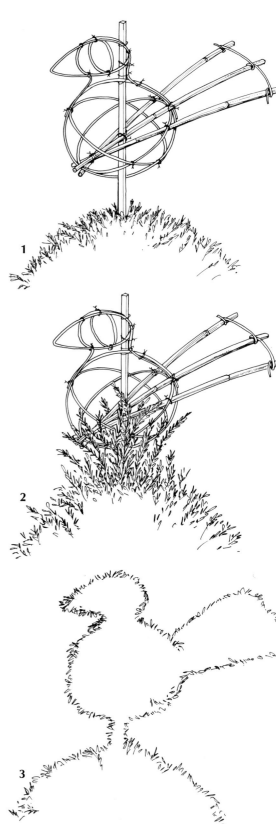

1

2

3

Representations of birds such as peacocks, pheasants, and blackbirds are among the most popular figurative shapes for topiary. Ingenious gardeners may find inspiration in many other subjects, animate and inanimate, whether they are forming a piece of topiary from a young plant or, in effect, carving a shape from a plant that is already partly or fully grown. For example, the growth pattern of a yew (*Taxus*) that is already well developed may even suggest a shape that can be worked on by pruning and training. Whatever the inspiration, the design must be reduced to a simplified shape that will endure despite annual growth and trimming.

Most shapes of any size are much improved if they appear to sit on a plinth or a base such as a hedge. Multiple planting is often used to speed up the formation of a base large enough for the shape that it is to support. If there is to be a plinth, the main shape is not started until this is near completion. Small specimens of topiary, for example in box (*Buxus*), are sometimes formed springing directly from the ground,

CREATING A BIRD SHAPE

1 Fashion a three-dimensional frame approximating to the desired shape and in late winter or early spring fix it securely in the plinth or hedge that forms the base.

2 In the following growing season and in subsequent years train in shoots, tying them to the frame. As the bird takes shape, pinch out or clip shoots to encourage dense growth.

3 Once the shape has been formed, trim it once or twice in summer to keep it sharply defined.

Left: In the United States the Ladew Gardens, Monkton, Maryland, contain some impressive specimens of topiary, including these lyre birds in yew.

but these generally look best when they are container-grown, the container providing the visual base.

The formation of the shape proper is much simplified by using a frame to which growths can be trained. The normal method is to make a three-dimensional outline of the shape in heavy-gauge wire, the shape itself being firmly fastened to a stake that is driven into the ground as near the center of the plinth as possible. When the base is a tall hedge the frame may need to be fastened to an upright which is itself tied firmly to branches in the interior of the hedge. Extensions of the basic shape, such as the tail of a bird, can be made using bamboo canes which are themselves tied to the frame. Inevitably there is an element of improvisation in making a frame to suit a specific shape, but it must be firm and last long enough for the basic shape to be formed. The best time to fix the frame is in late winter or early spring when the base is well developed and the training of the shape is about to begin.

Formative pruning and training

The base or plinth is formed as a simple geometric shape (see pp. 116-17). However, the trimming must leave a shoot or cluster of shoots at the apex which can be trained to form the figurative shape. It is quicker starting with several shoots, tied together with tarred string, but this is only satisfactory if the shape is to sit tightly on its base instead of on the end of a short stem.

The aim is to encourage dense growth to fill the frame and at the same time to train shoots to the outline. In the initial stages shoots are trained to the frame, to which they are tied with tarred string. This lasts long enough for the shoots to set in position. Plastic or metal ties are not suitable as they may remain visible, even after many years, and may also blunt tools if caught when the topiary is cut. A regime of training and trimming must be continued through each growing season until the shape is formed. Pinching back growth combined with the tying in of shoots will eventually produce a dense shape covering the frame beneath.

A-Z OF ORNAMENTALS

In the following listing, mainly of plants grown in temperate parts of the world, cross-references are given where relevant to methods of pruning and training covered elsewhere in this book. In all cases cut out dead and diseased wood when seen. The following abbreviations have been used in cross-referencing: Deciduous Shrubs (DS,), Evergreen Shrubs (ES), Trees (T), Hedges (H), and Group (G).

ABELIA Deciduous and evergreen shrubs which in cool temperate regions require a warm sheltered position. When grown as a bush A. x grandiflora requires little pruning (ES, G1, pp. 74-5). If trained against a wall, cut out some of the oldest branches in autumn, after flowering. Prune deciduous species (e.g. A. schumannii) in early spring.

ABELIOPHYLLUM A. distichum is a sprawling deciduous shrub which flowers in early spring on growths made in the previous year. Prune immediately after flowering (DS, G2, pp. 62-5). This species can be trained as a wall shrub with a permanent framework of branches.

ABIES Evergreen conifers, some attaining a great size. Train as branched trees, removing competing leaders (T, p. 48).

ABUTILON Evergreen shrubs and small trees, in cool temperate regions requiring a sheltered position or greenhouse treatment. Train A. megapotamicum and A. x milleri on canes or a system of wires. Train A. vitifolium with a central leader tied to a cane. Prune plants growing outdoors in mid-spring, cutting out damaged and a proportion of old wood. Prune specimens growing in the greenhouse in early spring, cutting back main stems by about half and shortening laterals to 3-4in (7.5-10cm).

ACACIA Deciduous and evergreen shrubs and small trees, which in cool temperate regions require sheltered positions in the open garden or greenhouse treatment. The most commonly grown are evergreen and require minimal pruning (ES, G1, pp. 74-5). If plants are too large for their position, cut back in late spring.

ACCA A. sellowiana is an evergreen fruiting shrub that only crops regularly in warm temperate regions. Elsewhere it benefits from being planted near the base of a sunny wall but should be allowed to grow freely (ES, G1, pp. 74-5).

ACER Mainly deciduous shrubs and trees, many with highly ornamental foliage and some with attractive bark. Wounds on most maples close slowly and all species are vulnerable to attack from the fungus coral spot. Most maples require little pruning. If shaping is necessary, do this while plants are young. Many maples bleed if pruned in spring. Cuts are best made in late summer or early autumn. Maintain the leader on the larger species, such as A. pseudoplatanus, and those with attractive bark, including A. griseum and A. pensylvanicum, to make a branched tree or a central-leader standard (T, pp. 46-7, 49), although most will eventually form branched-head trees. In general A. japonicum and A. palmatum require no pruning, even when densely branched (DS, G1, pp. 60-1). A. campestre can be trained as a branched-head standard (T, pp. 49-50) and is also suitable as a hedging plant (H, G2, p. 102).

ACTINIDIA Deciduous twining climbers, mainly grown for their foliage but see also kiwi

fruit, pp. 212-13. Train over large expanses of wall or fence or into vigorous trees. Spur prune excess growths in the same way as Wisteria (pp. 90-2) but do not prune after early winter to avoid bleeding.

AESCULUS Deciduous trees, including large, highly ornamental spring- and summer-flowering species such as the horse chestnut (A. hippocastanum). Train as central-leader standards (T, p. 49). A. parviflora is a suckering shrub, which requires no pruning (DS, G1, pp. 60-1) other than to restrict the spread of a clump. Cut out unwanted wood in winter.

AILANTHUS Fast-growing deciduous trees of large size. Train as branched trees or central-leader standards (T, pp. 46-7, 49). A. altissima can be cut back annually to near ground level in early spring for foliage effect (DS, G4, pp. 70-3).

AKEBIA Semi-evergreen vigorous twining climbers that can be allowed to sprawl, for example over a stump, or can be trained on a pergola or system of wires. Some tying is generally necessary. Cut out dead wood and weak growths in early spring.

ALBIZIA A. julibrissin is a deciduous fast-growing small tree grown for its attractive divided foliage and flowers. Train as a branched-head standard (T, p. 50), but in cool temperate regions it is generally necessary to give it the protection of a sunny wall.

ALLSPICE see CALYCANTHUS

ALMONDS, ORNAMENTAL see PRUNUS

ALNUS Deciduous trees and shrubs, those of medium and large size, such as A. cordata and A. glutinosa, best grown as branched trees or central-leader standards (T, pp. 46-7, 49). Treat shorter-growing species, such as A. viridis, as lightly pruned shrubs (DS, G1, pp. 60-1).

ALOYSIA A. triphylla (Lippia citriodora) is an aromatic shrub that requires wall protection in cool temperate regions. Treat as Deciduous Shrubs, Group 3, pp. 66-9.

AMELANCHIER Deciduous small trees and shrubs flowering freely in spring and with good autumn colors. Some, such as A. canadensis, are suckering shrubs that require little pruning except to control spread (DS, G1, pp. 60-1). Those that are non-suckering, such as A. lamarckii, can be grown as large shrubs with a minimum of pruning or trained as branched-head standards (T, p. 50). Prune, if necessary, after flowering.

AMPELOPSIS Deciduous climbers that attach themselves to supports by curling tendrils. Vigorous kinds, such as A. brevipedunculata, may need initial support but will clamber into trees or sprawl over hedges and fences. In the wild garden little pruning is required. They can be trained more rigorously, with a framework of rods tied in to a pergola or system of wires, annual growths being cut back to spurs in late autumn or early winter. Prone to bleeding if pruned in spring.

ANDROMEDA Low-growing evergreen shrubs requiring no regular pruning (ES, G1, pp. 74-5).

ARALIA Deciduous suckering shrubs or trees with large compound leaves. They require little pruning (DS, G1, pp. 60-1) but cut out unwanted suckers in early spring.

ARAUCARIA A. araucana is an evergreen coniferous tree. Retain the leader to make a branched tree or central-leader standard (T, p. 48). Remove completely any branches that begin to die back.

ARBOR-VITAE see THUJA

ARBUTUS Evergreen shrubs or small trees. No regular pruning is required (ES, G1, pp. 74-5) but, provided plants are in good health, they will regenerate if cut hard back in mid-spring.

ARCTOSTAPHYLOS A. pungens nevadensis and A. uva-ursi are prostrate evergreen shrubs that require no regular pruning (ES, G1, pp. 74-5).

ARISTOLOCHIA Deciduous and evergreen climbers, some of which require greenhouse treatment in cool temperate regions. To form well-branched plants, pinch out the growing points in the first year.

ARONIA Deciduous shrubs grown for flowers, brightly colored fruits, and autumn color. Vigorous plants produce numerous shoots from the base. When grown principally for their autumn color, cut out stems for which there are replacements in winter (DS, G1, pp. 70-1). Prune less rigorously for flowers and fruit.

ARTEMISIA Includes evergreen and semi-evergreen sub-shrubs and shrubs grown for their foliage. To keep compact and youthful, cut back in early to mid-spring (ES, G2, pp. 76-7).

ASH see FRAXINUS

ATRIPLEX Evergreen and semi-evergreen shrubs, mainly with grey or silvery foliage. Cut back in early to mid-spring to maintain compact growth (ES, G2, pp. 76-7).

AUCUBA Evergreen shrubs grown for their foliage and berries. They require no regular pruning (ES, G1, pp. 74-5). Overgrown specimens can be cut hard back in mid-spring. Cut out shoots that revert on variegated forms. Aucubas are better as informal hedges than trimmed formally. Cut back untidy growths with hand pruners in mid-spring.

AZALEA see RHODODENDRON

AZARA Evergreen shrubs, most requiring wall protection when grown in cool temperate regions. They require little pruning (ES, G1, pp. 74-5). A. microphylla can be fan-trained, unwanted laterals being cut back to the framework in late spring.

BALLOTA Includes sub-shrubs grown for their foliage. To keep plants compact, cut back by about half in mid-spring (ES, G2, pp. 76-7).

BARBERRY see BERBERIS

BAY, SWEET see LAURUS

BEAN TREE, INDIAN see CATALPA

BEAUTY BUSH see KOLKWITZIA

BEECH see FAGUS

BERBERIDOPSIS B. corallina is an evergreen twining climber that requires little pruning. Remove dead wood and unwanted growths in mid-spring.

BERBERIS Evergreen and deciduous shrubs grown mainly for their foliage and berries. They require little regular pruning (DS, G1, pp. 60-1 and ES, G1, pp. 74-5). If necessary, prune deciduous species in late winter or mid-summer (in the latter season dead wood can be distinguished) and evergreens after flowering or, when the aim is to retain a full display of berries, in mid-spring of the following year. Cut old branches to ground level or to vigorous young basal growths.

As hedges they are generally better shaped informally rather than formally (H, pp. 110-11). Trim evergreen kinds after flowering, deciduous kinds in late summer or early autumn.

BETULA Deciduous trees and shrubs requiring little regular pruning. Grow trees as branched specimens (T, pp. 46-7) or central-leader standards (T, p. 49), the latter method showing the attractive bark. Some species (e.g. *B. nigra*) are attractive when allowed to develop more than one trunk. Prune, if necessary, in late summer or autumn, not in late winter or spring, when wounds will bleed heavily.

BIGNONIA *B. capreolata* is a vigorous evergreen or semi-evergreen climber which clings to supports by means of twining leaf tendrils. In cool temperate regions it is best trained on a sunny wall and may require tying in to its support. In mid-spring cut out weak growths completely and prune laterals by a third to a half.

BIRCH see BETULA

BITTER SWEET, CLIMBING see CELASTRUS

BLACK LOCUST see ROBINIA

BLACKTHORN see PRUNUS

BLADDER SENNA see COLUTEA

BOTTLE BRUSH see CALLISTEMON

BOX see BUXUS

BROOM see CYTISUS, GENISTA, SPARTIUM

BROOM, BUTCHER'S see RUSCUS

BROUSSONETIA *B. papyrifera* is a deciduous large shrub or small tree requiring no regular pruning (DS, G1, pp. 60-1).

BRUCKENTHALIA Dwarf evergreen shrubs requiring the same treatment as heathers (ES, G2, pp. 76-7).

BUCKEYE see AESCULUS

BUCKTHORN, SEA see HIPPOPHAË

BUDDLEIA (BUDDLEJA) Deciduous and evergreen shrubs and small trees grown mainly for their flowers. Prune those that flower on the current season's wood (e.g. *B. davidii*), in early spring, cutting back to a low framework (DS, G3, pp. 66-9). Prune those that flower on the previous season's wood (e.g. *B. globosa* and *B. alternifolia*) after flowering (DS, G2, pp. 62-5). In cool climates the less hardy species, such as *B. crispa*, are suitable for framework training against a sunny wall. *B. alternifolia* is most effective when grown as a branched-head standard (T, p. 50).

BUPLEURUM *B. fruticosum*, an evergreen shrub, tends to become untidy when mature and then is best treated like Deciduous Shrubs, Group 4, pp. 70-3, being cut back to near ground level in mid- to late spring.

BUTTERFLY BUSH see BUDDLEJA

BUXUS Evergreen shrubs, and sometimes small trees, grown for their foliage, as hedging and for topiary. Little pruning is needed when grown as informal shrubs (ES, G1, pp. 74-5). To form a tree, select a single leader and eliminate rivals. For hedging and topiary, cut plants back hard in their first year (H, G1, pp. 100-1) and trim in mid- to late summer. Box tolerates being cut hard back, which should be done in mid-spring.

CALICO BUSH see KALMIA

CALLICARPA Deciduous shrubs and small trees that are grown mainly for their berries and autumn foliage. These can be grown with little pruning (DS, G1, pp. 60-1), but moderate thinning and cutting back of damaged growths in early spring is beneficial.

CALLISTEMON Evergreen shrubs grown mainly for their bottle-brush flowers. They require no regular pruning (ES, G1, pp. 74-5) except for the removal of old, spent and straggling shoots to the base. In cool temperate regions they benefit from the protection of a sunny wall, but allow to grow freely.

CALLUNA *C. vulgaris* and its many cultivars are low evergreen shrubs grown for their flowers and foliage. Trim off the previous season's flower heads in early to mid-spring or, in the case of those grown for their winter foliage color, in mid- to late autumn (ES, G2, pp. 76-7).

CALOCEDRUS *C. decurrens* is an evergreen coniferous tree. Train with a central-leader (T, p. 48).

CALYCANTHUS Deciduous shrubs grown mainly for their flowers. They tend to throw up new shoots from the base and are best treated like Deciduous Shrubs, Group 3, pp. 66-9, a proportion of the old wood being cut out in early spring.

CAMELLIA Evergreen shrubs and trees with glossy foliage and highly ornamental flowers. They require no regular pruning (ES, G1, pp. 74-5). Cut back straggling growths in mid-spring.

CAMPSIS Vigorous deciduous climbers, in temperate regions generally grown on a sunny sheltered wall. Require initial support but eventually self-clinging. Cut back to within 6in (15cm) of ground level at planting to promote growth from the base. In late winter and early spring cut back the previous season's growth. Flowers in mid- to late summer on the current season's wood.

CARAGANA Deciduous shrubs or small trees, mainly grown for their pea-like flowers. They require little pruning (DS, G1, pp. 60-1), although cutting back in the first year will encourage bushy growth. *C. arborescens* can be grown as a branched-head standard (T, p. 50) and is sometimes used as the stock for standards of other species, when it often suckers badly.

CARPENTERIA *C. californica* is an evergreen shrub, in cool temperate regions best grown in the shelter of a sunny wall, but allowed to develop naturally. It requires no regular pruning (ES, G1, pp. 74-5) but can be lightly trimmed after flowering.

CARPINUS Deciduous trees best grown as central-leader standards (T, p. 49). *C. betulus* makes an excellent hedge (H, G2, p. 102) and can be used for pleaching (pp. 106-7) and the making of arbors and tunnels (pp. 108-9). Trim these forms in mid-summer.

CARYA Fast-growing and ultimately large deciduous trees best grown as central-leader standards (T, p. 49). See also Pecan, p. 185.

CARYOPTERIS *C.* x *clandonensis* is a sub-shrub on which most of the top growth dies back in winter. Cut the previous year's growth hard back in early spring (DS, G3, pp. 66-9).

CASSINIA Heath-like evergreen shrubs. Prune in spring to keep compact (ES, G2, pp. 76-7).

CASSIOPE Evergreen dwarf or mat-forming shrubs that require no regular pruning (ES, G1, pp. 74-5).

CASTANEA For *C. sativa* grown for its nuts see Chestnut, p. 185. This tree is also grown for mainly ornamental purposes as a central-leader standard (T, p. 49). Note that mature specimens have a tendency to shed large limbs without warning. Remove suckers as they develop. Traditional coppicing exploits the suckering habit, commercial crops being cut about every 12 years.

CATALPA Deciduous trees best grown as branched-head standards (T, p. 50).

CEANOTHUS Evergreen and deciduous shrubs grown mainly for their blue flowers. In cool temperate regions the evergreen ceanothus are best trained against a warm wall or fence (see Climbers and Wall Shrubs, p. 93). Deciduous ceanothus bear flowers on the current season's wood. Prune in early spring (DS, G3, pp. 66-9).

CEDAR see CEDRUS

CEDAR, JAPANESE see CRYPTOMERIA

CEDRUS Evergreen coniferous trees, pyramidal when young but eventually flat-topped. It is important to retain a central leader (T, p. 48).

CELASTRUS Vigorous deciduous twining climbers that are best allowed to grow unrestricted in old trees. Pruning is normally limited to the removal of dead wood in summer.

CELTIS Fast-growing deciduous trees. Train as feathered trees or central-leader standards (T, pp. 46-7, 49).

CEPHALOTAXUS Evergreen coniferous shrubs or small trees requiring no regular pruning (ES, G1, pp. 74-5). Can be cut back hard in the same way as yew.

CERATOSTIGMA Evergreen and deciduous shrubs that flower on the current season's wood. They are normally cut back to ground level in winter. In mid-spring cut down all of the previous season's growths (DS, G3, pp. 66-9).

CERCIDIPHYLLUM *C. japonicum* is a deciduous large shrub or tree which naturally develops rival leaders. No regular pruning is required (DS, G1, pp. 60-1).

CERCIS Deciduous shrubs or small trees, normally bushy and requiring little pruning (DS, G1, pp. 60-1). They can also be trained as branched-head standards on a short trunk (T, p. 50). Trim after flowering to reduce the number of seed pods.

CHAENOMELES Deciduous spring-flowering shrubs. When grown as bushes little pruning is required (DS, G1, pp. 60-1). If any pruning is necessary, this should be done in late spring or early summer, after flowering. For pruning and training of *Chaenomeles* as wall shrubs see pp. 94-5.

CHAMAECYPARIS Evergreen coniferous trees. They are best given ample space to develop and trained as feathered trees (T, p. 48). *C. lawsoniana* is widely grown as a hedging plant (H, G3, p. 103). Trim in summer.

CHERRIES, ORNAMENTAL see PRUNUS

CHESTNUT, HORSE see AESCULUS

CHESTNUT, SWEET see CASTANEA

CHIMONANTHUS *C. praecox* is a deciduous shrub that flowers in winter. When grown as a bush little pruning is necessary (DS, G1, pp. 60-1). Prune badly placed shoots on wall-trained specimens in late winter after flowering.

CHIONANTHUS Deciduous shrubs or small trees. They require no regular pruning when grown as shrubs (DS, G1, pp. 60-1). Specimens can be trained as branched-head standards (T, p. 50).

CHOISYA *C. ternata* is an evergreen shrub that will break freely if cut back into old wood but requires minimal pruning (ES, G1, pp. 74-5). If necessary, trim in early summer, after flowering.

CHOKEBERRY see ARONIA

CISTUS Evergreen shrubs requiring minimal pruning (ES, G1, pp. 74-5). Bushy growth can be encouraged by pinching out the tips of young shoots in spring, but most *Cistus* will not respond when cut back into old wood.

CLADRASTIS Deciduous trees. Train as feathered trees or branched-head standards (T, pp. 46-7, 49). Prune in late summer to avoid bleeding.

CLEMATIS Deciduous and evergreen plants, mainly climbers that hoist themselves up by means of twining leaf stalks. In the following selection the name is followed by the appropriate pruning group as described on pp. 85-9.

C. alpina (including cvs such as 'Frances Rivis', 'Helsingborg' and 'Rosy Pagoda'), 2; C. armandii, 2; 'Barbara Jackman', 3; 'Beauty of Worcester', 1 or 3; 'Belle of Woking', 3; C. chrysocoma, 2; C. cirrhosa, 2; 'Comtesse de Bouchaud', 1; 'Countess of Lovelace', 3; 'Daniel Deronda', 1 or 3; 'Dr Ruppel', 3; 'Duchess of Edinburgh', 3; 'Duchess of Sutherland', 1 or 3; 'Elsa Späth', 1 or 3; 'Ernest Markham', 1 or 3; C. florida 'Sieboldii', 3; 'General Sikorski', 3; 'Gipsy Queen', 1; 'Gravetye Beauty', 1; 'Hagley Hybrid', 1; 'Henryi', 3; 'Huldine', 1; C. x jackmanii, 1; 'John Huxtable', 1; 'Lady Betty Balfour', 1; 'Lady Northcliffe', 1 or 3; 'Lasurstern', 1 or 3; C. macropetala (including cvs such as 'Blue Bird', 'Maidwell Hall', and 'Markham's Pink'), 2; 'Mme Julia Correvon', 1; 'Marie Boisselot', 1 or 3; 'Miss Bateman', 3; C. montana (including cvs such as 'Alexander', 'Elizabeth' and 'Tetrarose'), 2; 'Mrs Cholmondeley', 1 or 3; 'Nelly Moser', 3; C. orientalis, 1; 'Perle d'Azur', 1; 'Prins Hendrik', 3; 'Royal Velours', 1; 'Star of India', 1; C. tangutica, 1; 'The President', 1 or 3; 'Ville de Lyon', 1 or 3; C. vitalba, 1; C. viticella (including hybrid cvs such as 'Kermesina' and 'Purpurea Plena Elegans'), 1; 'Vyvyan Pennell', 3; 'William Kennett', 1 or 3.

CLETHRA Summer-flowering shrubs that require no pruning.

CLIANTHUS C. puniceus is an evergreen lax shrub best trained to wires against a sunny wall or in the greenhouse. Cut out any dead wood in early to mid-spring. On established plants remove one or two old stems in mid-summer, after flowering, and tie in young replacements.

COLLETIA Spiny late-flowering deciduous shrubs requiring no regular pruning (DS, G1, pp. 60-1).

COLQUHOUNIA C. coccinea is a deciduous shrub that flowers on the current season's wood. In cool temperate regions cut back hard in mid-spring (DS, G3, pp. 66-9),

COLUTEA C. arborescens is a deciduous shrub that flowers in summer on the current season's wood. Train a permanent framework of branches, cutting back to within a few buds of the old wood in early spring (DS, G3, pp. 66-9).

CONVOLVULUS C. cneorum is an evergreen shrub that is naturally bushy and compact (ES, G1, pp. 74-5). If it is necessary to prune long growths, cut these back to the base in spring.

CORDYLINE These evergreen palm-like shrubs, whether grown under glass or in the open garden, should be left unpruned unless the head is being cut back to promote the growth of propagation material.

CORNEL see CORNUS

CORNUS Deciduous and evergreen shrubs and trees grown for their flowers, colored stems and foliage. Prune hard in early spring those, such as C. alba and C.stolonifera 'Flaviramea', which are grown for their attractive colored stems or variegated foliage (DS, G4, p. 70-3). The species that make large shrubs or small trees, such as C. controversa, C. florida, C. kousa and C. mas, require no regular pruning (DS, G1, pp. 60-1), but for branched-head standards it is necessary to train in a leader (T, p. 50).

COROKIA Evergreen shrubs, often requiring a sheltered position, but not suitable for training against a wall. They require no regular pruning (ES, G1, pp. 74-5), but frost-damaged shoots

should be cut back in mid-spring.

CORONILLA The deciduous species C. emerus requires little pruning but tolerates being cut hard back. Take out old wood in winter. Evergreen species are wispy plants when young and benefit from light staking and pinching back of the young shoots to encourage more branched, sturdy growth. They require no regular pruning (ES, G1, pp. 74-5), but may be lightly trimmed in mid-spring.

CORYLOPSIS Deciduous shrubs or small trees. Although they may benefit from the shelter of a wall, they should be allowed to develop a natural shape (DS, G1, pp. 60-1). If cosmetic pruning is necessary or if removing old wood, prune in late spring, after flowering.

CORYLUS In addition to those grown for their nuts (see Cobnuts and Filberts, p. 184), several species and their cultivars are grown for their ornamental catkins and foliage. Train C. colurna as a central-leader standard (T, p. 49). The shrubby kinds generally sucker freely. They can be lightly trimmed after flowering (DS, G1, pp. 60-1) but respond well to periodic cutting back. For maximum foliage effect of such forms as C. maxima 'Purpurea', prune hard in late winter or early spring (DS, G4, pp. 70-3). C. avellana and C. maxima can be used for formal hedges (H, G2, p. 102) or traditional laid hedges (pp. 110-11).

COTINUS The deciduous C. coggygria can be grown as a large shrub or small tree carrying smoky flowers (DS, G1, pp. 60-1). For maximum foliage effect, but no flowers, cut back annually in early to mid-spring to a low framework of branches (DS, G4, p. 70).

COTONEASTER Evergreen and deciduous shrubs and small trees, many carrying conspicuous berries in autumn. No regular pruning is required (DS, G1, pp. 60-1 and ES, G1, pp. 74-5) and, if pruning is carried out, the natural habit should be respected. Some cotoneasters are suitable for wall training and should be treated in the same way as Pyracantha. Although evergreens are sometimes used as formal hedges (H, G3, p. 103), the display of berries is better if they are treated informally (pp. 110-11).

COTTONWOOD see POPULUS

CRATAEGUS Deciduous small trees or large shrubs grown mainly for their spring flowers, autumn coloring, and berries. Train as branched-head standards or central-leader standards (T, pp. 49, 50), the latter eventually developing a naturally branched head.

CRINODENDRON Evergreen shrubs or small trees, in cool temperate regions best protected by a wall, but allowed to develop freely (ES, G1, pp. 74-5). Cut out dead wood in spring.

CRYPTOMERIA C. japonica is an evergreen conifer forming a pyramidal tree and requiring little pruning (T, p. 48). C.j. 'Elegans', a form in which the juvenile foliage is retained, may need staking or it can be headed back to make the plant self-supporting. When using this form as a hedging plant (H, G3, p. 103), trim in late summer. The dwarf forms, often of dense habit, should normally be left unpruned.

CUNNINGHAMIA Evergreen coniferous trees. Train as feathered tree (T, p. 48).

x CUPRESSOCYPARIS x C. leylandii is a fast-growing evergreen coniferous tree. Retain the central leader to make a feathered tree clothed to ground level (T, p. 48). As a hedge (H, G3, p. 103), clip in mid- to late summer.

CUPRESSUS Evergreen coniferous trees on which it is important to retain the central leader (T, p.

48). C. macrocarpa, although often used for formal hedging, resents close clipping. C. sempervirens is one of the classic plants of Mediterranean gardens for formal hedges and topiary (H, G3, p. 103). Clip in summer.

CURRANT, FLOWERING see RIBES

CYDONIA For C. oblonga see Quince, pp. 180-81.

CYPRESS see CHAMAECYPARIS and CUPRESSUS

CYPRESS, LEYLAND see x CUPRESSOCYPARIS

CYPRESS, SWAMP see TAXODIUM

CYTISUS Mainly deciduous shrubs that are grown for their profuse flowering. Cut back after flowering to encourage young growths (DS, G2, p. 65). C. battandieri can be trained as a wall shrub but requires little pruning other than the removal of dead or damaged wood in mid-spring.

DABOECIA Evergreen sub-shrubs. To keep plants vigorous and compact, take off old flower stalks and most of the previous year's growth in mid-spring (ES, G2, pp. 76-7).

DAISY BUSH see OLEARIA

DAPHNE Deciduous and evergreen dwarf and medium-sized shrubs that usually require little pruning and frequently respond to it badly (ES, G1, pp. 74-5).

DAPHNIPHYLLUM Evergreen shrubs with inconspicuous flowers requiring no regular pruning (ES, G1, pp. 74-5).

DAVIDIA D. involucrata is a deciduous species that is best grown as a single-leader tree with a clear stem (T, p. 49), a method of training that allows the showy bracts to be seen to good effect.

DECAISNEA D. fargesii is a deciduous shrub that produces a number of upright stems from the base. No regular pruning is necessary (DS, G1, pp. 60-1), but old bare stems can be cut out at ground level in autumn or winter. In early to mid-summer cut out young shoots damaged by late frosts.

DENDROMECON Evergreen shrubs suitable for training against a sunny wall in cool temperate regions. Each year cut out a few of the oldest shoots.

DESFONTAINEA D. spinosa is an evergreen shrub often grown in the shelter of a wall, but best left to grow freely (ES, G1, pp. 74-5).

DESMODIUM Deciduous and evergreen shrubs that flower on the current season's growths. Treat in the same way as Perovskia, cutting back hard in spring (DS, G3, p. 66-9).

DEUTZIA Deciduous shrubs grown mainly for their flowers, which are produced on laterals growing on the previous year's wood. Take out old wood after flowering (DS, G2, pp. 62-3).

DIERVILLA Deciduous shrubs that flower in summer on the current season's wood. Cut back annually to near ground level in early spring (DS, G3, pp. 66-7).

DIOSPYROS D. armata is a slow-growing evergreen shrub requiring no regular pruning (ES, G1, pp. 74-5). D. lotus is a deciduous small tree and best trained as a branched-head standard of weeping habit (T, p. 51). For D. kaki and D. virginiana, which have edible fruit, see Persimmons, pp. 187-88.

DIPELTA Deciduous shrubs that flower on the previous season's wood (DS, G2, pp. 62-3).

DISANTHUS D. cercidifolius is a deciduous shrub that colors well in autumn. No regular

pruning is needed (DS, G1, pp. 60-1).
DISCARIA Spiny deciduous shrubs requiring no regular pruning (DS, G1, pp. 60-1).
DISTYLIUM *D. racemosum* is an evergreen shrub or small tree with a characteristic horizontal arrangement of branches. No regular pruning is required (DS, G1, pp. 60–1).
DOGWOOD see CORNUS
DORYCNIUM *D. hirsutum* is a dwarf sub-shrub, the stems of which often die back in winter. Remove them in spring.
DOVE TREE see DAVIDIA
DRIMYS Evergreen shrubs or small trees that require no regular pruning (ES, G1, pp. 74-5).

ECCREMOCARPUS *E. scaber* is a semi-woody climber, in temperate gardens grown on a sheltered wall or in the greenhouse, often as an annual. If maintained for more than one year, cut out dead stems in early to mid-spring.
EDGEWORTHIA Deciduous shrub with fragrant flowers that requires no regular pruning (ES, G1, pp. 74-5).
EHRETIA Small deciduous trees. Train as feathered trees (T, pp. 46-7).
ELAEAGNUS Evergreen and deciduous shrubs, grown mainly for their attractive foliage. Most require only cosmetic pruning (DS, G1, pp. 60-1 and ES, G1, pp. 74-5), although in general they tolerate cutting back into old wood, which may be necessary with overgrown specimens. Prune deciduous kinds in early spring and evergreen kinds in mid-spring. When evergreen kinds are grown as informal hedges, cut back individual stems in late summer. On variegated forms of *E. pungens* cut out shoots with pure green foliage as soon as they develop.
ELDER see SAMBUCUS
ELM see ULMUS
EMBOTHRIUM Evergreen shrubs or small trees that require no regular pruning (ES, G1, pp. 74-5). However, straggling growths can be cut back in mid-summer, after flowering.
EMMENOPTERYS *E. henryi* is a deciduous small tree. Train as a central-leader standard (T, p. 49).
ENKIANTHUS Naturally bushy deciduous or semi-evergreen shrubs that require minimal pruning (DS, G1, pp. 60-1), although they tolerate being cut back into old wood.
ERICA Evergreen shrubs and sub-shrubs, most of the summer- and autumn-flowering dwarf kinds requiring annual cutting back of the previous season's growth to keep them compact and free-flowering (ES, G2, pp. 76-7). *E. arborea, E. lusitanica, E. terminalis,* and *E.* x *veitchii* normally require no pruning.
ERIOBOTRYA An evergreen tree or large shrub sometimes grown for its fruit but in cool temperate gardens mainly for its foliage. As a fruiting tree, grow as a central-leader standard (T, p. 49). As a foliage plant (ES, G1, pp. 74-5), it may require light trimming and the removal of damaged leaves in mid-spring.
ESCALLONIA Evergreen or semi-evergreen shrubs or small trees, most of those commonly grown being evergreen (ES, G1, pp. 74-5). Prune, if required, in late summer or early autumn, after flowering. As hedges, escallonias are best cut hard back at planting (H, G1, pp. 100-1) and trimmed annually in late summer or early autumn, after flowering.
EUCALYPTUS Evergreen trees and shrubs, most cultivated species being grown as central-leader

standards with a minimum of pruning (T, p. 49) or as shrubs or stooled plants that are maintained at the juvenile stage, for the sake of the foliage, by regular cutting back in spring (p. 73).
EUCOMMIA *E. ulmoides* is a deciduous tree, best trained as a central leader standard (T, p. 49).
EUCRYPHIA Evergreen and deciduous shrubs and trees that flower in summer. They require no regular pruning (DS, G1, pp. 60-1 and ES, G1, pp. 74-5), but bushy growth can be encouraged by pinching out the leading shoots on young plants.
EUONYMUS Deciduous and evergreen shrubs, often with conspicuous fruits. The deciduous kinds, which often color well in autumn, require no regular pruning (DS, G1, pp. 60-1). The evergreens (ES, G1, pp. 74-5) include many variegated forms. Any shoots that revert should be cut out. Trailing and climbing forms (at the flowering stage *E. fortunei* becomes bushy) generally need tying in to suppports.
EXOCHORDA Deciduous shrubs of suckering habit. Prune, if necessary, in summer, after flowering. Some suckers may be trained in as replacement growths but remove any that are unwanted as they develop.

FABIANA *F. imbricata* is an evergreen shrub grown for its foliage and flowers. In cool temperate regions it benefits from the shelter of a warm wall but allow it to grow freely (ES, G1, pp. 74-5). Prune, if necessary, after flowering; it will regenerate even when old wood is cut back.
FAGUS Deciduous trees of which the most widely grown is *F. sylvatica* and its various forms. It is best grown as a central-leader standard (T, p. 49). Mature specimens may unexpectedly shed large branches. Beech is an excellent hedging plant, retaining its old leaves in winter (H, G2, p. 102).
FALLOPIA Deciduous twining climbers that can be trained on a system of wires, over a pergola or into trees. They require no regular pruning.
x FATSHEDERA The bigeneric hybrid x *F. lizei* is a sprawling evergreen grown as ground cover or trained against a wall (ES, G1, pp. 74-5). If necessary, cut back in mid-spring but no regular pruning is necessary.
FATSIA *F. japonica* is an evergreen shrub that requires little pruning (ES, G1, pp. 74-5) but, if size needs to be restricted, cut out old wood in mid-spring.
FEIJOA see ACCA
FILBERT see CORYLUS
FIR see ABIES and PICEA
FIR, DOUGLAS see PSEUDOTSUGA
FIRETHORN see PYRACANTHA
FONTANESIA Deciduous privet-like shrubs requiring no regular pruning (DS, G1, pp. 60-1).
FORSYTHIA Deciduous shrubs that flower profusely in spring on wood produced the previous year. Prune after flowering (DS, G2, pp. 62-5). *F. suspensa* is a lax shrub that is suitable for training against a wall and should be pruned back annually to a permanent fan-shaped framework. Forsythias can be shaped as formal flowering hedges (H, G2, p. 102).
FOTHERGILLA Deciduous shrubs grown mainly for their flowers and fine autumn colors. They require no regular pruning (DS, G1, pp. 60-1).
FRANKLINIA *F. alatamaha* is a deciduous shrub that colors well in autumn. No regular pruning

is required (DS, G1, pp. 60-1).
FRAXINUS Deciduous trees. Train as central-leader standards (T, p. 49). On weeping forms retain the leader for as long as possible and create a clear stem to a height of 6-10ft (1.8-3m).
FREMONTODENDRON *F. californica* is an evergreen shrub native to southern California foothills. Drought resistant. Best on hillsides and supported by a stake. It requires little pruning (ES, G1, p. 74-5) other than the removal of damaged growths in mid-spring.
FUCHSIA Deciduous trees and shrubs which flower profusely on the current season's wood. Prune hardy varieties that are grown outdoors to near ground level in early to mid-spring (DS, G3, pp. 66-9) and cut back fuchsias grown as informal hedges at the same time. To encourage bushy growth of fuchsias grown under glass pinch out growing points. For training tender fuchsias as standards see p. 132.
FURZE see ULEX

GARRYA *G. elliptica*, the most widely grown of these evergreen shrubs, often benefits from the protection of a wall, but should be set back from it and allowed to grow freely. No regular pruning is required (ES, G1, pp. 74-5) but, if it is necessary to restrict size, cut back growths in mid-spring.
GAULTHERIA Evergreen shrubs that require no regular pruning (ES, G1, pp. 74-5).
GENISTA Deciduous or nearly leafless shrubs that flower profusely in late spring or summer. Most are best treated like *Cytisus*, stems being cut back to young growth after flowering (DS, G2, p. 65). *G. aetnensis* can be trained as a branched-head standard (T, p. 50).
GHOST TREE see DAVIDIA
GINKGO *G. biloba* is a deciduous tree allied to the conifers. Remove any rival leads to form a central-leader standard (T, pp. 49, 50).
GLEDITSIA Deciduous trees, grown mainly for their foliage. Train as central-leader or branched-head standards (T, p. 49), pruning, if necessary, in early spring.
GOLDEN CHAIN see LABURNUM
GORDONIA Evergreen shrubs and small trees that require no regular pruning (ES, G1, pp. 74-5).
GORSE see ULEX
GORSE, SPANISH see GENISTA
GREVILLEA Evergreen shrubs and trees, in cool temperate regions grown under glass or close to a sunny wall, but not trained against it. No regular pruning is needed (ES, G1, pp. 74-5). Prune straggling and frost-damaged shoots in mid-spring.
GRINDELIA *G. chiloensis* is an evergreen sub-shrub which in mild conditions requires no pruning (ES, G1, pp. 74-5). If growths are damaged in winter, cut these back in mid-spring.
GRISELINIA Evergreen shrubs and trees that require no regular pruning (ES, G1, pp. 74-5). They are used for hedging (H, G3, p. 103), but are more suitable as informal windbreaks, pruners being used to remove individual shoots in early summer.
GUM TREE see EUCALYPTUS
GYMNOCLADUS Deciduous trees best trained as central-leader standards (T, p. 49).

HALESIA Deciduous spring-flowering trees and shrubs, generally requiring little pruning. *H. carolina* is best allowed to develop as a densely branched shrub (DS, G1, pp. 60-1), or a branched-head tree on a short trunk (T, p. 50), this latter method of training being suited also to *H. monticola*.

x HALIMIOCISTUS Evergreen bigeneric hybrids between *Halimium* and *Cistus*. They do not respond well to pruning. Take out dead wood and trim off the dead flowers of the previous season in mid-spring (ES, G1, pp. 74-5).

HALIMIUM Evergreen shrubs grown for their rose-like flowers. Pruning is generally resented and little is needed (ES, G1, pp. 74-5). Cut out dead wood in spring and, if necessary, lightly trim straggly growths.

HAMAMELIS Deciduous shrubs grown for their winter flowers and autumn foliage and requiring no regular pruning (DS, G1, pp. 60-1). Most plants are grafted and tend to sucker.

HAWTHORN see CRATAEGUS

HEATH see ERICA

HEATHER see CALLUNA

HEBE Evergreen shrubs, often grown for their attractive foliage as well as their flowers. Normally, they require little pruning (ES, G1, pp. 74-5). Deadhead and lightly trim those that bloom early in the year as soon as flowering is over and those that flower in late summer and autumn in mid-spring of the following year. Shoots break freely from old wood and hard cutting back may be necessary if there has been severe frost damage.

HEDERA Evergreen self-clinging climbers grown for their foliage. On mature specimens the adult growths, which carry the flowers, are bushy and not self-clinging. Trim, if necessary, in late spring and early summer. This will maintain plants at the juvenile stage. See also p. 84.

HEIMIA *H. salicifolia* is a deciduous shrub that requires no regular pruning (DS, G1, pp. 60-1).

HELIANTHEMUM Dwarf evergreen shrubs that require no regular pruning (ES, G1, pp. 74-5). If pruning is necessary to encourage tight growth, trim after flowering.

HELICHRYSUM Evergreen shrubs and sub-shrubs grown mainly for their silver foliage. Some species do not require regular pruning and should only be trimmed after flowering; others may be pruned back to the previous year's wood in early to mid-spring (DS, G4, pp. 70-3).

HEMLOCK see TSUGA

HIBISCUS *H. syriacus* is a deciduous shrub flowering in late summer on the current season's wood. It requires no regular pruning (DS, G1, pp. 60-1), but cut out dead and damaged wood in mid-spring. Straggly plants respond to hard pruning.

HIPPOPHAË Deciduous shrubs grown mainly for their long-lasting berries. They require no regular pruning (DS, G1, pp. 60-1).

HOHERIA Evergreen and deciduous shrubs or small trees that flower in summer. No regular pruning (DS, G1, pp. 60-1 and ES, G1, pp. 74-5).

HOLBOELLIA Evergreen twining climbers that can be left unpruned. If necessary, remove old stems after flowering.

HOLLY see ILEX

HOLODISCUS Deciduous shrubs that carry flowers on growths produced the previous season. Prune after flowering (DS, G2, pp. 62-5).

HONEYSUCKLE see LONICERA

HYDRANGEA Deciduous and evergreen shrubs and climbers producing flowers on the previous year's growths. Some medium to large shrubs, such as *H. villosa, H. quercifolia*, and *H. sargentiana* need no regular pruning (DS, G1, pp. 60-1). Prune those that flower on the current season's wood, such as *H. paniculata* and *H. arborescens*, in spring (DS, G3, pp. 66-9). The mophead and lacecap hydrangeas (*H. macrophylla*), which flower on growths produced the previous year, are pruned selectively in mid-spring (DS, G2, pp. 64-5). Train self-clinging climbers such as *H. petiolaris* on walls or into trees. Cut back unwanted growths in summer.

HYPERICUM Includes deciduous and evergreen shrubs grown for their flowers. Most require no regular pruning (DS, G1, pp. 60-1 and ES, G1, pp. 74-5), but cut out winter-damaged growths in spring. *H. calycinum* and *H. inodorum* 'Elstead' can be trimmed over with shears in spring to maintain them in good condition.

IDESIA *I. polycarpa* is a deciduous tree best trained as a central-leader standard (T, p. 49).

ILEX Mainly evergreen shrubs and trees grown for their foliage and berries. Train hollies as branched trees (T, pp. 46-7) or grow as shrubs with a minimum of pruning (ES, G1, pp. 74-5). When grown as hedges (H, G3, p. 103) and topiary specimens, trim in late summer. Hedges tolerate being cut hard back, but the work should be staged over more than one season (p. 109).

ILLICIUM Aromatic evergreen shrubs requiring no regular pruning (ES, G1, pp. 74-5).

INDIGOFERA Deciduous shrubs that flower freely on the current season's wood. Prune in spring as *Perovskia* (DS, G3, p. 67), or leave unpruned apart from cosmetic trimming.

ITEA Evergreen and deciduous summer-flowering shrubs requiring no regular pruning (DS, G1, pp. 60-1, and ES, G1, pp. 74-5).

IVY see HEDERA

JAPONICA see CHAENOMELES

JASMINE see JASMINUM

JASMINUM Evergreen and deciduous shrubs and climbers grown for their flowers, which are generally borne on the previous season's wood. When necessary, prune shrubs after flowering (DS, G2, pp. 62-5). Train the lax shrub *J. nudiflorum* against a wall, cutting out flowered stems as soon as flowering is over. *J. officinale* is a vigorous twining climber which is difficult to control. Reduce tangles by taking out some old stems after flowering.

JOVELLANA *J. violacea* is a small evergreen shrub which in cool temperate regions usually loses its foliage in winter. Cut back in mid-spring as *Perovskia* (DS, G3, pp. 66-7).

JUDAS TREE see CERCIS

JUGLANS see Walnut, p. 185.

JUNE BERRY see AMELANCHIER

JUNIPER see JUNIPERUS

JUNIPERUS Evergreen conifers, including prostrate and bushy shrubs and tall trees. The shrubs require no regular pruning (ES, G1, p. 75). Train tall-growing columnar species (e.g. *J. virginiana*) as branched trees (T, pp. 46-7).

KALMIA Evergreen summer-flowering shrubs that require no regular pruning (ES, G1, pp. 74-5).

KALOPANAX Deciduous tree. Train as branched tree (T, pp. 46-7).

KERRIA *K. japonica* is a deciduous suckering shrub. Prune immediately after flowering (DS, G2, p. 65).

KOELREUTERIA *K. paniculata* is a deciduous tree or large shrub. Train as a central-leader standard, which will eventually develop a branched head (T, p. 49). As a shrub it requires no regular pruning (DS, G1, pp. 60-1).

KOLKWITZIA *K. amabilis* is a deciduous shrub that flowers on the previous year's wood. Prune after flowering (DS, G2, pp. 62-5).

+ LABURNOCYTISUS A graft hybrid best grown as a central-leader standard or branched-head standard (T, pp. 49, 50).

LABURNUM Deciduous trees and shrubs grown for their pendulous pea-like flowers. Train as central-leader or branched-head standards (T, pp. 49-50) or as large shrubs (DS, G1, pp. 60-1). *L. anagyroides* and its hybrids can be trained on pergolas and spur pruned (p. 108). When cut in spring, laburnums may bleed badly. Remove large branches in summer and spur prune in early winter.

LAPAGERIA An evergreen twining climber that is popular as a greenhouse plant, but can be grown outdoors in cool temperate areas in a sheltered position. Train on a system of vertical and horizontal wires or large-gauge trellis. Cut out dead and weak growth in mid-spring.

LARCH see LARIX

LARIX Deciduous conifers best grown as central-leader standards (T, p. 49).

LAUREL, BAY see LAURUS

LAUREL, CHERRY see PRUNUS

LAUREL, COMMON see PRUNUS

LAUREL, MOUNTAIN see KALMIA

LAUREL, PORTUGAL see PRUNUS

LAUREL, SPOTTED see AUCUBA

LAURUS *L. nobilis* is an evergreen large shrub or small tree requiring no pruning other than occasional light trimming in mid-spring (ES, G1, pp. 74-5). As hedges (H, G3, p. 103) trim in summer. Topiary specimens, such as mop-headed standards, should also be trimmed in summer, using hand pruners to cut back whole shoots.

LAURUSTINUS see VIBURNUM

LAVANDULA Evergreen shrubs grown for their fragrant flowers and aromatic foliage. Keep compact by pruning in spring (ES, G2, p. 76-7).

LAVATERA Deciduous shrubs grown for their flowers, which are produced on the current season's growth. Cut back in mid-spring, as *Perovskia* (DS, G3, p. 67).

LAVENDER see LAVANDULA

LEDUM Low-growing evergreen shrubs requiring no regular pruning (ES, G1, pp. 74-5).

LEPTOSPERMUM Evergreen shrubs grown mainly for their flowers. They require no regular pruning (ES, G1, pp. 74-5). Although in cool temperate regions benefiting from the protection of a warm wall, they should be allowed to grow freely. They thrive near sea on West Coast.

LESPEDEZA Deciduous shrubs that flower on the current season's growth. Cut back old growths in spring, as *Perovskia* (DS, G3, p. 67), or leave unpruned except for cosmetic trimming.

LEUCOTHOË Evergreen shrubs requiring no regular pruning (ES, G1, pp. 74-5).

LEYCESTERIA Deciduous shrubs that carry hanging flowers on the current season's wood. Prune in the same way as *Perovskia* (DS, G3, p. 67), in spring, cutting to ground level stems that carried flowers the preceding summer. Another method is to remove all but a few strong non-flowered shoots that develop in summer. These flower early the following year and further growths produced from spring onwards extend the flowering season.

LIGUSTRUM Deciduous and evergreen shrubs and small trees. *L. lucidum* may be grown as a branched-head standard (T, p. 50) or, like most other species, as shrubs that are allowed to develop with minimal pruning (DS, G1, pp. 60-61 and ES, G1, pp. 74-5). *L. ovalifolium* is a common hedge plant (H, G1, pp. 100-1), which needs frequent clipping throughout summer. Overgrown hedges and specimens of *Ligustrum* usually respond well to hard cutting back in mid-spring. Cut out green-leaved shoots on variegated forms that revert.

LINDEN see TILIA

LINDERA Mainly deciduous shrubs and small trees grown for their foliage and requiring no regular pruning (DS, G1, pp. 60-1).

LING see CALLUNA

LIQUIDAMBAR Deciduous trees, generally with good autumn coloring. Train as branched trees or central-leader standards (T, pp. 46-7, 49).

LIRIODENDRON Fast-growing deciduous trees of medium or large size best grown as central-leader standards (T, p. 49).

LOMATIA Evergreen shrubs requiring no regular pruning (ES, G1, pp. 74-5).

LONICERA Deciduous and evergreen shrubs and twining climbers. Prune deciduous shrubby species, such as *L. fragrantissima*, after flowering. The evergreen *L. nitida* needs little pruning (ES, G1, pp. 74-5) unless it is grown as a formal hedge (H, G1, pp. 100-1), when it needs frequent clipping throughout summer.

Climbing honeysuckles fall into two groups. Those in the first group, which includes *L. japonica*, flower on the current season's growth. These can be clipped over annually in early to mid-spring. Those in the second group include *L. x americana*, *L. x brownii*, *L. periclymenum*, *L. sempervirens*, *L. x tellmanniana* and *L. tragophylla*. Their flowers are borne on laterals produced on the previous season's growth. They can be allowed to grow freely but often form tangled masses above bare stems. If possible, cut out some old growths after flowering.

LUPIN see LUPINUS

LUPINUS *L. arboreus* is a semi-evergreen shrub grown for its flowers. Remove spent flower heads and prune in early spring, less severely but similarly to shrubs in Group 3, pp. 66-9.

MAACKIA Slow-growing deciduous shrubs or small trees requiring no regular pruning (DS, G1, pp. 60-1).

MAGNOLIA Deciduous and evergreen trees and shrubs grown for their magnificent flowers. Shrubby deciduous magnolias, such as *M. x loebneri*, *M. x soulangeana* and *M. stellata*, require no regular pruning (DS, G1, pp. 60-1). Train larger deciduous species, such as *M. campbellii*, *M. dawsoniana*, *M. kobus*, and *M. salicifolia*, as branched trees or branched-head standards (T, pp. 46-7, 50). If pruning of deciduous species is necessary, it is best done in

summer. The evergreen *M. grandiflora* can be grown in the open as a large shrub or small tree. In cool temperate regions this plant benefits from being grown against a sunny wall. Ensure a generous allocation of space, train up the central leader and tie in main branches. Some backward- and forward-facing branches may need to be removed in mid-spring. Most magnolias regenerate readily, even from old wood.

MAHONIA Evergreen shrubs grown for their foliage and flowers. Some mahonias require no regular pruning (ES, G1, pp. 74-5). However, *M. lomariifolia* and *M. x media* 'Charity' are examples of mahonias that become straggly if not regularly pruned. Cut flowered shoots hard back in early spring. Plants will break well from two-year-old wood. *M. aquifolium* suckers freely and is often used as ground cover. It can be trimmed over to near ground level in mid-spring each year or at intervals of a few years.

MAIDENHAIR TREE see GINKGO

MALLOW, TREE see LAVATERA

MALUS Deciduous trees and shrubs grown for their flowers and ornamental fruits. Train as central-leader or branched-head standards (T, pp. 49, 50). Plants are usually grafted. Remove suckers promptly. See also Apples, pp. 138-53.

MANDEVILLA *M. suaveolens* is a deciduous twining climber. It requires no regular pruning other than the removal of weak growths and dead wood in mid-spring.

MANUKA see LEPTOSPERMUM

MANZANITA see ARCTOSTAPHYLOS

MAPLE see ACER

MAY see CRATAEGUS

MENZIESIA Small to medium deciduous shrubs grown mainly for their flowers. They require no regular pruning (DS, G1, pp. 60-1).

MESPILUS see Medlar, pp. 180-1.

METASEQUOIA *M. glyptostroboides* is a strong-growing deciduous coniferous tree of conical shape. Train as a branched tree (T, pp. 46-77). As a hedge, maintain the leaders to a height of approximately 6ft (1.8m) before cutting back (H, G3, p. 103). Clip in mid-summer.

MEZEREON see DAPHNE

MICHELIA Evergreen trees or shrubs grown mainly for their flowers. The shrubby species (e.g. *M. figo*) require no regular pruning (ES, G1, pp. 74-5). Train larger species as central-leader standards (T, p. 49).

MONKEY PUZZLE see ARAUCARIA

MORUS Deciduous small- to medium-sized trees. Train as central-leader standards (T, p. 49), although the tendency of the head to branch will eventually assert itself. Mulberries are prone to bleeding. Keep pruning to a minimum and do not prune between mid-winter and late spring. For the black mulberry (*M. nigra*) see Mulberries, p. 182.

MUTISIA Evergreen climbers that attach themselves by tendrils at the ends of the leaves. They can be allowed to develop naturally on walls or fences and over robust plants. *M. decurrens* resents being cut back, and no regular pruning of others is required except to remove excess growth of very vigorous species in mid-spring.

MYRICA Deciduous and evergreen aromatic shrubs that require no regular pruning (DS, G1, pp. 60-1 and ES, G1, pp. 74-5).

MYRICA Deciduous and evergreen aromatic shrubs that require no regular pruning (DS, G1, pp. 60-1 and ES, G1, pp. 74-5).

MYRTLE see MYRTUS

MYRTUS Aromatic evergreen shrubs, many of which have white flowers. They require no regular pruning (ES, G1, pp. 74-5). In mild temperate regions *M. communis* is often grown as a wall shrub, either planted some distance from the base and allowed to grow freely or trained against the wall. The surface of trained plants can be trimmed over once or twice in a year, between mid-spring and mid-summer.

NANDINA *N. domestica* is an evergreen bamboo-like shrub, the leaves of which colour well in autumn. No regular pruning is required (ES, G1, pp. 74-5). If pruning is necessary, take out whole stems.

NEILLIA Deciduous shrubs that sucker more or less freely. Prune after flowering, cutting out old stems that have flowered (DS, G2, pp. 62-5).

NERIUM *N. oleander* is an evergreen shrub grown mainly for its flowers, which needs greenhouse conditions in cold temperate regions. It can be left unpruned (ES, G1, pp. 74-5), but to keep compact shorten flowering shoots and laterals after flowering.

NOTHOFAGUS Evergreen and deciduous fast-growing trees and shrubs. Train as branched trees or central-leader standards (T, pp. 46-7, 49).

NOTOSPARTIUM Deciduous broom-like shrubs, largely leafless as mature plants. No regular pruning is required (DS, G1, pp. 60-1). Old specimens may be rejuvenated by cutting back to young growths at the base.

NYSSA Deciduous trees that color well in autumn. Train as branched trees or central-leader standards (T, pp. 46-7, 49).

OLEA see Olive, p. 186.

OLEANDER see NERIUM

OLEARIA Evergreen shrubs with daisy-like flower-heads that require no regular pruning (ES, G1, pp. 74-5). Plants, however, can be cut back hard and this is best done in mid-spring. Olearias can be used for formal hedges (H, G3, p. 103), but are better treated informally (pp. 110-11).

OSMANTHUS (Incl. x *Osmarea*.) Evergreen shrubs, most bearing fragrant white flowers. They require no regular pruning (ES, G1, pp. 74-5), but respond well to hard cutting back, which is best done between mid- and late spring. *O. decorus* and *O. heterophyllus* are among those that make good hedges (H, G3, p. 103). Summer is the best time to trim, but clipping at this season removes most of the flowering wood.

OSTRYA Deciduous medium-sized trees. Train as branched trees or central-leader standards (T, pp. 46-7, 49).

OXYDENDRUM *O. arboreum* is a deciduous small tree notable for its autumn coloring. Train as a branched tree or a central-leader standard (T, pp. 46-7, 49).

PAEONIA Shrubby species, which are deciduous, requiring little pruning other than the removal of dead, damaged, and diseased wood in spring as buds swell. (DS, G1, pp. 60-1).

PAGODA TREE, JAPANESE see SOPHORA

PALIURUS *P. spina-christi* is a deciduous shrub or small tree which naturally forms a tangle of thorny branches. Train as a branched-head standard (T, p. 50) or grow as a bush with a minimum of pruning (DS, G1, pp. 60-1). However, plants respond to drastic pruning, which should be carried out in early spring.

PALM, CABBAGE see CORDYLINE

PARROTIA *P. persica* is a deciduous large shrub or small tree with a densely branched spreading head. Allow to develop with no trunk or train as a branched-head standard (T, p. 50).

PARROTIOPSIS *P. jacquemontiana* is a deciduous shrub or small tree requiring no regular pruning (DS, G1, pp. 60-1).

PARROT'S BILL see CLIANTHUS

PARTHENOCISSUS Deciduous climbers, most, like *P. quinquefolia* and *P. tricuspidata*, self-clinging by means of adhesive pads. Allow plants to develop naturally on sound walls, fences, and tree trunks. *P. inserta* has twining tendrils, not adhesive pads, and can be trained on trees, pergolas, or a system of horizontal wires. Cut back excess growth in early winter. Later pruning may cause plants to bleed. An alternative method of training is to spur prune, cutting back annually in early winter to a permanent framework of rods.

PASSIFLORA *P. caerulea* belongs to a large genus of evergreen climbers, equipped with twining tendrils, that are grown for their flowers and, in some cases, edible fruits. Space out main stems on a support, but allow to grow naturally. In mid-spring thin out main stems, if necessary, and shorten laterals to about 6in (15cm). See also Passion Fruit, p. 211.

PASSION FLOWER see PASSIFLORA

PAULOWNIA Deciduous trees grown for their flowers and foliage. Train as central-leader standards (T, p. 49). Mature specimens develop a branched head. Paulownias can be cut down to near ground level annually in mid-spring, like shrubs in Group 4, pp. 70-3, to produce luxuriant foliage.

PEACHES, ORNAMENTAL see PRUNUS

PEONY see PAEONIA

PERNETTYA Evergreen shrubs, often suckering, grown as ground cover and for their berries. They require no regular pruning (ES, G1, pp. 74-5).

PEROVSKIA Sub-shrubs on which the growth normally dies back in the winter. Cut back hard in early spring (DS, G3, p. 67).

PHELLODENDRON Fast-growing deciduous trees. Train as central-leader standards (T, p. 49), although they eventually develop a branched head.

PHILADELPHUS Deciduous small and large shrubs that flower most freely on laterals growing from one-year-old wood. Cut out some of the oldest flowered wood annually, after flowering (DS, G2, pp. 62-5). Prune to maintain a high proportion of young growth on forms of *P. coronarius* such as 'Aureus' that are grown mainly for their foliage.

PHILLYREA Evergreen shrubs or small trees grown for their attractive foliage and fragrant flowers. As free-growing plants they require little pruning (ES, G1, pp. 74-5). Formerly, they were much used for formal hedges (H, G3, p. 103) and topiary. Trim hedges and shaped specimens in late summer.

PHLOMIS Low-growing evergreen sub-shrubs and shrubs. Cut back old and damaged growths in early spring, treating them like the deciduous shrubs in Group 3, pp. 66-9.

PHOTINIA Evergreen and deciduous large shrubs or small trees, deciduous kinds often coloring well in autumn and some of the evergreens having red or bronze young leaves.

They require little pruning (DS, G1, pp. 60-61 and ES, G1, pp. 74-5), but tipping back in summer of the evergreen *P. x fraseri* will encourage denser growth. Evergreen photinias can be used for hedging (H, G3, p. 103).

PHYGELIUS Deciduous shrubs and sub-shrubs. Treat as *Perovskia* (DS, G3, p. 67), cutting back to near ground level in early to mid-spring.

PHYLLODOCE Dwarf evergreen shrubs requiring no regular pruning (ES, G1, pp. 74-5).

PHYSOCARPUS Deciduous shrubs grown mainly for their flowers. They produce new growth freely from the base. Prune after flowering (DS, G2, pp. 62-5).

PICEA Evergreen conifers requiring little pruning other than the removal on some specimens of competing leaders to form branched trees, generally of narrow conical shape (T, p. 48). Dwarf forms are naturally dense and compact (ES, G1, p. 75).

PICRASMA *P. quassoides* is a deciduous shrub or small tree grown for its foliage and requiring no regular pruning (DS, G1, pp. 60-1).

PIERIS Evergreen shrubs grown for their foliage, often copper or red when young, and their flowers. No regular pruning is required (ES, G1, pp. 74-5) but, if necessary, cut back damaged growths in late spring.

PILEOSTEGIA *P. viburnoides* is an evergreen climber that clings by aerial roots. Cut back unwanted growth in mid-spring or pinch back laterals in summer.

PINE see PINUS

PINE, NORFOLK ISLAND see ARAUCARIA

PINUS Evergreen conifers. Train as branched trees or central-leader standards (T, pp. 46-7, 49). On mature specimens lower branches tend to die back. If the central leader is damaged, train in a strong shoot from the whorl below the damage as the replacement leader. Dwarf pines of spreading habit may have more than one leader. To promote dense growth pinch out candles in spring (ES, G1, p. 75).

PIPTANTHUS Evergreen shrubs which in cool temperate regions benefit from the protection of a wall, although best allowed to grow freely. Pinch out the tips of shoots on young plants to get bushy growth. No regular pruning is required (ES, G1, pp. 74-5) but, if necessary, thin and remove damaged growths in mid-spring.

PITTOSPORUM Evergreen shrubs or small trees requiring little pruning (ES, G1, pp. 74-5). Shoots break readily from old wood. If necessary, prune in mid-spring. When used for hedging, cut back young plants moderately hard in the first year (H, G1, pp. 100-1) and trim established hedges in mid-spring and again in mid-summer.

PLANE see PLATANUS

PLATANUS Deciduous trees. Train as central-leader standards (T, p. 49). Trees respond to regular lopping and pollarding (pp. 54-5) by producing numerous growths, but these are often weakly attached to the tree.

PLATYCARYA *P. strobilacea* is a deciduous tree. Train as a central-leader standard (T, p. 49).

PLUMS, ORNAMENTAL see PRUNUS

PODOCARPUS Evergreen coniferous trees and shrubs. Shrubby species such as *P. nivalis* require no regular pruning (ES, G1, pp. 74-5). Train tall-growing species such as *P. totara* as branched trees or as central-leader standards (T, p. 48). Some species (e.g. *P. andinus*) are suitable for hedging (H, G3, p. 103). Trim in mid-summer.

POLYGONUM see FALLOPIA

PONCIRUS *P. trifoliata* is a dense and thorny

deciduous shrub with orange-blossom flowers. No regular pruning is required (DS, G1, pp. 60-1).

POPLAR see POPULUS

POPULUS Deciduous trees, some of which are very fast growing. Train as branched trees or central-leader standards (T, pp. 46-7, 49). Pollard poplars with golden or variegated foliage (e.g. *P. alba* 'Richardii' and *P. x candicans* 'Aurora') for maximum effect (p. 55). Carry out any pruning of poplars in early winter to avoid the risk of trees bleeding. *P. alba* and some other species sucker freely. Remove suckers regularly.

POTATO-TREE, CHILEAN see SOLANUM

POTENTILLA Deciduous shrubs that flower over a long season. No regular pruning is required (DS, G1, pp. 60-1).

PRIVET see LIGUSTRUM

PROSTANTHERA Aromatic evergreen shrubs requiring no regular pruning (ES, G1, pp. 74-5).

PRUNUS Deciduous and evergreen shrubs and trees, including some important fruit trees and numerous ornamentals. The deciduous ornamentals are grown mainly for their flowers. Train medium- to large-sized trees (e.g. *P. avium, P. maackii, P. padus,* and *P. serotina*) as central-leader standards (T, p. 49). Train the Japanese cherries and ornamental flowering almonds and peaches as branched-head standards (T, p. 50). Prune shrubby species such as *P. glandulosa* and *P. triloba* after flowering (DS, G2, pp. 66-9). *P. cerasifera* and *P. spinosa* can be made into formal hedges (H, G1, pp. 100-1) or incorporated in traditional laid hedges (H, pp. 110-11).

Evergreen shrubby species (e.g. *P. laurocerasus* and *P. lusitanica*) are grown mainly for their foliage and as free-growing specimens require no regular pruning (ES, G1, pp. 74-5). When used as formal hedging plants (H, G3, p. 103) or topiary (*P. lusitanica* is suitable for training as a standard), trim in summer. These large-leaved species are, however, more effective as informal hedges and windbreaks (H, pp. 110-11).

For Prunus with edible fruit see Apricots, pp. 171-72; Cherries, pp. 159-65; Peaches, pp. 166-70; Plums, pp. 155-58.

PSEUDOLARIX Deciduous coniferous trees. Train as branched trees or central-leader standards (T, p. 48).

PSEUDOTSUGA Evergreen coniferous trees. Train as branched trees or central-leader standards (T, p. 48).

PTELEA Aromatic deciduous shrubs and small trees requiring no regular pruning (DS, G1, pp. 60-1).

PTEROCARYA Fast-growing deciduous trees. Train as feathered trees (T, pp. 46-7) or allow to branch from near ground level.

PTEROSTYRAX Deciduous shrubs or small trees requiring no regular pruning (DS, G1, pp. 60-1).

PUNICA see Pomegranates, pp. 187-88.

PYRACANTHA Evergreen shrubs grown for their foliage, flowers, and berries. When grown as free-standing plants, they require little pruning (ES, G1, pp. 74-5). When trained as wall shrubs, they respond well to trimming (see pp. 94-5). Cutting of hedges, best done in summer, will reduce the crop of berries (H, G3, p. 103).

PYRUS The ornamental pears are small to medium-sized deciduous trees, most of which are best trained as central-leader standards (T, p. 49). Train *P. salicifolia* 'Pendula' as a branched-head weeping tree (T, p. 51). For pears grown for their fruit see Apples and Pears, pp. 138-53.

QUERCUS Deciduous and evergreen trees and shrubs. Grow large species (e.g. *Q. robur*) as branched trees or central-leader standards (T, pp. 46-7, 49). Shrubby species require no regular pruning (DS, G1, pp. 60-1 and ES, G1, pp. 74-5). The evergreen *Q. ilex* can be used as a hedging plant (H, G3, pp. 100-1) and for simple large-scale topiary. Clip in late summer.
QUINCE, FLOWERING see CHAENOMELES

RAPHIOLEPIS Evergreen shrubs that require no regular pruning (ES, G1, pp. 74-5).
REDWOOD, COAST see SEQUOIA
REDWOOD, DAWN see METASEQUOIA
REDWOOD, GIANT see SEQUOIA
REHDERODENDRON *R. macrocarpum* is a deciduous tree grown for its flowers and fruit. Train as a central-leader standard (T, p. 49).
RHAMNUS Deciduous and evergreen shrubs or small trees, mainly grown for their foliage. In general they can be grown with a minimum of pruning (DS, G1, pp. 60-1 and ES, G1, pp. 74-5). *R. purshiana* can be grown with a central leader to make a branched tree (T, pp. 46-7).
RHODODENDRON A large group of ornamentals, including evergreen and deciduous shrubs and trees, grown mainly for their flowers. Evergreen rhododendrons require no regular pruning (ES, G1, pp. 74-5). However, they benefit from dead-heading and many respond well when cut hard back immediately after flowering. *R. ponticum* makes a good informal hedge (H, pp. 110-11). Many deciduous azaleas need little pruning (DS, G1, pp. 60-1), but when there are strong basal growths these can be used to replace old wood, which should be cut out after flowering. Remove suckers on all grafted plants promptly.
RHODOTYPOS *R. scandens* is a deciduous shrub that flowers on wood produced in the previous season. Prune after flowering as *Kerria* (DS, G2, p. 64).
RHUS Deciduous shrubs and small trees grown mainly for their autumn foliage and conspicuous fruits. They can be grown satisfactorily with very little pruning (DS, G1, pp. 60-1). For maximum foliage effect of *R. glabra* 'Laciniata' and *R. typhina* 'Laciniata' form a low permanent framework of branches and cut back other wood each spring (DS, G4, pp. 70-3).
RIBES Deciduous and evergreen shrubs grown mainly for their flowers. Evergreen kinds (e.g. *R. laurifolium*) require no regular pruning (ES, G1, pp. 74-5). Deciduous kinds (e.g. *R. sanguineum*) flower mainly on one-year-old wood. Prune after flowering (DS, G2, pp. 62-5). As a hedging plant *R. sanguineum* can be trimmed formally after flowering (H, G2, p. 102) but is better treated informally (H, pp. 110-11). *R. speciosum* is suitable for training against a wall. Tie in young growths as replacements each year. For *Ribes* with edible fruits see Black Currants (p. 196), Gooseberries (pp. 190-92), and Red and White Currants (pp. 193-95).
ROBINIA Deciduous trees grown mainly for their pea-like flowers. Train as branched trees or central-leader standards (T, pp. 46-7, 49).
ROSA see Roses, pp. 18-39.
ROSE, GUELDER see VIBURNUM
ROSE OF SHARON see HIBISCUS
ROSE, ROCK see CISTUS and HELIANTHEMUM
ROSE, SUN see CISTUS
ROSEMARY see ROSMARINUS

ROSMARINUS *R. officinalis* is an aromatic evergreen shrub that requires no regular pruning (ES, G1, pp. 74-5), but damaged specimens will generally break when cut back to old wood. Pinch out the growing points of young plants to encourage bushy growth.
ROWAN see SORBUS
RUBUS The deciduous ornamental brambles are grown mainly for their flowers or winter stems. Prune white-stemmed kinds (e.g. *R. cockburnianus*) after flowering, cutting out old stems completely (DS, G4, p. 71). Those grown for their flowers (e.g. *R. deliciosus*, *R. odoratus*, and *R. 'Tridel'*) bloom on the previous season's wood (DS, G2, pp. 62-5) and should also be pruned after flowering. For fruiting kinds see Blackberries (pp. 200-2) and Raspberries (pp. 197-99).
RUE see RUTA
RUSCUS Evergreen suckering sub-shrubs. They require no regular pruning (ES, G1, pp. 74-5).
RUTA Aromatic evergreen shrubs and sub-shrubs that become untidy unless cut back in mid-spring (ES, G2, pp. 76-7).

SAGE see SALVIA
ST JOHN'S WORT see HYPERICUM
SALIX Deciduous trees and shrubs grown mainly for their foliage, catkins, weeping habit or colored stems in winter. Train large species (e.g. *S. alba*) as central-leader standards (T, p. 49), although all tend eventually to develop branched heads. Train weeping forms on a clear stem (T, p. 51). Dwarf and prostrate species usually require no regular pruning (DS, G1, pp. 60-1) but, if necessary, cut out old wood after flowering. Cut back willows grown for their colored stems (e.g. *S. alba* 'Britzensis', *S. a. vitellina*, *S. daphnoides*, and *S. irrorata*) in spring (DS, G4, pp. 70-3).
SALVIA Aromatic, mainly evergreen shrubs and sub-shrubs which tend to become untidy unless cut back in mid-spring (ES, G2, pp. 76-7). Pinch out the growing tips of shoots to encourage dense growth.
SAMBUCUS Short-lived deciduous shrubs and small trees grown for their flowers, foliage, and fruit (Elderberry, p. 183). Cut out some of the oldest wood in winter or, for maximum foliage effect (e.g. of *S. nigra* 'Aurea' and *S. racemosa* 'Plumosa Aurea'), cut back to ground level or to a low framework in spring (DS, G4, pp. 70-3).
SANTOLINA Aromatic evergreen dwarf shrubs that become untidy unless cut back in spring (ES, G2, pp. 76-7).
SARCOCOCCA Evergreen shrubs that require no regular pruning (ES, G1, pp. 74-5).
SASSAFRAS *S. albidum* is a deciduous tree. Train as a central-leader standard (T, p. 49), although the tree will eventually form a branched head.
SCHIMA Evergreen shrubs grown mainly for their flowers. They require no regular pruning (ES, G1, pp. 74-5).
SCHISANDRA Deciduous and evergreen twining climbers. Some thinning out of old wood in winter is beneficial.
SCHIZOPHRAGMA Deciduous climbers that support themselves by means of aerial roots. Little pruning is needed other than the removal of unwanted extension growth. Some tying may be necessary, especially in the first few years.
SCIADOPITYS *S. verticillata* is an evergreen coniferous tree. Train as a central-leader standard (T, p. 48).

SENECIO A large genus that includes evergreen shrubs with daisy-like flower heads. No regular pruning is required (ES, G1, pp. 74-5). However, shrubs respond well if cut back hard. If this is necessary, it should be done in mid-spring.
SEQUOIA *S. sempervirens* is a fast-growing evergreen coniferous tree. Train as a branched tree or central-leader standard (T, p. 48). Mature trees are flat-topped. In autumn and winter remove suckers from the base.
SEQUOIADENDRON *S. giganteum* is a very large evergreen coniferous tree. Train as a branched tree or central-leader standard (T, p. 48).
SHADBUSH see AMELANCHIER
SHEPHERDIA Deciduous shrubs grown mainly for their berries. They require no regular pruning (DS, G1, pp. 60-1).
SINOJACKIA Deciduous shrubs or small trees that usually branch from near ground level. Although there may be numerous crossing branches, no regular pruning is required (DS, G1, pp. 60-1).
SKIMMIA Evergreen shrubs grown for their foliage and berries. They require no regular pruning (ES, G1, pp. 74-5).
SMILAX Deciduous and evergreen scramblers and climbers equipped with tendrils. They require no regular pruning.
SMOKE TREE see COTINUS
SNOWBERRY see SYMPHORICARPOS
SNOWDROP TREE see HALESIA
SNOWY MESPILUS see AMELANCHIER
SOLANUM Includes semi-evergreen lax shrubs and scramblers suitable for training on walls and other supports. *S. crispum* is an untidy scandent shrub suitable for fan training. *S. jasminoides* scrambles by making rapid extension of growth. Both species need tying in and the cutting out of weak growths in mid-spring.
SOPHORA Deciduous evergreen trees and shrubs grown for their foliage and flowers. Train large species such as *S. japonica* as central-leader standards (T, p. 49). The evergreen shrubby species require no regular pruning (ES, G1, pp. 74-5). However, in cool temperate regions *S. microphylla* and *S. tetraptera* benefit from training against a sunny wall. If necessary, prune wall-trained specimens after flowering.
SORBARIA Vigorous deciduous shrubs that flower on the current season's wood. Prune in early spring as *Buddleja davidii* (DS, G3, pp. 66-9), but with a stronger framework. Regularly replace weak framework branches with strong basal growths.
SORBUS Deciduous trees and shrubs grown for their flowers, berries, and autumn color. Train as central-leader standards or, in the case of less vigorous species (e.g. *S. cashmiriana*), as branched-head standards (T, pp. 46-7, 50). Shrubby species require no regular pruning.
SPARTIUM *S. junceum* is a deciduous shrub that bears pea-like flowers on the current season's growth. Prune in mid-spring (DS, G3, pp. 66-9).
SPIRAEA Deciduous shrubs grown mainly for their flowers. The following flower on the current season's shoots: *S. x bumalda*, *S. douglasii*, *S. japonica*, and *S. menziesii*. Prune these in spring (DS, G3, pp. 66-9). Others, including *S. 'Arguta'*, *S. prunifolia*, and *S. thunbergii*, flower from the previous year's shoots and are pruned after flowering (DS, G2, pp. 62-5).
SPRUCE see PICEA
STACHYURUS Deciduous shrubs grown mainly for their early flowers. They require no regular

pruning (DS, G1, pp. 60-1), but old branches can be replaced by strong basal growths.
STAPHYLEA Deciduous shrubs with seeds enclosed in bladders. They can be grown with little pruning (DS, G1, pp. 60-1), but strong basal growths can be used to replace old branches.
STAUNTONIA *S. hexaphylla* is an evergreen climbing twiner. It can be left unpruned or old wood can be cut out after flowering.
STEPHANANDRA Deciduous shrubs grown for stems and foliage more than flowers, which are produced on the previous season's wood. Prune after flowering (DS, G2, pp. 62-5) or, for maximum effect of foliage and stems, but at the expense of flowers, in spring (DS, G4, pp. 70-3).
STEWARTIA (syn. STUARTIA) Deciduous shrubs and small trees grown for their flowers, autumn coloring, and bark. Train the larger species (e.g. *S. pseudo-camellia*) as central-leader standards (T, p. 49). Shrubby species require no regular pruning (DS, G1, pp. 60-1).
STRAWBERRY TREE see ARBUTUS
STRANVAESIA Evergreen shrubs and small trees grown for their foliage, flowers, and berries. They require no regular pruning.
STYRAX Deciduous shrubs and small trees with attractive flowers. Train the larger species (e.g. *S. hemsleyana*) as branched trees (T, pp. 46-7). Shrubby species require no regular pruning (DS, G1, pp. 60-1).
SUMACH see RHUS
SWEET GUM see LIQUIDAMBAR
SYCAMORE see PLATANUS
SYCOPSIS Evergreen shrubs and small trees. Require no regular pruning (ES, G1, pp. 74-5).
SYMPHORICARPOS Suckering deciduous shrubs grown mainly for their berries. The display of berries will be reduced if plants are pruned after flowering. Remove old and weak shoots in early spring.
SYRINGA Deciduous shrubs or small trees grown mainly for their flowers. *S. vulgaris* requires no regular pruning (DS, G1, pp. 60-1), but can be renovated by cutting hard back (Renovation, pp. 78-9). Species and hybrids that regularly produce strong new shoots low down (e.g. *S. meyeri, S. microphylla, S. x prestoniae* and *S. reflexa*) are best pruned on a light renewal system (DS, G2, pp. 62-5).

TAMARISK see TAMARIX
TAMARIX Deciduous shrubs grown mainly for their flowers. Prune those that flower on the previous season's wood (*T. parviflora* and *T. tetranda*) after flowering (DS, G2, pp. 62-5) and those that flower on the current season's wood (*T. gallica* and *T. pentandra*) in early spring (DS, G3, pp. 66-9). The late-flowering tamarisks make attractive hedges and windbreaks (H, G1, pp. 100-1, 110-11). Trimmed in spring, they will flower in late summer or autumn.
TAXODIUM Deciduous coniferous trees. Train as branched trees (T, p. 48).
TAXUS Evergreen coniferous trees and shrubs. Train trees with a central leader (T, p. 48). The shrubs require no regular pruning (ES, G1, pp. 74-5). Yews are much used for hedging (H, G3, p. 103) and topiary, annual clipping in summer giving a close-textured surface.
TEUCRIUM Includes evergreen shrubs and sub-shrubs. In cool temperate regions they are commonly grown in the protection of a sunny wall, *T. fruticans* lending itself to fan training. No

regular pruning is required (ES, G1, pp. 74-5) but, if necessary, thin and remove weak and damaged wood in mid-spring.
THORN, ORNAMENTAL see CRATAEGUS
THUJA Evergreen conifers, the trees being of conical shape. Train as branched trees or central-leader standards (T, p. 48). Both *T. occidentalis* and *T. plicata* are suitable for hedging (H, G3, p. 103). The numerous dwarf forms require no regular pruning (ES, G1, p. 75).
TILIA Deciduous trees with fragrant flowers. Train as central-leader standards (T, p. 49). Lindens are the most commonly used trees for pleaching (pp. 106-7).
TRACHELOSPERMUM Twining evergreen climbers that flower on the old wood. They require little pruning.
TRUMPET CREEPER see CAMPSIS
TSUGA Evergreen coniferous trees of conical shape. Train as feathered trees or central-leader standards (T, p. 48). *T. heterophylla* is suitable for hedging (H, G3, p. 103). Clip in late summer.

ULEX Spiny evergreen shrubs, often flowering over a long season. Encourage bushy growth by cutting back young plants in their first spring. Treat established plants like Deciduous Shrubs, Group 2, pp. 62-5, cutting back in late spring, after flowering. Leggy plants can be cut back into old wood and will make fresh growth.
ULMUS Deciduous trees. Train as central-leader standards (T, p. 49). Formerly it was a common practice to lop or pollard elms, but the branches that develop as a result of this treatment are weakly attached (T, p. 55).

VACCINIUM Deciduous and evergreen shrubs, some of which are grown for their edible fruit (see Blueberries, p. 203) and others for their ornamental value. Little pruning is required (DS, G1, pp. 60-1, and ES, G1, pp. 74-5). If necessary, prune deciduous kinds in winter and evergreen kinds in mid-spring.
VIBURNUM Deciduous and evergreen shrubs grown mainly for their flowers and berries. They require little pruning (DS, G1, pp. 60-1 and ES, G1, pp. 74-5) but when deciduous species produce strong basal shoots these can be used to replace old wood. Prune those that flower in winter after flowering and those that flower in summer in early spring. Trim hedges of *V. tinus* (H, G1, pp. 100-1) in mid-spring.
VINCA This genus includes evergreen trailing shrubs. No pruning is required, but when grown as ground cover vincas may be cut back every two or three years in early spring as part of general garden maintenance.
VIRGINIA CREEPER see PARTHENOCISSUS
VITEX Includes deciduous shrubs grown mainly for their flowers. They can be grown with minimal pruning (DS, G1, pp. 60-1), but in cold temperate regions *V. agnus-castus* and *V. negundo* require the protection of a sunny wall. Prune wall-trained plants in early to mid-spring, cutting back the previous summer's growth to leave two to three buds from the framework branches.
VITIS Deciduous and evergreen climbers that climb by means of tendrils. The ornamental species are grown mainly for their foliage. (See also Grapes, pp. 204-10). If space allows, they

can be left unpruned. Cut out excess growth in early winter. Vines pruned in late winter or spring will bleed. Ornamental vines can be pruned in the same way as those grown for fruit on the rod-and-spur system, with laterals cut back to two or three buds in early winter.

WATTLE see ACACIA
WEIGELA Deciduous shrubs that flower in summer on shoots produced in the previous season. Prune after flowering (DS, G2, pp. 62-5).
WHITEBEAM see SORBUS
WHITE FORSYTHIA see ABELIOPHYLLUM
WILLOW see SALIX
WINTER SWEET see CHIMONANTHUS
WISTERIA Deciduous twining climbers. See Wisteria, pp. 90-2.
WITCH HAZEL see HAMAMELIS
WOODBINE see LONICERA
WORMWOOD see ARTEMISIA

YEW see TAXUS
YUCCA Evergreen shrubs and small trees with sword-like leaves. No pruning is required.

ZELKOVA Deciduous trees. Train as branched trees or central-leader standards (T, pp. 46-7, 49). *Z. abelicea* is best left to develop naturally as it often produces strong basal shoots.

PINCH PRUNING

This book deals mainly with woody plants that are pruned and trained to be ornamental or fruitful over a long life. Among ornamentals, however, there are a number of sub-shrubs and perennials that are readily shaped and when treated in this way can provide impressive, if short-term, displays in the garden, home or greenhouse. The stems of sub-shrubs, including popular summer bedding and pot or greenhouse plants such as fuchsias, geraniums, and coleus, will eventually become woody, especially when the growth is checked by root restriction or exposure to cold. But while growths are young, they are soft-stemmed and pruning is simply done by pinching out growing points. This pinching out or stopping, as it is sometimes called, stimulates the development of side shoots and, if carried out regularly, results in dense bushy growth. The selective use of this method of pruning on sub-shrubs and perennials such as certain types of chrysanthemums allows considerable freedom in the shaping of plants.

Many home gardeners will grow these forms for purely ornamental purposes and when this is the case the dimensions of a shape are not critical. If the aim is to exhibit competitively, training must take into account show schedules. These will specify, for example, the height of clear stem required of a standard and an exhibit that does not conform to the schedule is likely to be penalized.

Left: Cascade chrysanthemums can be trained in several ways. One method is to grow them as pillars, an even denser effect being achieved with several plants in the same container.

Above: Two cascade chrysanthemums trained on a substantial framework are needed to make a large fan.

Top: The cascade training of chrysanthemums can be done with single specimens or groups, a row of several plants grown together forming an impressive flowering screen.

CASCADE CHRYSANTHEMUMS

It is only since the 1930s that cascade chrysanthemums have been known in the West, but there is a long history of their cultivation in Japan. If these cultivars are allowed to grow without training, they make bushy plants to a height of up to 5ft (1.5m) and are covered with small daisy-like flowers in late autumn. However, they are very amenable to training and, if young plants are regularly pinched out and shaped, they can create spectacular floral displays. They can even be grown on frames to make figurative sculptures of living material. Good cultivars in the relatively limited color range include 'The Bride' (white), 'Gold Cascade' (bronzy yellow), 'Shinotome' (deep pink) and 'Yellow Spray' (bright yellow).

The easiest way of raising plants is to take cuttings of named cultivars two to three weeks before the end of winter, keeping them in a well-lit greenhouse at a minimum temperature of 7°C (45°F). Four to six weeks later pot on, using 3in (7.5cm) pots before moving on into 5in (12.5cm) pots.

Training a cascade

During the formative outdoor training of a cascade, and subsequently when the plant is flowering under glass, a stable staging must be provided that will allow the growth, 6ft (1.8m) or more in length, to spill down from the container. Plants are restricted to one or two leading shoots at an early stage and then regularly pinched out during the growing season while being trained down a cane or similar guide of about 5ft (1.5m) in length angled from the raised container to ground level. Cuttings planted in late winter and pinched out until the first week or two of autumn will begin flowering in late autumn and continue for about six weeks. After flowering, selected plants can be retained to provide cuttings for the following year.

This method of downward training can be adapted to various decorative purposes. For example, a number of plants can be grown in the same container, which can be suspended as a large hanging basket. Another possibility is to group several containers at the top of a frame, the combined growth of the plants creating a flowered curtain. The amateur, however, will probably be limited in what he or she does by the problems of moving heavy and unwieldy items, as is necessary when plants are brought under glass in autumn.

By the time cuttings are potted on all but one or two leading shoots should be pinched out. Plants must be protected from frost, but they can be placed in frames in mid- to late spring. At the end of spring move plants into their final pots. A container 1ft (30cm) in size filled with a loam-based soil mixture will be reasonably stable and can accommodate one or two plants. At this stage use short split canes to stake plants temporarily so that they are angled outwards.

As soon as the risk of frost has passed, move plants outdoors to prepared staging and, if the sun is strong, provide shade for the first few days. However, good exposure to sunlight is essential, the plants being trained towards the light, preferably in a sheltered position backed by a wall or hedge. At this stage the cane or similar training guide should be fixed in position

Right: Cascade chrysanthemums can be grown as either continuous or interrupted pillars, the latter in effect being a vertical sequence of balls on a standard.

between the container and the ground. One method is to attach the guide at one end to a strong wire collar at the rim of the pot and at the other to a stake in the ground.

With the guide in position the stem can be untied from the temporary light stake, gently turned down and tied to the guide. By reducing the watering at this stage so that the plants are slightly limp there will be less chance of shoots being snapped. Tie or clip the stem at the top of the guide and at every 4-6in (10-15cm) as it grows.

The terminal bud must be allowed to develop until it has reached the ground, but a full cascade can only be made by regularly pinching back lateral growths when they have made two or three leaves and by regular feeding with a balanced liquid fertilizer. If the terminal growth is damaged, tie in a strong lateral as a replacement. Inspect plants about twice a week and pinch out shoots as necessary until about the second week of autumn, when plants are moved under glass. The work of the growing season can be spoiled if this is not carried out with care. Move on a still warm day, having first untied the cascade from the guide.

Once pinching out has finished, begin regular applications of a high-potash feed, which will improve flower color when flowering occurs about eight weeks later.

Standards, pillars, and fans

When forming standards, pillars, and fans the essential difference from the cascade form is the direction of training. To make a standard, train a plant up a stake, taking off side shoots as they develop except for those 6-8in (15-20cm) below where the growing point is removed. Keep a compact head by pinching out side shoots.

To make a substantial pillar train up three plants in a container that is at least 1ft (30cm) in size, using a strong central stake that is about 6ft (1.8m) in height. The side shoots at the base may need to be pinched back more severely than those near the top to create a pillar of more or less uniform diameter.

A suitable framework for a fan consists of three strong canes radiating in the same plane which support a half moon of netting. Use two plants per pot, stopping them when they are a few inches high and then pinching out regularly and tying in leaders and laterals to fill all spaces.

Left: A cascade chrysanthemum grown as a cascade is trained down a cane, the pot containing the plant or plants being firmly held on a staging.

TRAINING A CASCADE

1 Take cuttings of named cultivars towards the end of winter.

2 Once cuttings have rooted, pot them on, keeping them in a well-lit greenhouse and not letting the temperature fall below 7°C (45°F).

3 Restrict plants to 1 or 2 leading shoots. Move plants to an outdoor staging when all risk of frost is past. Train the leading shoots down a cane, pinching out side shoots regularly.

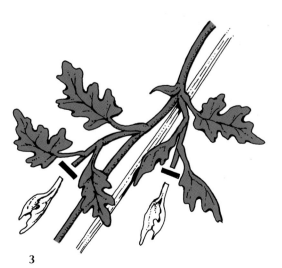

1   2

3

FUCHSIAS

All but the hardy fuchsias need some pinching out to make good bushy plants. An elaboration of this method of pruning, combined with training, is used to create more ambitious forms. Regular pinching out delays flowering, which normally starts six to ten weeks after the last stop, depending on whether flowers are single or fully double. In winter trained fuchsias should be kept in good light and above 10°C (50°F). Some fuchsias have leaves arranged in threes rather than in opposite pairs and growers generally prefer to make standards and other trained forms from such plants because a shapely head can be built up more quickly.

Training a standard
The clear stem of a standard is 2½-3ft (76-90cm) high, of a half-standard 1⅔-2ft (51-60cm), of a quarter-standard 1-1¼ft (30-38cm), and of a table standard 10-12in (25-30cm). The method of training for all is essentially the same, but for a full or half-standard a vigorous cultivar is needed, such as 'Annabel', 'Mrs Lovell Swisher', 'Snowcap', 'Tennessee Waltz' or 'Hidcote Beauty'.

To form a standard start with a strong rooted cutting planted in spring and give it support as soon as it starts to grow to prevent the stem developing a kink. While vertical growth is being made, tie the stem at intervals of 2in (5cm), if necessary replacing the ties as the stem thickens.

Plants must be potted on regularly for any crowding of the roots will result in hard wood and will encourage flowering. An ultimate pot size of 9in (23cm) is adequate for the tallest standards. In the formative stage the leaves on the stem should be retained; they will be lost naturally as the standard develops or can be removed as the head is formed. Retain all side shoots on ordinary standards, but with weeping standards a strong stem will be formed more quickly if side shoots are retained in the early stages but pinched back to two or three pairs of leaves. Once the stem has reached the desired height, with the head making about a third of the total height, take out the top.

The bushy head is formed by regularly pinching out side shoots on the top 6-8in (15-20cm) of the stem when they have made two or three pairs of leaves. Any other side shoots must be removed completely.

TRAINING A STANDARD
1 Train a rooted cutting vertically without check, retaining leaves.

2 Pinch out the growing point when the stem has reached the desired height.

Top right: A standard-trained fuchsia can be combined with a varied and attractive underplanting.

Training pyramids, fans and espaliers
The pyramid is generally considered the most difficult form in which to train a fuchsia. It takes two years to build up a well-shaped specimen and in the first year all flower buds should be removed. The shape is built up by growing a vigorous cultivar that makes strong lateral growths, pinching out the top to stimulate the development of side shoots every 9in (23cm) or so, followed by training in a replacement leader until the desired height has been reached.

With an espalier, side shoots are retained at the level of the horizontals, but all others must be rubbed out. If the growth-rate of side shoots slows, train the laterals temporarily at an angle above the horizontal, tying them horizontal again when they have made sufficient growth. Stop laterals and the leader when they have made the required amount of growth.

The fan needs stopping at four pairs of leaves. When side shoots develop, retain two pairs that are growing in the same plane as the frame. Stop these laterals at one pair of leaves and the subsequent shoots at one or two pairs of leaves. Pinch out any further growth as required to fill in the whole frame, tying in growths.

COLEUS

Like fuchsias, the cultivars of *Coleus ×
hybridus* are sub-shrubs, the stems becoming
woody and hard as they mature. However,
the young soft tips are easily pinched out, a
method of pruning that is worth carrying out
systematically, even when growing plants as
bushes. The framework of a neat bushy plant
is created by removing the growing point
when five pairs of leaves have been formed,
and subsequently pinching back side shoots
to two or three pairs of leaves. Further
pinching back will form a well-shaped plant,
densely covered in foliage, and will delay
the production of the flower spikes. Once
flowe s form the plant will deteriorate so the
spikes should be pinched out as soon as they
are noticed.

A few named cultivars are particularly
vigorous growers and can be trained as
impressive standards with a clear stem to a
height of 4ft (1.2m) or more. 'Pineapple
Beauty', which has yellow leaves with a red-
brown blotch near the base, is one of the
most suitable, and for lighter standards
'Glory of Luxembourg', 'Royal Scot', 'Spire',
and 'Walter Turner'. These cultivars can also
be trained as fans, the method being a simple
adaptation of bush pruning but with growth
trained to a framework in a single plane.

Named cultivars must be propagated
vegetatively. Plants raised from seed tend to
run to flower in their first year and are best
treated as annuals.

Although in temperate regions *Coleus* are
usually grown outdoors during the summer
and established plants will withstand
temperatures down to 10°C (50°F), ideally
they should be maintained at 16-24°C
(60-70°F) throughout the year. Strong
sunlight can bleach the leaves and tall plants
are vulnerable to wind damage.

Training a standard or half-standard
Take cuttings in late summer or early
autumn, choosing young short-jointed
shoots, and pot on as soon as the root system
is established. Do not exceed a pot size of
5in (12.5cm) for winter and an ultimate size,
the following spring, of 9in (23cm).

Grow plants on without check, watering
and feeding regularly. Nitrogen-rich
fertilizers will prevent the development of
bright colors in the foliage, so once the
necessary growth has been made the feeding
must be reduced to get the maximum

decorative effect. Staking is essential to
ensure the development of a straight stem.
Tie securely but check regularly, retying if
necessary to prevent any constriction of the
thickening stem.

Do not take off leaves growing directly
from the stem, but remove side shoots as
soon as they are large enough to get hold of.
When, however, the plant is approaching
the required height, leave about four side
shoots just below the point at which the top
is taken out. The formation of a flower spike
will effectively limit the height to which the
stem may be grown. Remove the spike and
the top two pairs of leaves. The cultivar
'Pineapple Beauty' can normally be grown
on without showing signs of flowering and
the growing point can then be taken out
when the stem is 4-5ft (1.2-1.5m) high.

Regular pinching back of side shoots is
necessary to build up a dense head. In the
early stages stop shoots after the first pair of
leaves. Later it may be enough to stop shoots
at two or more pairs of leaves, according to
the way the shape of the head is developing.

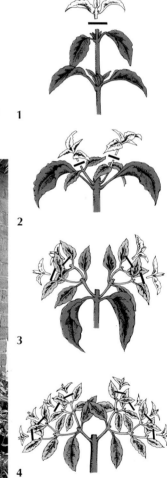

FORMING THE HEAD
1 Pinch out the tip
when the stem has
reached the desired
height.

2-4 Successive
pinching back (only 2
side shoots are shown)
will eventually produce
the dense head.

1

2

3

4

Left: Regular pinching
out has produced an
attractive, dense head
on this full standard of
Coleus blumei
'Pineapple Beauty'.

PELARGONIUMS (GERANIUMS)

The zonal pelargoniums, more often known as geraniums, and the regal pelargoniums (Martha Washington geraniums) are tender evergreen sub-shrubs that should be maintained at a winter temperature of 7-10°C (45-50°F), but can be moved outdoors in summer. Numerous cultivars of these hybrid pelargoniums are available, some of which are vigorous enough to be grown on their own stems as standards. Cultivars with thin or brittle stems, including the ivy-leaved kinds, should be grafted on to vigorous cultivars.

Above: Standards of pelargoniums and heliotrope (*Heliotropium arborescens*) are combined with low-growing pelargoniums.

Right: More rigorous training at an early stage was needed to make satisfactory standards of these variegated pelargoniums.

TAKING A CUTTING
Take cuttings of vigorous pelargonium cultivars from mid-spring to summer and keep plants growing without flowering until the following year.

Forming a standard
The height to which a standard can be grown will depend to some extent on the vigor of the cultivar. Full standards can be grown to a height of 4-5ft (1.2-1.5m), but a more usual height is 2½-3ft (76-90cm), with a clear stem of about 2⅓ft (71cm). Half-standards and table standards are proportionally smaller, but in all cases the aim should be to form a well-balanced plant.

Grow standards from strong rooted cuttings of named cultivars. Tip cuttings can be taken in early to mid-spring and right into summer. The aim generally is to encourage vigorous growth through one season without flowering so that the plant is at the required height by early spring of the following year.

To avoid any check to growth in the first year pot on as required, cuttings planted in spring being moved to 8in (20cm) pots by early autumn. By the time plants are about 8in (20cm) high they must be staked. Tie in as growth is made to ensure the development of a straight stem.

To maintain vigorous upright growth it is necessary to feed regularly with a balanced liquid fertilizer and to remove side shoots as they develop, except for those that form above the height required for the clear stem. Leaves growing directly from the stem can be allowed to die back naturally. Stop feeding geraniums early in autumn and throughout the winter keep plants on the dry side.

Provided that the plant has reached the desired height, the growing point can be removed in early spring of the second year, after repotting. Pinch out to three or four leaves the topmost side shoots that have been retained above the stem height. Further pinching out is necessary when the new shoots have made three or four leaves, but subsequently little pruning will be needed except to ensure the development of a well-shaped head.

Flower buds will form once pinching out has finished and the display can be prolonged by removing faded flowers.

MISCELLANEOUS ORNAMENTALS

The training of standards, combined with pinching out to form a bushy head, can be applied to a number of shrubs or sub-shrubs that in temperate regions need greenhouse protection in winter.

An attractive example is heliotrope or cherry pie (*Heliotropium arborescens*). Cuttings taken in mid-summer can be trained up to form a standard, the tip being pinched out when the plant has reached the desired height. The laterals that develop as a result of this pinching out themselves need at least one pinching out, at four or five leaves, to produce a full head.

The Paris or Boston daisy or marguerite (*Chrysanthemum frutescens*) is another example. Standards can form large heads and when they do so they need firm staking.

The subject of grafting is beyond the scope of this book, but the most satisfactory way of producing some standards involves training up a vigorous cultivar of a plant and grafting to it a selected cultivar, which is then pinched out to form a well-shaped head. Plants on which this technique is used include the Christmas poinsettia (*Euphorbia heterophylla*).

Above: *Lantana camara*, a shrub that has become a weed in many tropical countries, makes an attractive standard in the greenhouse.

Far left: In cool temperate regions, heliotrope (*Heliotropium arborescens*), a shrub with fragrant flowers, makes a useful standard for the greenhouse or for summer bedding.

Left: The Paris or Boston daisy (*Chrysanthemum frutescens*) is one of the most commonly grown sub-shrubs trained as standards. It has a very long flowering season.

TREE FRUITS

The development of genetically dwarf and compact trees and dwarfing rootstocks mean that already some fruit trees are grown with a minimum of traditional pruning and training. These trends are likely to continue, and in the long term may completely revolutionize the way fruits are grown. In the meantime, pruning and training remain important aspects of fruit growing. In the first years of growth they establish the framework of the tree, according to the desired form, and as the tree matures, pruning maintains a healthy stable tree and promotes the growth of fruit-bearing wood.

Pruning and training are, however, only part of the program that results in productive long-lived trees. There must be good growing conditions, with adequate supplies of nutrients and moisture; if necessary, there must be shelter, control of pests and diseases, and the right pollinators must be present to ensure a good set of fruit. To succeed, this program needs to be directed at fruit trees selected to suit the regional growing conditions, grown in forms suitable to the space available, and on the right rootstocks.

Above: Bush trees on dwarfing roostocks generally require less demanding pruning than most other forms.

Far right top: Well pruned fruit trees will remain productive for many years.

Above right: The fan form is suitable for a number of fruit trees, including, as shown here, plums.

Far right middle: Dwarfing and semi-dwarfing rootstocks are now available for plums.

Right: Apples grown on dwarfing rootstocks can be grown as single-tier espaliers.

Far right bottom: There are many variants of the restricted forms of apples and pears.

Forms of tree

There is generally a choice in the way a fruit tree can be grown. The forms that are covered in the following pages fall into two broad categories: unrestricted forms that are grown in the open garden including bush trees, half-standards and standards, and the central-leader spindlebushes much used in the commercial growing of apples and pears; and where space is limited, restricted forms such as cordons, espaliers, fans and dwarf pyramids, all grown on dwarfing to semi-dwarfing rootstocks.

Pruning

The unrestricted forms are pruned in late winter, except for cherry, peach, nectarine and plum trees; the risk of a canker disease gaining entry through cuts postpones their pruning until late spring. In general, fruit trees are easy to manage and are capable of yielding large crops but, other than the dwarf and semi-dwarf bushes, they are difficult to accommodate in a small or even medium-sized garden.

The restricted forms are pruned in summer by the Modified Lorette System to control growth rigorously and to produce useful crops, although lighter than those produced by the unrestricted forms. Trained against walls and fences or as screens separating one part of a garden from another, they are ornamental as well as being productive.

Rootstocks

Although some fruit trees, figs among them, are grown on their own roots, many other fruits are budded or grafted on to selected rootstocks that influence vigor. For apples, the most widely grown of the temperate fruits, there is a finely graded range of rootstocks, from the extremely dwarfing to the vigorous standard-size. As a general rule, the more dwarfing the rootstock, the better the growing conditions required. On poor soils, approximately the same result might be achieved using a semi-vigorous rootstock as would be achieved on fertile ground with one that is dwarfing.

All other things being equal, it is the rootstock that determines the ultimate size of a tree, and normal pruning cannot satisfactorily correct the over-vigorous growth of a tree that is growing on an unsuitable rootstock.

APPLES AND PEARS

Apples and pears are indispensable fruits of the temperate garden and a long history of cultivation has resulted in a very large number of dessert and culinary cultivars. Although there are some differences in detail – for example, pears will in general tolerate harder pruning than apples – methods of cultivation, including pruning and training, are the same for both fruits. This applies to them whether grown as bush trees and other unrestricted forms in the open garden or as restricted forms, such as cordons and espaliers, that are particularly useful where space is limited.

One point on which there is considerable difference is the range of rootstocks available. Pears grown on the quince stocks Quince A (moderately vigorous) and Quince C (less vigorous) show some dwarfing; these trees are often short-lived. Newer rootstocks, OHF.69, OHF.333, and OHF.513, have been tested; they produce semi-dwarf trees.

Apple rootstocks are available in a range that extends from the extremely dwarfing to the vigorous: P.22, M.27, M.9, M.26, M.8, M.7, MM.106, MM.111, and M.2. When ordering trees from a mail-order nursery, ask about the rootstocks used, the size of tree they will make, and their suitability for local weather and soil conditions.

Below: The fan is a highly ornamental, restricted form which nowadays is not used very much for apples and pears. Each rib is treated as though it were a cordon and pruned by the Modified Lorette System.

PRUNING FOR FRUIT

From an early stage the restricted forms are pruned in summer to encourage the formation of fruit-bearing wood. The most widely used method of pruning for these forms is known as the Modified Lorette System (see pp. 145–47).

Unrestricted forms of apples and pears grown in the open are mostly pruned in winter but in early spring in the north. The formative stages of their pruning and training are described on pages 142–43. Pruning to encourage the development of fruiting wood begins between the second and fifth year, depending on the rootstock (in general the more dwarfing the rootstock, the earlier trees come into fruit) and to some extent on the cultivar. The method followed depends on the fruiting habit of the cultivar.

Most apples and pears are spur-bearers, carrying fruit on stubby shoots, the spurs, that develop on older wood. Trees can be made more productive by spur pruning, which induces the development of spurs. Spur-bearers also bear fruit on two-year-old wood, and a system of renewal pruning ensures that fruited wood is replaced by young laterals. These two systems are frequently used on the same tree, with laterals that do not have room to extend being spur pruned, while those on the outside of the tree are pruned by the renewal method.

Semi-dwarf super-spur apple trees have double the number of fruit-bearing spurs and produce fruit from the second year. Some apples and pears are tip-bearers, carrying much of their fruit at the tips of shoots grown during the previous summer. Pruning should encourage such growth.

Spur pruning

Once the framework of a spur-bearing cultivar has been established, the leaders should be left unpruned unless the tree is growing weakly, in which case cutting back will help to stimulate growth. To initiate the formation of spurs, cut back a maiden lateral in winter to four or five buds. This will make new growth from the top few buds the following growing season, while most of the lower buds will usually develop into flower buds, distinguished by being rounder and plumper than wood (shoot) buds.

In the second winter the previous summer's growth is cut back to the topmost

Below: A multiple vertical cordon. The same general principles are followed for both oblique and vertical multiple cordons. Apples and pears are commonly grown as oblique cordons, which makes it possible to grow tree fruits in a small space.

SPUR PRUNING

1 Cut back a maiden lateral to 4 buds in the first winter.

2 In the second winter cut back the lateral to the topmost flower bud. It will carry fruit in the following growing season.

3 A branching system will develop in subsequent years.

Left: This pruned branch of a spur-bearing apple shows a spur system developing on 3-year-old wood, fruit buds on 2-year-old wood, and extension growth that has been pruned back in winter. Where there is room to extend spur systems along a branch, cut back to 3 or 4 wood buds on the previous summer's growth, rather than to the top flower bud.

flower bud. If there is room for a longer spur system, cut back to three or four wood buds on the previous summer's extension growth. Spur systems, whether formed naturally or as a result of pruning, are self-renewing, flower buds forming behind the fruit.

Renewal pruning

In the first winter select laterals with room for growth, generally on the outside of the tree, and leave them unpruned. By the following winter there will be new growth from the end bud of each lateral and, on the older wood below, a number of flower buds. Cut back each lateral to the topmost flower bud, in effect cutting off the new growth. In the following growing season the retained wood should carry fruit. In the third winter a proportion of these fruited laterals, about half if there is room, can be retained as elongated spur systems; but cut back the rest, leaving about an inch (2.5cm) of stub. In the next growing season the cycle is completed when a new lateral develops from this stub.

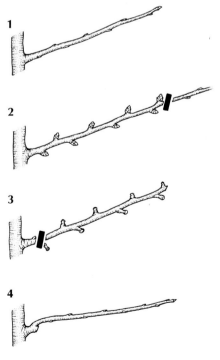

RENEWAL PRUNING

1 In the first winter select, but leave unpruned, a strong well-placed lateral.

2 In the second winter cut back the lateral above the topmost flower bud; remove the extension growth made in the previous season.

3 In the third winter cut back the fruited lateral to leave a 1in (2.5cm) stub.

4 In its first winter do not prune the strong new lateral that grows from the stub.

Spur thinning

As trees mature their spur systems eventually become crowded or too long, generally resulting in fruit of poor quality and size. The remedy is to shorten and thin the spur systems, an operation for late winter to early spring, whether the tree is an unrestricted form or a restricted form that is summer pruned by the Modified Lorette System. When cutting out a proportion of the fruit buds, remove the weakest and any on the underside of branches.

Pruning tip-bearers

Tip-bearers among apples include 'Granny Smith', 'Tydeman's Red', 'Cortland', and 'Rome Beauty', although most apples can produce fruit buds on terminal shoots in some seasons. When grown as restricted forms, these should be summer pruned in the same way as all other cultivars. When grown as unrestricted forms that are pruned in late winter to early spring, the best course is to leave unpruned maiden laterals up to 9in (23cm) in length, so that the fruit bud at the tip can develop. Shorten longer laterals to four buds, to encourage the development of short sub-laterals the following year, and on the same principle prune leaders lightly. Although tip-bearers are naturally gaunt, the suggested pruning may cause overcrowding and winter thinning of laterals may be needed.

Above, top and bottom: When their spur systems become crowded, apples and pears are unlikely to produce fruit of good size and quality. To overcome this, thinning should be carried out in winter with the use of pruners. Take out a proportion of buds that are crowded and also buds on the underside of branches, where fruit might be starved of light.

Right: Espalier-trained pears, like all apples and pears grown in restricted forms, are summer pruned to check excessive vigor and to stimulate the formation of flower buds close to the main stem.

Right: Tip-bearing and partial tip-bearing apples and pears carry fruit buds at the end of shoots.

BUSHES AND STANDARDS

Left: Most pruning of apples and pears grown in unrestricted forms is carried out during the winter.

The pruning and training of apples and pears as bush trees, half-standards and standards is essentially the same. These are all unrestricted forms grown in the open, consisting of a goblet-shaped head on a clear stem, the difference between them lying in the length of the stem or trunk. The height to the first permanent branches of a bush is between 1¾-2½ft (53-76cm). However, dwarfing or semi-dwarfing rootstocks, ranging from the extremely dwarfing M.27 to the semi-dwarfing M.26, make it possible to grow dwarf bush apples with a stem of about 1½-2ft (46-60cm). There are no truly dwarfing rootstocks for pears.

For half-standards and standards, which have trunk heights of about 4ft (1.2m) and 6ft (1.8m), suitable apple rootstocks range from the semi-dwarfing MM.106 to the vigorous MM.111 and M.2. Semi-dwarf trees on OHF.69, OHF.333, and OHF.513 also perform well. The most commonly used rootstock for pears is the semi-vigorous Quince A, although Quince C is suitable on fertile soils and with vigorous cultivars.

Half-standards and standards eventually yield heavy crops, but their size presents several problems for the home gardener: they are difficult to accommodate in all but a large garden; they are slow to start bearing; and a ladder is needed to work on them.

The age at which bush trees begin to fruit depends on growing conditions as well as variety and rootstock. However, trees that are bought as maidens will generally set fruit buds two or three years later, and begin to bear reasonable crops in a further year or so. By starting with two- or three-year-old trees partly formed by the nursery, it is possible to have reasonable crops after only two or three years. Older plants are slow to establish themselves.

Bush trees, half-standards and standards need staking for the first four or five years, while dwarf bushes need a permanent stake. In all cases, the top of the stake should be just below the head of the tree.

Formative pruning

Basic pruning on these unrestricted forms is carried out in the dormant season, late winter, or early spring in the north.

The first stage in forming the goblet-shaped head is to cut back a maiden to encourage the development of strong shoots that will become the primary branches (the nursery may have done this). For a bush tree make the cut at a bud about 2½ft (76cm) above the ground, while for a dwarf bush cut at about 2ft (60cm). On an unbranched

maiden make a sloping cut immediately above a bud which has three or four good buds below it. For a branched maiden make the cut immediately above the topmost of three or four well-placed shoots.

In the second dormant season, having started with an unfeathered maiden, select three or four strong branches as the primaries. Choose branches that have formed wide angles with the stem; narrow-angled branches are weaker and more likely to break when carrying a crop. The topmost leader is often nearly upright and therefore unsuitable, in which case the top needs to be headed back. Bear in mind the need to create a balanced head, with branches well spaced. Cut out superfluous branches

FORMING A BUSH TREE

1 When planting in early spring of the first year cut back a branched maiden to the topmost of 3 or 4 laterals, about 2½ft (76cm) from the ground, or in the case of an unbranched maiden above a bud with 3 or 4 good buds beneath it.

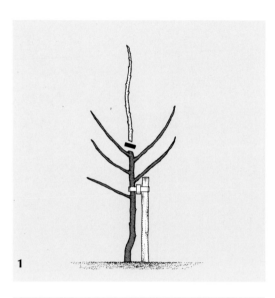

2 In the second winter select 3 or 4 wide-angled branches as the primaries, cutting back strong branches by a half and weaker branches by about two-thirds to outward-facing buds. Remove unwanted branches.

3 In the third winter there should be 6 to 8 branches to form the permanent framework of the tree. Cut these back to outward-facing buds, by about half if they are strong and by two-thirds if they are weak. Formative pruning may need to be continued for a year or two.

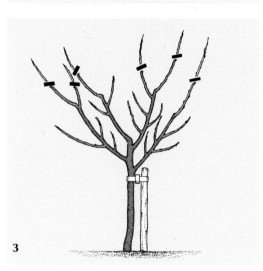

completely and then shorten the branches that are being retained. Cut back strong branches by a half and weaker branches by about two-thirds, cutting to an outward-facing bud.

In the case of cultivars with very upright growth, such as 'Delicious', tying down growths while they are young and flexible will help to form a tree with wide-angled branches.

The hard pruning of the primary branches encourages the development of strong secondaries, and in the third winter select about four of these to add to the permanent framework of branches. Cut back the previous season's growth of the framework branches by about half or, in the case of weak branches, by two-thirds, cutting to outward-facing buds to keep the center open. Prune any other laterals back to four or five buds.

Light formative pruning will need to be continued for at least another year and, in the case of weak growers, for a few more seasons after that. Leave laterals on the outer part of the tree unpruned.

To get the necessary height, a maiden that is to make a standard or half-standard needs to be grown on for a year or two before it is cut back. During this phase leave side shoots on as they will help thicken the stem, but in summer pinch back vigorous laterals to six leaves. In the second dormant season after planting, cut back the leader following the same principles as for a bush tree, but for a half-standard select a bud at about 4½ft (1.4m) and for a standard at 6½ft (2m). For a year or two laterals below the head can be left on while the trunk thickens up, but pinch back vigorous growth in the summer. If not already removed, take off all laterals below the head once the tree begins to flower. For other pruning follow the same procedure as for a bush tree.

Pruning the bearing tree

A healthy young tree that is bearing well needs only light pruning in the dormant season, mainly to encourage the formation of fruit buds. Most cultivars are spur-bearers and are pruned to encourage the formation of spurs and also on the renewal system. As the tree matures spur systems will need to be thinned. Tip-bearing cultivars need a different treatment (see pages 138–40 for

pruning spur bearers, spur thinning, renewal pruning and pruning tip-bearers).

Excessive winter pruning will encourage vegetative growth at the expense of fruit production. However, it is important to keep the tree open-centered and to take out crossing and rubbing branches as well as dead, diseased or damaged wood. Trees of very spreading habit, such as 'Golden Delicious', may need to be pruned to inward-facing buds, or to upright replacement laterals if branches are too low.

On very vigorous trees summer pruning will help to check growth and improve the chances of wood and fruit ripening well. Carry out the operation over a period of six to eight weeks, cutting back to about five leaves the current season's growth of laterals that are more than 1ft (30cm) long.

Family trees

The family tree seems an attractive option if there is only room for one fruit tree in a garden. They are produced at the nursery, where four or five cultivars, chosen as suitable pollinators for one another, are grafted on to the same rootstock and normally offered as semi-dwarf bush trees.

The pruning and training is, in principle, the same as for other bush trees. However, very often inequalities of vigour between the two cultivars become apparent as the tree matures and it becomes difficult to maintain a balanced head. In many cases it is as easy to accommodate in a small garden three or four compatible cordons as it is to grow a family tree successfully.

Above: There is a limited choice of rootstocks for pears, which make reasonably vigorous bush trees. The cultivar 'Packham's Triumph', shown here, comes into blossom in early spring.

Far left: On this apple tree the formative pruning has been done in the nursery. It is not advisable to buy trees more than 3 years old.

SPINDLEBUSH TREES

Spindlebush apples and pears are cone-shaped trees grown on dwarfing or semi-dwarfing rootstocks and trained on a central leader that carries evenly spaced branches to its full height. The lower branches, which are permanent and trained near the horizontal, carry fruiting laterals pruned on the renewal system (see p. 139). The upper branches are kept shorter and replaced when they become unproductive or too dominant. The tree must be permanently staked to a height of about 6ft (1.8m). Spindlebush trees start bearing early, but they must be well maintained.

Formative pruning
Begin, if possible, with a branched maiden, as illustrated, which already has three or four laterals, the lowest not less that 2ft (60cm) from the ground, which can form the first tier of branches. If starting with an unbranched maiden, cut back to a bud at about 3ft (90cm). Make all cuts on laterals to downward-facing buds.

Cut back the central leader annually until it has reached a height of 7-8ft (2.1-2.4m), each time cutting to a bud on the opposite side to the previous year's bud in order to keep the leader straight. When the maximum desired height has been reached, cut back the extension growth annually to a lateral, and tie this in as the new leader.

In late summer of the second and third years more laterals can be tied down to form permanent branches. When tying down branches it is best to use thick, soft string which should be secured to wire pegs.

Pruning the bearing tree
As the tree comes into bearing the emphasis shifts to regular renewal pruning. A proportion of the upper branches are cut out each year when they are three or four years old. A stub about 1in (2.5cm) long is left, from which a new lateral develops. Unproductive fruiting laterals and spurs on the lower branches are also pruned in the same way.

Above: Spindlebush apples, which are grown on dwarfing or semi-dwarfing rootstocks, start bearing early, but require skilled pruning and training to continue producing good crops.

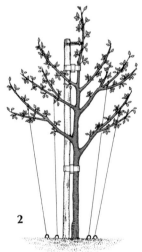
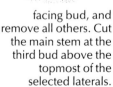
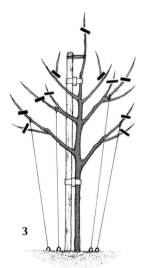

FORMING A SPINDLEBUSH
1 In the dormant season select 4 or 5 laterals of a newly planted branched maiden to form the first tier of branches. The lowest should be not less that 2ft (60cm) from the ground. Reduce the selected laterals by about half, cutting at a downward-facing bud, and remove all others. Cut the main stem at the third bud above the topmost of the selected laterals.

2 By late summer of the first year train the new central leader to the stake. Tie down 3 or 4 laterals which form wide angles with the stem, holding them 20-30° above the horizontal until they set. More laterals can be tied down in subsequent years. Cut out upright laterals forming narrow angles with the main stem.

3 In the second winter cut back the central leader by about a third. Remove strings from branches that have set, and loosen retained ties if they constrict. Cut out upright laterals and any competing with the central leader, and reduce laterals by a quarter, cutting to a downward-facing bud.

CORDONS

Below: The cordon is a very useful form for apples and pears in the small garden. The single or multiple stems are furnished with fruiting spurs, summer pruning being used to check growth.

Bottom: The oblique training of apple and pear cordons helps to control their vigor and makes it easy to manage trees without the use of steps.

The cordon is a restricted form consisting in essence of a main stem furnished with short-growing fruiting spurs. Apples are normally grown on dwarfing or semi-dwarfing rootstocks (vigorous rootstocks are only suitable on poor soils). Pears are usually grafted on to Quince A or Quince C rootstocks.

The cordon can be grown vertically or at an angle, and as a single stem or as two or more parallel arms. The single oblique cordon is the most common form and has several advantages: a number of trees can be grown in a small space; trees can be easily reached over their whole length; and training towards the horizontal checks vigor but encourages the production of fruit buds.

Cordons require permanent support. In the open garden use a system of posts and wires, spacing wires 2, 4 and 6ft (60, 120 and 180cm) above ground level. Use the same spacing for wires on walls or fences, running them 4-6in (10-15cm) out from the surface to allow the free circulation of air. The cordons are tied to bamboo canes, which should be attached to the wires before planting. Allow 2½-3ft (76-90cm) between cordons.

Formative pruning and training
It is preferable to start with a branched maiden, on which the pruned back laterals will develop fruiting spurs. The tree will probably start bearing in its third year.

At planting, between late autumn and early spring (the latter in the north), set the cordon at an angle of 45 degrees, ensuring that the union is above ground and the scion is uppermost. In the northern hemisphere, slope cordons in north-south rows to the north, and in the southern hemisphere to the south. In east-west rows slope the cordons to the east.

Tie the cordon to the cane at two points, and cut back laterals to four buds. In the growing season tie in extension growth of the leader and begin the summer pruning as outlined for the bearing cordon.

If there are flowers in the spring after planting, remove them, taking care to avoid damaging the shoot behind the blossom.

Summer pruning: the Modified Lorette System
This system is the most widely used method of pruning bearing cordons and is started in the second year. In mid-summer – apples

Above: Cordons can be grown vertically but, as with these old pear trees, a high wall is required and their vigor is less easily controlled.

PRUNING AND TRAINING

1 At planting, between late autumn and early spring (early spring in the north), set the branched maiden at 45°, ensuring the union is above ground and the scion uppermost. Tie the cordon to the cane at 2 points. Cut back laterals to 4 buds.

2 Remove flowers in the second year, but leave the basal rosette of leaves intact.

3 Begin summer pruning by the Modified Lorette System in mid- to late summer of the second year. Shorten to 3 good leaves above the basal cluster all mature laterals growing directly from the stem that are more than 9in (23cm) long. Cut back to one leaf beyond the basal cluster any sub-laterals growing from existing spur systems.

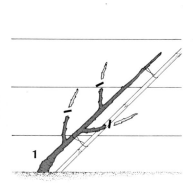

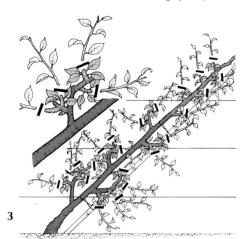

Right: Although most apples and pears that are grown as cordons are now trained as oblique singles, forms that were popular in the past include oblique and vertical multiple cordons.

generally about a week later than pears – cut back mature laterals growing directly from the main stem at three leaves, not counting the basal cluster. Shorten mature laterals arising from spur systems more drastically, cutting at the first leaf beyond the basal cluster. Delay cutting immature laterals, which are lighter in leaf and bark than mature shoots, until early autumn.

Sometimes secondary growths develop after the mid-summer pruning. Remove these, cutting back to a bud or leaf on mature wood, just before leaf fall. If secondary growth is a recurrent problem, delay the summer pruning by two or three weeks or follow the advice for winter pruning.

When the leader has passed the top wire, cut it back in late spring to within 6in (15cm) of the wire. Annual cutting back in mid-summer of all but about one inch (2.5cm) of the year's growth will keep the cordon at the same height throughout its life.

A longer stem can be accommodated by lowering the cordon. However, this operation is most often used to check an over-vigorous cordon, limiting the amount of extension growth made and encouraging the production of fruit buds. The cordon should be lowered in stages, by about five degrees at each stage, to not less than 35 degrees.

4 In autumn, just before leaf fall, remove secondary growths that have developed since the summer pruning. Cut back to a leaf or bud on mature wood.

5 When the leader has reached the required height and passed the top wire, cut back in late spring, leaving about 6in (15cm) above the wire.

6 In mid-summer of subsequent years cut back all but one inch (2.5cm) of the leader's growth. Continue to summer prune, cutting back to 3 leaves mature laterals growing from

the main stem that are more than 9in (23cm) long, and shortening to one leaf beyond the basal cluster any sub-laterals growing from existing side shoots and spurs.

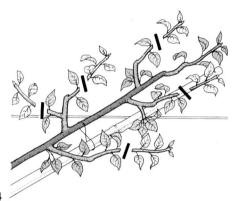

4

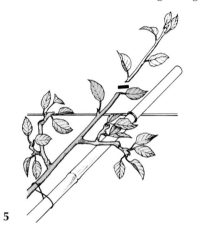

5

6

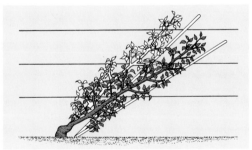

LOWERING A CORDON

To check an over-vigorous cordon or to accommodate a longer cordon, lower it but to not less than 35°. Lower 5° at a time, tying the cordon in to a new cane already fixed in position.

Winter pruning the bearing cordon

This is normally confined to simplifying crowded spur systems on mature trees (see p. 140). In mild areas with a high rainfall, secondary growth after summer pruning may be so prolific that the best course is to prune in winter. In such cases cut to three buds on laterals and one bud on sub-laterals.

Sometimes a young cordon produces insufficient laterals or laterals that are poorly spaced along the stem. Cutting back the previous summer's growth of the main stem by up to a third will encourage the development of new side shoots.

Winter is the best time to renovate neglected cordons, the aim being to restrict laterals to short fruiting spurs. After the initial renovation return to a program of normal summer pruning.

ESPALIERS

The espalier is a restricted form consisting of a central stem supporting several tiers of paired horizontal branches all trained in the same plane. Espaliers generally have four or five tiers, but more are possible and single-tier espaliers are sometimes used as an edging to beds. Except on poor soils, apples are normally grown on dwarfing or semi-dwarfing rootstocks. Pears are grown on either Quince A or Quince C. Partially trained espaliers are sometimes available from nurseries. These start bearing sooner than those planted as maidens.

Espalier trees need support throughout their lives, whether they are grown against walls or trained on a system of posts and wires in the open. The height of the wires above ground level should correspond to the tiers of the espalier, which are usually 1¼-1½ft (38-46cm) apart.

Below: The Modified Lorette System of summer pruning apples and pears encourages the formation of fruiting spurs.

Formative pruning and training
In early spring cut back a newly planted, unbranched maiden about 1¼ft (38cm) above the ground, making the cut to the topmost of three good buds. Growth from the top bud will extend the central stem, while growth from the two lower buds, one facing to the left, the other to the right, will develop as the two arms of the bottom tier.

In summer train the topmost shoot vertically to a cane. Horizontal training in the first summer would check the growth of the arms too severely. Train them on canes at 45 degrees to the horizontal. If growth is unbalanced, check a vigorous arm by

lowering slightly and encourage a weaker arm by raising it. In late autumn carefully lower the two arms to the horizontal and tie them to the wires. If growth has been weak, shorten leaders by about a third to upward-facing buds, but otherwise leave them unpruned.

To create the next tier, prune back the central leader about 1½ft (46cm) above the bottom branches. Yet again there must be three buds below the cut, one to extend the central stem and two, facing in opposite directions, to form the arms. Shorten surplus laterals to three buds. Throughout the subsequent summer train the leaders as for the first tier, with the arms at 45 degrees, until they are lowered to the second wire in late autumn.

Follow this pattern of building up tiers until the required number has been formed.

Pruning the bearing espalier
The arms of an espalier are like horizontal cordons, the fruit being borne on spur systems. As with cordons, summer pruning starts in the second year and the Modified Lorette System should be used. In essence this means cutting back mature laterals longer than 9in (23cm) arising from the tiers to three leaves above the basal cluster, and any laterals on side shoots or spurs to one leaf. To stop the central stem and the horizontal arms extending too much, prune them back in late spring, cutting almost all of the preceding summer's growth. On mature trees, thin crowded spur systems in winter.

FORMING AN ESPALIER
1 After planting in early spring, cut back a newly planted, unbranched maiden at the topmost of 3 good buds about 1¼ft (38cm) above the ground.

2 During summer train the shoots to canes, the topmost vertically and the arms at 45°.

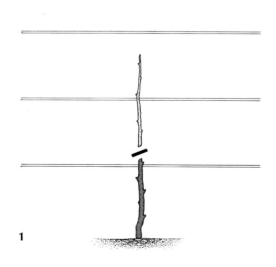

1

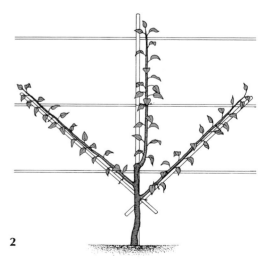

2

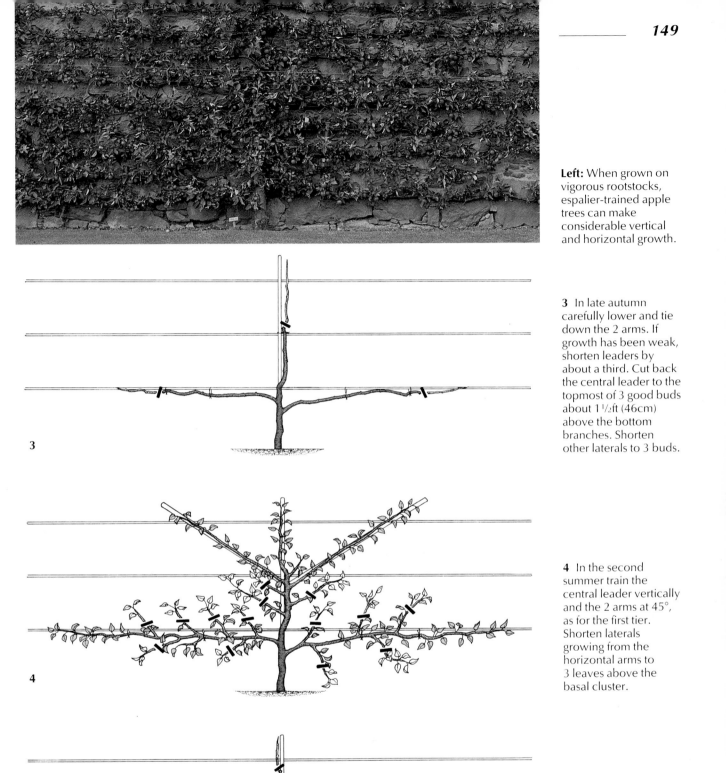

Left: When grown on vigorous rootstocks, espalier-trained apple trees can make considerable vertical and horizontal growth.

3 In late autumn carefully lower and tie down the 2 arms. If growth has been weak, shorten leaders by about a third. Cut back the central leader to the topmost of 3 good buds about 1 1/2ft (46cm) above the bottom branches. Shorten other laterals to 3 buds.

4 In the second summer train the central leader vertically and the 2 arms at 45°, as for the first tier. Shorten laterals growing from the horizontal arms to 3 leaves above the basal cluster.

5 In late autumn of the second year carefully lower and tie down the 2 topmost arms, pruning back by a third if growth is weak. Cut the central leader back at the topmost of 3 good buds about 1 1/2ft (46cm) above the second tier.

DWARF PYRAMIDS

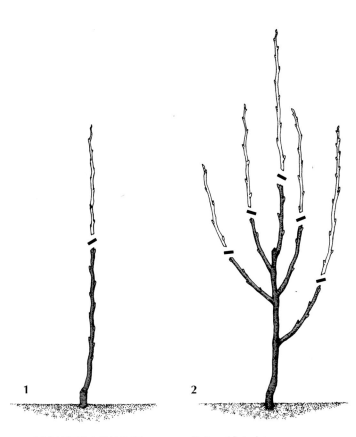

FORMING A DWARF PYRAMID

1 Between late autumn and late winter cut back an unbranched maiden to a bud about 1³/₄ft (51cm) above ground level.

2 In the second winter cut back the central leader, retaining 8-10in (20-25cm) of the previous summer's growth. Repeat this operation annually until the tree has reached about 7ft (2.1m). Thereafter cut back the leader to its origin annually in late spring. Retain 3 to 5 well-spaced side branches and cut them back to downward-facing buds about 8in (20cm) from the main stem.

3 In mid- to late summer of the second year begin pruning using the Modified Lorette System. Leave leaders unpruned, but shorten laterals to 3 leaves and sub-laterals to one leaf beyond the basal cluster.

4 In the third and subsequent years continue pruning annually in mid- to late summer by the Modified Lorette System, cutting laterals back to 3 leaves and sub-laterals to one leaf beyond the basal cluster. Cut back branch leaders to 6 leaves beyond the basal cluster.

This restricted form, initially developed by commercial growers, has been taken up successfully by amateur gardeners. The aim is to create a tapering central-leader tree about 7ft (2.1m) high. To encourage the production of side branches during the formative stage, the central leader is cut back annually. By zigzagging, one year cutting to a bud on one side of the stem and the next to a bud on the opposite side, the central stem will maintain more or less straight growth. The branches of the dwarf pyramid are pruned in summer, each branch being treated as though it were a cordon.

Suitable rootstocks for apples are the dwarfing M.26 and, on good soils, the even more dwarfing M.9 and M.27. For pears Quince C is preferable to Quince A, which is too vigorous except on poor soils. Provided the right rootstock is used and growth is properly controlled, these central-leader trees can be close planted.

All trees grown as dwarf pyramids need some support for the first four or five years, and apples on M.27 and M.9 must have support throughout their lives. If trees are grown in rows, an alternative to staking is to run two horizontal wires along the row, one at a height of 1½ft (46cm) and the other at 3ft (90cm) above the ground. The trees can be tied to these as they develop.

Formative pruning
Starting with an unbranched maiden, plant between late autumn and late winter (early spring in the north) and cut back the stem to a bud about 20in (51cm) above ground level. Treat a branched maiden in the same way but, if laterals are longer than 6in (15cm), cut these back to downward-facing buds at 4-6in (10-15cm).

The topmost of the four or five shoots that develop during the following summer becomes the central leader. In the second winter cut this back, retaining 8-10in (20-25cm) of new growth. This pruning should be repeated annually until the tree is about 7ft (2.1m) tall. Shorten branch leaders and any laterals to about 6-8in (15-20cm). A pyramid shape is required, with the base branches longer than those at the top.

Pruning the mature tree
The side branches are summer pruned by the Modified Lorette System (see pp. 145–47).

Begin summer pruning in the second year, dealing with pears in mid-summer and apples about two weeks later. Leave the leaders unpruned, but cut back laterals to three leaves and sub-laterals to one leaf beyond the basal cluster. Leave pruning of immature shoots with light green leaves and bark until early autumn. Follow this method of pruning in subsequent summers and, starting in the third year, cut back branch leaders to six leaves beyond the basal cluster.

When the central leader has reached the required height, cut back the previous season's growth annually in late spring. This is also the best time to shorten any branches at the top of the tree that are competing with the central leader or any branch leaders that are too long. Cut these back to downward-facing buds.

Winter pruning is limited to thinning crowded spur systems (see p.140), and restoring the shape of the tree if necessary.

MAINTAINING THE SHAPE
The shape of the mature dwarf pyramid is maintained by cutting back the previous year's growth of the central leader in late spring, and at the same time shortening vigorous branches, making cuts at downward-facing buds. In winter it may be necessary to thin crowded spur systems.

FANS, ARCHES, AND TUNNELS

Old gardening manuals, and sometimes old gardens, reveal the range of forms in which apples and pears have been grown in the past. These are, generally, variations of the restricted forms, often elaborated for their ornamental value. The simplest of these variations are fans and cordons grown to form arches and tunnels.

Fans

Although the fan is mainly used for stone fruits such as peaches and cherries, apples and pears can also be grown in this way. Even when using dwarfing or semi-dwarfing rootstocks, apple fans need a minimum wall or fence height of about 7ft (2.1m), and pears on Quince A or Quince C require about 8ft (2.4m).

The initial pruning and training is very similar to that outlined for a peach fan (see pp.168–70). In the first year the main stem of a maiden is cut back in the dormant season to a bud about 1¼ft (38cm) above ground level, and in the following summer two strong shoots are trained out at an angle of 45 degrees. These are cut back in the second winter, and in the following summer selected shoots are trained in as ribs of the fan. It will take several more years of cutting back and training in to complete the fan.

Summer pruning by the Modified Lorette System, treating each rib as though it were a separate cordon (see pp.145–47), controls the growth of the fan and promotes the development of fruiting spurs.

Arches and tunnels

A fruiting arch is one of the easiest ways of accommodating a pair of trees in a very small garden. If there is room for no other fruit trees, the selection of cultivars must take account of their pollination requirements. The two trees are simply grown as vertical cordons that are arched over to meet each other at the top.

It is essential from the outset to have a firm and durable structure of wood or metal on which to train the cordons and, as part of the reason for having an arch is to ornament the garden, the support should also be pleasing to the eye.

A series of arches can be used to form a tunnel. A much slower method of covering the framework of an arbour or tunnel is to train espalier trees on either side.

Above left and above: Apples and pears can be trained as fans, either against walls (above) or in the open garden (above left) on a framework of wires. However, they require generous spacing and for this reason are not suitable for small gardens.

Left: One method of forming a fruit tunnel is to train 2 rows of cordon apples or pears to a permanent framework that arches over a path.

Left: The arcure method of training is not widely practiced today, but is an interesting variant of the cordon, with the tree trained in a sequence of arcs.

Left and above: An alternative to the fruit tunnel composed of a series of cordons is one made from 2 rows of espaliered apples or pears trained over a permanent framework.

Above middle: In the 19th century, pears and apples were often trained in a variety of vase shapes, the methods used being adaptations of the techniques for growing cordons and espaliers. This shape is called "le bateau" after its resemblance to the ribs of a boat.

PLUMS

Below: When plums such as the popular 'Victoria' are grown as bushes or standards they require little pruning once the framework is formed.

Although plums are an important group of stone fruits, they have been rather neglected by home gardeners, largely because until recently the commonly available rootstock, Myrobalan, was so vigorous. The development of the semi-dwarfing St Julien A and *Prunus besseyi* rootstocks has made it possible to grow more compact trees, and work on the even more recent Pixy indicates that it has considerable potential as a dwarfing rootstock on fertile ground.

The introduction of these three new rootstocks, resulting in more manageable trees that can be given protection, will help to overcome other problems associated with plums, in particular damage to Japanese plum flower buds in winter and frost damage to blossom in spring.

Brown rot and bacterial canker are two serious diseases of plums. The risk of infection is reduced if pruning is done in late spring and summer, rather than in autumn and winter, and if pruning cuts are treated immediately with a wound paint. However, formative pruning is usually carried out in early spring to allow a long growing season.

If suckers are produced, remove them as soon as they are seen. They should be taken off at the point where they are growing out from the rootstock.

The pruning methods outlined here apply to European and Japanese plums. Although culinary plums will tolerate some shade, dessert plums, especially 'Gage' cultivars, need warmth and sunlight to develop their flavor fully and do well when fan trained on a sunny wall.

BIRD DAMAGE
Cut back bird-stripped shoots to an undamaged bud in spring (left). The shoots will remain bare if left unpruned (right).

BUSHES AND STANDARDS
The pruning of these forms to create a goblet-shaped head is similar; where they differ is in the height of the trunk. The stem of a bush is 2½-3ft (76-90cm), that of a half-standard about 4½ft (1.4m), and that of a standard about 6ft (1.8m).

All of these forms need staking for the first four or five years at least. For bushes on St Julien A or Pixy use a single stake, but larger-headed plants, especially if they are on more vigorous rootstocks, are best supported by two vertical stakes with a crossbar. The single stake or the crossbar should be just below the lowest branches. Position stakes before planting.

Formative pruning
Trees can be planted when available from the nursery, usually in early spring. Irrespective of when the tree is planted, delay pruning until late spring when the buds start to break. Maiden trees may need to be grown on for a year to reach the height of stem needed to make a half-standard or standard. The purpose of the initial pruning is to encourage the development of strong primary branches.

The illustrations show the formation of a half-standard from a weakly branched maiden. Starting with an unbranched maiden, cut at an appropriate height, for a bush at about 3ft (90cm), and to the topmost of four or five good buds. On a branched maiden there may be laterals that can be used to form the primary branches. In this case cut the stem immediately above the topmost selected lateral, and reduce each lateral needed for the head by about two-thirds, pruning at an outward-facing bud. Subsequent pruning is essentially as illustrated for the half-standard.

Pruning the mature tree
In subsequent years little pruning is necessary except for some thinning. Plums, however, are naturally more crowded in their growth than, for example, apples and pears. If a plum has spreading or drooping branches, more upright growth can be encouraged by pruning lightly to upward-facing buds in late spring or early summer.

Shoots from which the buds have been stripped by birds should be cut back to a sound bud in early spring.

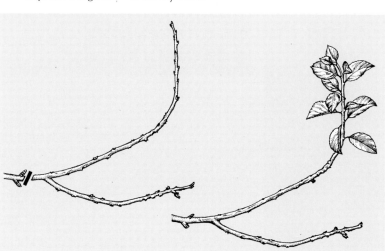

FORMING A HALF STANDARD

1 After planting the dormant plum tree, delay pruning until late spring. Starting with a weakly branched maiden that has been staked and tied, cut back to the topmost of 4 or 5 good buds. Retain temporarily any other laterals, pruning back to about 3in (7.5cm).

2 During the first summer 4 or 5 primary branches should develop. Leave these unpruned but pinch back growth on the laterals that were shortened in late spring and any others that develop below the head, leaving no more than 4 or 5 leaves.

3 In late spring of the second year select 4 well-spaced branches with wide angles as the permanent branches. Cut each back by a half to two-thirds at an outward-facing bud. Remove all other laterals, including those retained the previous year to help thicken the stem.

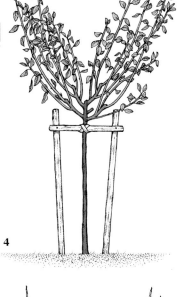

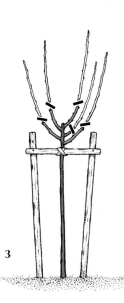

4 In late spring of the third year select up to 8 strong outward-growing secondary branches to make up a balanced head. Cut these back by a half to two-thirds of the growth made the previous year, pruning to outward-facing buds.

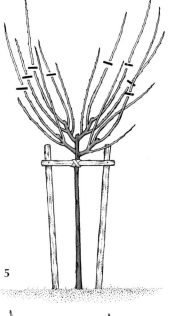

5 At the same time prune back laterals on the inside of the tree to about 4in (10cm), but laterals on the outside of the head which are not needed for the framework can be left unpruned. They will carry flowers the following year. With weaker-growing varieties it may be necessary to continue cutting back leaders in late spring for another year or two.

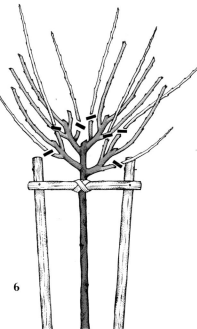

6 The fully formed tree needs little pruning. To prevent the center becoming crowded, shorten laterals on the inside of the bush to about 4in (10cm) in summer. Cut out also any exceptionally vigorous or crossing growths.

PYRAMID PLUMS

THE PYRAMID PLUM
1 As buds begin to break cut back the central stem of a branched maiden at about 5ft (1.5m), or 3 or 4 buds above the topmost lateral. Cut unbranched maidens cut to a bud at about 3ft (90cm). Remove completely any laterals from the bottom 1½ft (46cm) of the stem, and reduce remaining laterals by about half, cutting to downward-facing buds.

By using the semi-dwarfing St Julien A or the other available rootstocks, such as *Prunus besseyi* or Pixy, plums can be successfully grown as relatively compact pyramids. The formative pruning creates a 6- 8ft (1.8-2.4m) high, cone-shaped tree on a central trunk, and the shape is maintained by subsequent summer pruning. Staking to a height of about 7ft (2.1m) is necessary for the first five years.

Pruning and training
If possible, start with a branched maiden, planting in early spring. Early planting is advisable, but delay pruning until bud burst in late spring. To form a pyramid plum follow the illustrated steps. Cut all shoots to downward-facing buds to encourage the

development of near-horizontal branches. Branches growing vigorously away from the horizontal may need to be tied down to ensure controlled growth.

Annual cutting back of the central leader will encourage the growth of evenly spaced laterals to the full height of the pyramid. By zigzagging, one year cutting to a bud on one side of the stem and the next to a bud on the opposite side, the leader will grow more or less straight and upright.

In addition to the regular summer pruning, some thinning out of crossing branches may be necessary. Cut out completely any vigorous upright branches that would unbalance the pyramid shape and compete with the leader.

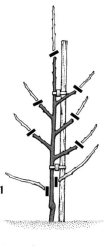

2 In mid-summer shorten the growth made, except that of the central leader, reducing laterals growing directly from the stem to about 8in (20cm) and sub-laterals to 6in (15cm).

3 Until the tree reaches the desired height, cut back the main stem annually in late spring by two-thirds of the growth made the previous year. When no further extension is wanted, maintain the tree at the desired height by cutting back the leader annually in late spring.

4 The pattern of summer pruning that has already been established is continued throughout the life of the tree, branch leaders being cut back to 8in (20cm) and laterals to 6in (15cm).

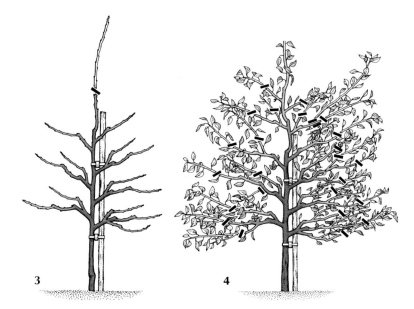

Left: On the semi-dwarfing St Julien A rootstock plums are not easy to grow as cordons or espaliers. The restricted forms may prove more successful when grown on the newer and more dwarfing Pixy.

FAN-TRAINED PLUMS

Left and below: Plums are early flowering and their blossom can suffer serious frost damage. Trees fan-trained on walls or fences are more easily protected than those growing in the open garden. The most suitable rootstock is St Julien A.

Dessert plums, especially 'Gage' cultivars, need good growing conditions to produce fruit with their full depth of flavor. In cool temperate areas the best way to produce such high-quality fruit is to fan-train trees against a warm sunny wall.

St Julien A has proved a satisfactory rootstock for fans, trees grown on it requiring a wall or fence about 6½ft (1.9m) high and with room for a spread of 15-18ft (4.6-5.5m). The dwarfing rootstock Pixy is also showing promise and cultivars grown on it require less space, about 12ft (3.7m) of wall or fence with a minimum height of 6ft (1.8m).

Formative pruning

In the initial stages the fan training of a plum is the same as for a peach. The aim is to build up a radiating pattern of ribs carrying evenly distributed, fruit-bearing laterals. A permanent system of horizontal wires is necessary, the first starting about 1¼ft (38cm) from the ground and above that spaced at intervals of 6in (15cm). Some nurseries offer trees that have been partly trained, and the training should be continued according to the stage the tree has reached.

Starting with a maiden, plant in early spring, but delay pruning until late spring. Cut the maiden back to a lateral or, in the case of an unbranched maiden, a bud about 2ft (60cm) above the ground. Below this lateral or bud there must be either two good buds, one facing to the left and the other to the right, or two well-placed laterals. These will form the first two ribs of the fan. Cut back the laterals by two-thirds to an upward-facing bud and take out completely all the other laterals.

In early summer attach two canes to the wires radiating out on either side of the main stem at an angle of 45 degrees, and train the growths made by the selected buds or laterals to these. When these shoots are about 1½ft (46cm) long, cut the central leader back to their junction and pinch back any other shoots to one leaf.

In late spring of the second year cut back the two ribs at buds 1-1½ft (30-46cm) from the main stem. This pruning results in the growth of laterals that provide further ribs for the fan. In summer select four strong growths on each side, one to extend the existing rib, one on the lower side to be trained almost horizontally, and two evenly spaced on the upper side. Train each to a cane fixed to the wires. The fan should now have a total of eight ribs; if there are other shoots, cut them back at one leaf.

In the third spring cut back the eight ribs by one-third to upward-facing buds. In the summer the extension growths will need to

FORMING THE FAN

Begin by cutting back a branched maiden to a lateral at about 2ft (60cm), which has below it 2 laterals or buds, one facing left and the other right, that will form the first 2 ribs of the fan.

1 In mid-summer train the arms of the fan to bamboo canes fixed to the wires at an angle of 45°. When the arms are about 1½ft (46cm) long, cut the central leader back to the topmost lateral and pinch back any other shoots to one leaf.

2 In spring of the second year cut back the 2 ribs at buds 1-1½ft (30-46cm) from the main stem.

3 In summer select 4 strong growths on each side to form evenly spaced, radiating ribs and tie these in to bamboo canes fixed to the wires. Cut back other shoots at one leaf. In the following spring cut back the ribs by a third and during the growing season train in new shoots where there is space.

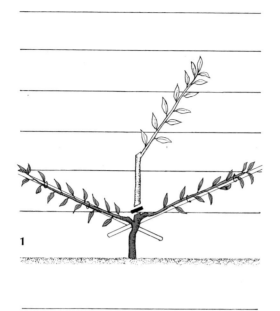

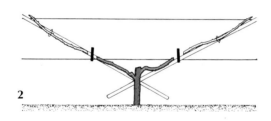

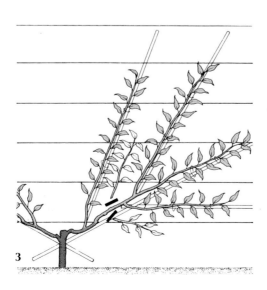

be tied in to canes fixed to the wires. In this and the following summer tie in new shoots to the wires wherever there is available space. Some subsequent filling in of ribs may also be necessary. Always leave the center until last as upright growth may be disproportionately vigorous.

Pruning the established fan

Plums bear fruit on growth made the previous year and on short spurs on older wood. However, as wood ages it tends to become bare, and so the aim in pruning a bearing plum fan is to strike a balance between encouraging spur formation and replacing old unfruitful branches with younger, more productive growth.

In early spring rub out shoots that are growing in to the wall or fence. The ideal spacing between laterals is about 4in (10cm). Thin to this spacing if laterals are too close. The development of fruit-bearing spurs is initiated in summer by pinching back to six or seven leaves any new shoots, including breastwood, not needed for the framework. After the crop has been picked, shorten these same shoots still further by cutting them back to three leaves.

Cutting out of unfruitful wood and any very vigorous upright growths is best done after harvesting, but must be completed by the end of summer.

SPUR SYSTEMS
Pinch back new shoots not needed for the framework to 6 or 7 leaves in mid-summer, and to 3 after harvest.

SWEET AND DUKE CHERRIES

Above: The sweet cherry makes a large tree when grown as either a bush, half-standard or standard, and is not suitable for small gardens.

Sweet cherries make large trees and, as most are self-sterile (there are a few self-fertile cultivars such as 'Stella' and 'Lapins'), they will not bear crops unless at least two compatible cultivars are grown close together. Duke cherries (pollinated by either sweet or sour varieties) are grown in the same way as sweet cherries, but are intermediate in character between them and the less vigorous sour or tart cherries, which need a different system of pruning.

Most cherry trees are still grown on Mahaleb and Mazzard rootstocks. Sweet cherries are much too vigorous to be trained in the more restricted forms, such as dwarf pyramids and cordons, because, even with constant pruning, it is difficult to maintain the form. The recent use by some nurseries of a semi-dwarfing rootstock, G.M. 61, and other rootstocks which are still at an experimental stage, may make sweet cherries a more manageable fruit for the small garden. G.M. 61 should produce a tree under 15ft (4.5m).

The risk of the fungus disease perennial canker gaining entry through cuts is reduced if pruning is carried out in late spring and summer, rather than winter, when the disease is most active.

BUSHES AND STANDARDS

The same method of pruning applies to bushes, half-standards and standards, and the system used for sweet and Duke cherries is much the same as for plums (see pp. 154–55). All need staking for the first four or five years, with the top of the stake reaching to just below the head of the tree.

Formative pruning

Cherries are generally available as one- or two-year trees, which should be planted between late autumn and late winter (or in early spring in the north). However, delay pruning until the buds begin to open.

For a bush, cut back the tree to the topmost of four or five strong laterals at about 2^1/$_2$ft (76cm); for a half-standard make the cut at about 4^1/$_2$ft (1.4m), and for a standard at about 6^1/$_2$ft (1.9m). New trees that are going to be trained as half-standards or standards may need to be grown on for a year to reach the required height.

To encourage the development of an open-centered tree prune back each of the selected laterals by about half to outward-facing buds. Any lower laterals should be pinched back to four leaves. They can be retained while the trunk thickens and pinched back annually until removed completely in the third or fourth year.

The leaders forming the head need to be cut back by about a half in the second spring, but by the third spring they need only light pruning that leaves about 2ft (60cm) of the previous season's growth. Cut out completely vigorous upright laterals in the center of the head, and prune laterals competing with the leaders to three buds. Other laterals can be left unpruned, provided there is room.

Pruning the bearing tree

Some thinning of crowded and crossing branches, and the removal of dead, diseased or damaged wood, are all the pruning a mature tree needs.

FAN TRAINING

Each fan-trained sweet cherry requires 15-20ft (4.6-6.1m) of wall or fence to a height of about 10ft (3m). Before planting, the horizontal wires needed to support the fan should be fixed in place spaced about 6in (15cm) apart.

FORMING A FAN

1 In early spring cut back an unbranched maiden to a bud at about 1¼ft (38cm). Make the cut at a bud that is pointing left or right, with another bud beneath it pointing in the opposite direction.

1

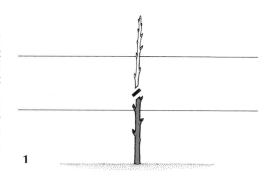

2 As shoots develop from the selected buds tie them to canes fixed to the wires at an angle of 45°. Remove any other shoots on the main stem.

2

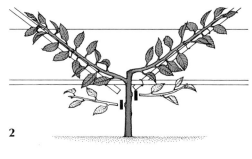

3 In early spring of the second year cut the arms back to buds about 1ft (30cm) from the main stem.

3

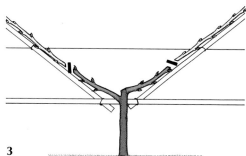

4 During the summer of the second year train in 4 to 6 strong shoots growing from the cut-back arms. Tie these ribs of the fan to bamboo canes fixed to the wires, so that they radiate outwards and are evenly spaced.

4

Formative pruning and training

This is essentially the same as for fan-trained peaches (see pp.168-70). Cutting back the central stem encourages the development of strong laterals that form the ribs of the fan, and training of these in a single plane creates a well-spaced framework that carries fruiting spurs. Cherries, however, are more vigorous than peaches and therefore their framework of ribs can be built up more quickly.

The illustrations show how to produce a fan from an unbranched maiden. A branched maiden generally has a pair of suitable laterals, and it is not uncommon for there to be two well-spaced laterals on each side, in which case all four can be used to form primary ribs. Cut back the central stem to the topmost selected lateral and remove all laterals that are not wanted as ribs. Then shorten the laterals that are to be retained, cutting at upward-facing buds 1½-2ft (46-60cm) from the main stem.

Subsequent pruning and training is essentially as illustrated, but if starting with two ribs on either side retain only two laterals on each of these.

Pruning the bearing tree

In spring rub or cut out shoots growing into the wall. Breastwood may have to be treated in the same way, but it can sometimes be trained in or simply retained if it is not causing an obstruction.

The major pruning activity is to form fruiting spurs by restricting vegetative growth in summer. Pinch back shoots to five or six leaves, about 6in (15cm), and in early autumn shorten them yet again, cutting back to three buds, about 4in (10cm).

Little other pruning or training is needed except for general maintenance. On mature trees it may be necessary to thin or shorten fruiting spurs and this should be done in spring. If after a number of years the fan begins to overtop its wall, cut back ribs to weaker laterals lower down. Check ties at the end of the growing season and retie if branches are constricted.

FORMING FRUITING SPURS

Restricting vegetative growth encourages the development of fruiting spurs. In summer pinch back sub-laterals to 5 or 6 leaves, about 6in (15cm). In early autumn shorten the same shoots again, cutting back to 3 buds, about 4in (10cm).

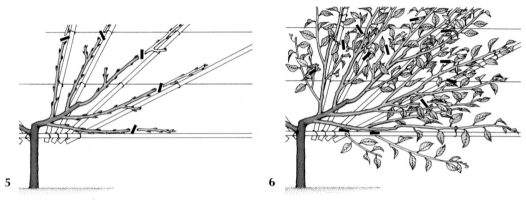

5

6

5 In early spring of the third year prune all leaders, cutting back to a bud so that 1½-1¾ft (46-53cm) of the growth made during the previous year is retained.

6 In the summer of the third year continue to fill in the fan, selecting and tying in 3 to 6 shoots from each cut-back rib. Cut out completely any shoots that are not needed and shorten sub-laterals to about 4in (10cm).

7 If the fan is not complete by early spring of the fourth year, cut back selected leaders to stimulate the growth of laterals, which can be trained in where needed during the summer.

7

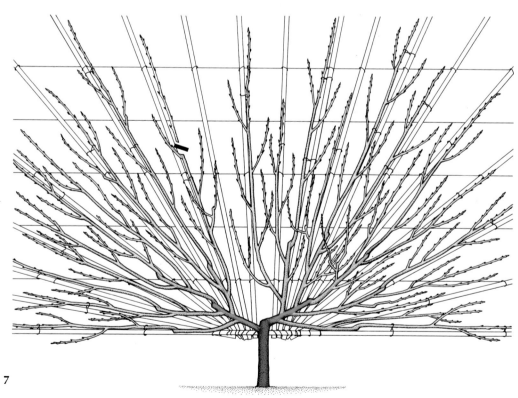

SOUR (TART) CHERRIES

The sour or tart cherry is less vigorous than most standard-size sweet cherries. The most commonly grown cultivar is the self-fertile 'Montmorency', which makes a bush 10-15ft (3-4.5m) high.

'Meteor' grows to only 10-12ft (3-3.7m). Still smaller at 6-8ft (1.8-2.4m) is the 'Morello'-type 'North Star', a naturally dwarf, very hardy sour cherry. These trees should be pruned in spring rather than winter to avoid canker disease. Consult the relevant Cooperative Extension Agent for regional pest control information.

Right: The sour or morello cherry is less vigorous than the sweet cherry. It is often fan trained against a wall or fence, but can also be grown as a bush or pyramid-shaped central-leader tree.

BUSH TREES
In the open garden the sour cherry is generally grown as a bush rather than as a half-standard or standard. The aim of pruning is to create a balanced head on the bearing tree, in which young wood regularly replaces older wood that has already fruited. Trees need staking for the first four or five years, with the top of the stake at about 3ft (90cm), just below the head of the tree.

Formative pruning
Most nurseries ship one- or two-year cherry trees, often partially pre-pruned. If the tree has four or five strong, well-placed laterals

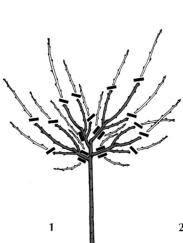

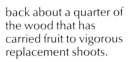
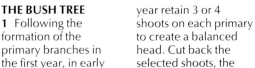

THE BUSH TREE
1 Following the formation of the primary branches in the first year, in early spring of the second year retain 3 or 4 shoots on each primary to create a balanced head. Cut back the selected shoots, the least vigorous by about two-thirds, the most vigorous by half.

2 In late summer of the third year, immediately after harvesting, cut back about a quarter of the wood that has carried fruit to vigorous replacement shoots.

3 More drastic pruning may be necessary on older trees, in late summer cutting back 3- or 4-year-old wood to vigorous new shoots.

they can form the primary branches. Cut back the central stem just above the topmost selected lateral, which should be at a height of about 3½ft (1.1m), and remove any lower laterals not needed for the head of the bush. Shorten the selected laterals by about two-thirds, cutting at outward-facing buds.

If starting with an unbranched maiden make the initial cut above four or five well-placed buds.

Over the next two or three years the head is built up by cutting back in early spring the previous summer's growth by a half to two-thirds. To build up a balanced, uncluttered head most pruning should be to outward-facing buds.

Pruning the bearing tree

As almost all fruit is carried on wood produced the previous summer, the aim of pruning is to encourage the development of young shoots. In late summer, after the crop has been picked, cut back about a quarter of the wood that has fruited to vigorous replacement shoots. To maintain an adequate proportion of young wood on older trees it may be necessary to cut back three- or four-year-old wood to a vigorous shoot produced during the summer. These larger wounds should be treated with a wound paint. Avoid very drastic pruning.

PYRAMID TREES

In the open garden an alternative to the bush is the pyramid, with a central stem grown to a height of 6-9ft (1.8-2.7m). Summer pruning is necessary to maintain the pyramid shape, with the lower branches longer than those higher up, and to keep the tree compact. The pyramid needs to be staked for the first five or six years.

Formative pruning

The early stages in the pruning of a sour cherry as a pyramid are the same as for a plum pyramid. In early spring cut back the leader of a branched maiden at about 5ft (1.5m), removing all laterals below 1½ft (46cm) and shortening those that are retained by half. In mid- to late summer of the same year shorten the extension growths made during the season to 8in (20cm), cutting to downward-facing buds within the leaf axils. Shorten to six leaves the laterals that have developed from the main branches.

PYRAMID TREES

1 In the first 3 years prune the leaders in early spring, cutting back to downward-facing buds.

2 On mature trees replace some of the older wood by cutting back to 1 year old laterals or young shoots in early spring.

3 If the tree is bare and unproductive, after harvesting cut back some of the older wood to strong young shoots.

In early spring of the second year shorten the central leader by two-thirds of the growth made in the previous summer. In subsequent years continue shortening in this way until the tree has reached the desired height. This height is maintained by cutting back all but an inch (2.5cm) of the central leader's annual growth in late spring.

In late summer, starting in the third year, by which time the tree should have yielded its first crop, begin a program of annual replacement pruning. Cut back laterals which have fruited and are not required to extend the branch framework to strong young shoots of the current season's growth. These will fruit in the following summer.

Pruning the bearing tree

The late summer pruning, carried out immediately after harvesting beginning in the third year, should maintain an adequate supply of new wood. However, more drastic pruning is necessary when a tree is bearing poorly. This should be done in late summer, cutting back to young wood up to a third of the main branches, shortening them by between a quarter and a third.

FAN TRAINING

The sour cherry can be trained as a fan against a wall or fence (fans being easier to protect from birds than trees in the open, and because they produce good crops even when not exposed to direct sun). A fan needs 12-15ft (3.7-4.6m) of wall space and a minimum wall height of about 7ft (2.1m). Before planting fix horizontal wires about 6in (15cm) apart, with the first wire about 1-1⅓ft (30-41in) above ground level.

Formative pruning and training

The initial pruning is much the same as for a fan-trained peach (see pp. 168–70), the aim being to build up a framework of well-spaced ribs. Maidens are usually branched, and two strong, suitably placed laterals 1-1⅓ft (30-41cm) from the ground can be used to form the first ribs.

In early spring cut back the main stem above the topmost selected lateral and remove unwanted laterals. The two selected laterals, having been cut back by about a third to upward-facing buds, should be trained at an angle of 45 degrees and tied to bamboo canes fixed to the wires. By the end of the growing season each rib should have produced extension growth and three more laterals, providing in total four ribs on either side. In early spring of the following year shorten these by about a third, and during the growing season tie in suitably placed new laterals to fill the available wall space. The building up of the framework may need to be continued into the following year. If at the outset the maiden is not well-branched, follow the method shown in the illustrations.

Above left and above: The sour cherry can be fan trained against a wall or on a system of wires in the open garden. The best results are achieved by cutting back a branched maiden to stimulate growth of strong primary branches.

FORMING THE FAN
1 Cut to a lateral about 2ft (60cm) above the ground in early spring with 2 laterals left below. During the summer train the topmost shoot vertically and tie the 2 side shoots to bamboo canes fixed to the wires at 45°. In mid-summer cut the central shoot back to the topmost side shoot.

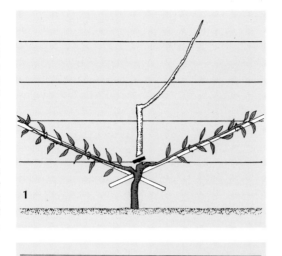

2 In early spring of the second year reduce the length of the side shoots to 1-1½ft (30-46cm).

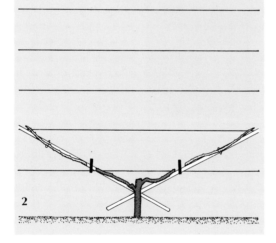

3 In the summer of the second year select 4 shoots on each arm, including the extension growth on the original ribs, as further ribs of the fan. As they extend, tie them to bamboo canes radiating outwards from the main stem. In the following spring cut these ribs back by about a third, making the cut at downward-pointing buds. During the growing season tie in suitable new laterals to fill out the fan.

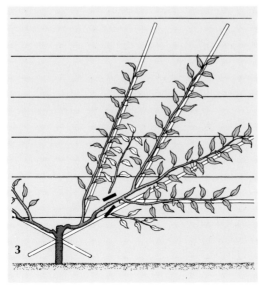

Pruning the bearing tree
As with the bush tree, the aim is to ensure a constant supply of young wood to replace older wood that has already carried fruit. In spring and early summer thin the young shoots growing on the framework branches so that they are spaced about 4-6in (10-15cm) apart. The flexible young shoots that are retained should be tied to the wires and allowed to extend throughout the growing season. Leave one shoot at the base of each lateral which will bear fruit in the summer. As soon as the crop has been picked cut back the shoot that has borne fruit to the replacement shoot at its base.

On older trees, fruiting sometimes declines except at the edges of the fan. The best remedy is to take out some three- or four-year-old wood in late summer or early spring, cutting back to a young lateral. On a vigorous, healthy tree up to a quarter of the older wood could be removed in a year.

PRUNING THE BEARING FAN
In late summer, when the crop has been picked, cut back each of the laterals that has carried fruit to a young replacement shoot at its base.

PEACHES

Perennial canker, brown rot and peach leaf curl are serious diseases of peaches, nectarines and almonds. To minimize the risk of disease entering through pruning cuts, prune in late spring and summer, rather than in winter. Consult a Cooperative Extension Agent for regional pest control information.

BUSH TREES
As long as frost-pockets and wind-swept sites are avoided, peach and nectarine trees should bear well (they are self-fruitful) when grown in open bud form.

Formative pruning
The formative pruning is very much the same as for a bush plum (see pp.154–55), the aim being to build up a framework of primary and secondary branches by cutting back the central stem, and then for several years annually pruning the leaders.

If possible, start with a branched maiden planted early in the dormant season, but leave pruning until late spring. If the tree has not been pre-pruned, cut back the central stem to 2-2½ft (60-76cm) above the ground, making the cut just above the

Above: In cool areas peaches are often fan trained against sunny walls. The blossom can be protected against frost, and reflected warmth from the wall helps ripen the fruit.

Far right: The dense mopheads of genetically compact peaches do not require pruning.

The peach, nectarine (a smooth-skinned sport of the peach) and almond are all pruned and trained in the same way. They flower in early spring and thrive in all regions except where winters are very severe – below −23°C/−10°F. They can be grown in bush form or as fans on sunny walls or fences, where they benefit from reflected warmth and can best be protected from frost.

The development of genetically compact peaches has made it possible to grow dwarf ornamental varieties in tubs on terraces. In cool temperate climates almonds are grown more for their ornamental blossom than for their fruit.

Various dwarfing rootstocks have been tried on peaches, with mixed results. Citation and Lovell rootstocks produce semi-dwarf trees, 8-12ft (2.4-3.7m) tall. Pruning can keep standard-size peach trees within bounds. Genetically dwarf peaches make a compact mophead, when budded on Lovell rootstock, to a height of about 4-6ft (1.2-1.8m). They need little or no pruning and, as they are suitable for growing in containers, they can be moved under cover from late autumn to spring.

THE BUSH TREE
1 In late spring cut back the central stem of a branched maiden at 2-2½ft (60-76cm), just above the topmost selected lateral. Shorten these laterals by two-thirds. Remove unwanted shoots.

2 Early in the second spring select 8 to 10 leaders to form the framework. Cut them by half to outward-facing buds. Remove awkwardly placed shoots and cut back any others to 4in (10cm).

3 In late spring of the third year take out any diseased, damaged or dead wood and thin crowded shoots. Cut back leaders by half, to outward-facing buds, and remove any shoots below the head.

1

topmost of four to six laterals selected for their potential as primary branches. Cut these laterals by two-thirds at outward-facing buds and remove completely any unwanted laterals. This will result in the development of side shoots and extension growth.

In the following spring select eight to ten leaders to form the framework of the tree, cutting them back by a half at outward-facing buds. Other shoots can be cut back to about 4in (10cm). The process of building up the framework may need to be continued for four or five years.

Pruning the bearing tree

Pruning must encourage the replacement of old wood by vigorous new growths. However, large cuts should be avoided as these can provide an entry for disease. Each spring carry out general maintenance pruning, taking out crowded or crossing laterals and dead or damaged wood. Then cut some of the older, bare wood back to suitably placed laterals. Other branches can be left unpruned except for any that have been pulled down by the weight of previous crops. Cut these back to well-placed laterals.

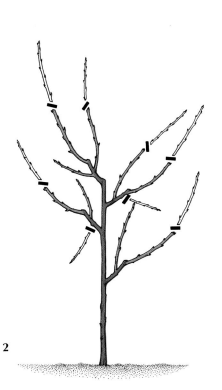

2

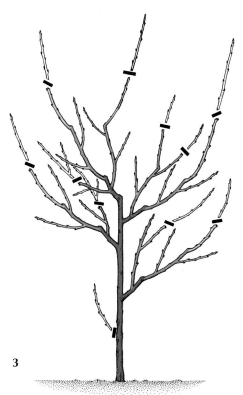

3

THE BEARING TREE
In late spring remove any damaged, diseased and dead wood and thin, crowded and crossing laterals. Cut back 1 or 2 older branches to vigorous young growth. Avoid excessive pruning.

FAN-TRAINED PEACHES

In creating a peach or nectarine fan the aim is to establish a short trunk and a radiating pattern of evenly spaced ribs. On the St Julien A rootstock (although commonly used, peaches are short-lived on this rootstock) a fan needs a minimum wall or fence height of 6ft (1.8m) and space for lateral spread of up to 15ft (4.6m). Before planting fix horizontal wires 6in (15cm) apart, starting about 16in (41cm) above the ground.

Formative pruning
The first step in forming a fan is to cut back a maiden in late spring, so as to encourage the development of side shoots at an appropriate height to form the ribs of the fan. In subsequent years the shortening of the ribs or leaders encourages the development of more shoots. Those that are needed to fill out the fan are tied in during the growing season to bamboo canes fixed to the wires at an angle of about 45 degrees.

Peaches are best planted early in the dormant season, but delay initial pruning until early spring. If a maiden has two strong laterals near the bottom wire, one to the left and the other to the right, cut the central stem to the topmost of these. These laterals can form the first of the ribs and should be trained in to bamboo canes.

FORMING A FAN
In early spring cut back a branched maiden at a lateral about 2ft (60cm) above the ground. Below this there should be laterals or buds on either side of the main stem that are potential ribs of the fan. Cut all other laterals back to one bud.

1 Train the topmost lateral vertically and in mid-summer cut it back to the topmost side shoot. As the side shoots lengthen, tie them to bamboo canes.

2 In early spring of the second year cut back the 2 arms to wood or triple buds 1-1½ft (30-46cm) from the stem.

3 During the growing season select 4 shoots on each arm to form ribs and tie to the bamboo canes. Pinch back other shoots to one leaf.

4 In early spring of the third year shorten leaders by about a third, cutting to downward-facing buds. Repeat this and the training in of new shoots until the fan is complete.

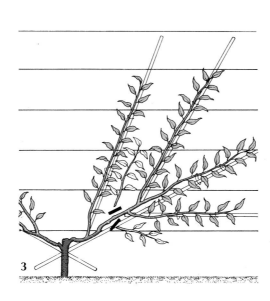

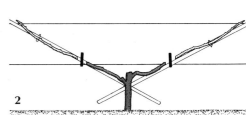

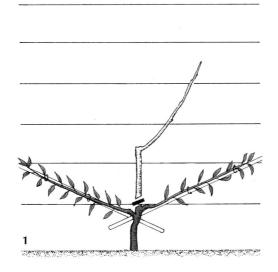

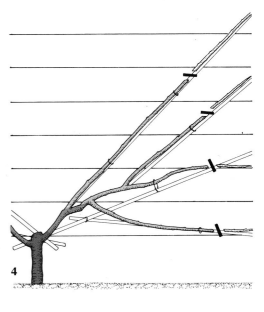

When a maiden is weakly branched cut back the main stem to a lateral at about 2ft (60cm). Below this lateral there must be two other laterals or wood buds, growth from which can be trained out to left and right of the main stem to form the first ribs. Wood buds are slender and pointed while flower buds are fat and round. Sometimes it may be necessary to cut to a triple bud, which consists of a wood bud and two flower buds.

Initially three shoots are allowed to develop, one either side and one vertically. In mid-summer cut back the vertical shoot to the topmost of the lengthening side shoots. During the first growing season train the two laterals to the angled bamboo canes as soon as they are about 1 1/2ft (46cm) long. In late spring of the second year cut back the two arms to wood or triple buds 1-1 1/2ft (30-46cm) from the main stem. From the shoots that develop during the growing season select four from each arm as ribs of the fan. They need to be well spaced and tied in to bamboo canes, one extending the arm, two angled more sharply above it, and one trained almost horizontally below it. As other shoots develop, pinch them back to one leaf.

In the third year the number of ribs is increased. In late spring shorten leaders by about a third, cutting at downward-facing

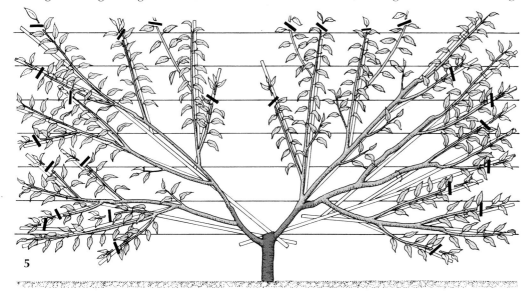

5

5 During summer of the third year train in extension growth and, where there is space, new shoots to fill out the fan. In late summer pinch back at about 1 1/2ft (46cm) any new laterals not needed as ribs and tie them in. They will carry blossom the next year.

RENEWAL PRUNING OF A FAN

1 In late spring select a couple of replacement shoots on each fruit-carrying lateral, one near the base and a reserve near the middle. Leave these unpruned along with the shoot that will extend the fruit-carrying lateral, but pinch back all other laterals to 2 leaves.

2 When the replacement and reserve laterals are 1 1/2ft (46cm) long, and the extension of the fruiting lateral has 6 leaves, stop all 3 by pinching out the growing points. Immediately after harvesting, cut each fruited lateral back to the replacement at its base or to the reserve.

1 2

wood buds. During summer allow the leaders to extend and, where there is space, train new shoots to radiate outwards, tying them to bamboo canes. Trees will begin bearing the following year on shoots produced along the ribs. These laterals need to be spaced 4-6in (10-15cm) apart on the upper and lower side of the ribs. Pinch back superfluous laterals to one leaf, and any that are growing into the wall that cannot be tied back parallel with the ribs should be cut out. In late summer stop the new laterals not needed for the ribs of the fan by pinching out the growing point where new growth has made 1½ft (46cm), and tie to canes.

Pruning the bearing tree

To maintain a fruitful fan it is essential to follow an annual program of pruning in which laterals that have fruited are taken out and replaced by selected new shoots. In late spring deal with shoots that are growing into the wall or outwards from the fan. Where there are few laterals these can sometimes be retained and tied in parallel with the ribs. Most of them will need to be removed, but if there are flower buds at the base then cut back leaving the buds and one or two leaves.

The laterals that are to bear fruit in the summer will be carrying blossom and side shoots. Select a side shoot at the base as the replacement and another in the middle as a reserve. Allow these two shoots and growth at the tip of the fruiting lateral to extend, but pinch back other side shoots to two leaves. When the replacement and reserve laterals are 1½ft (46cm) long, and the extension of the fruiting lateral has six leaves, stop all three by pinching out the growing points.

To obtain fruit of a good size some thinning is necessary, and this should be done in two stages. In early summer, when the fruit is about the size of hazelnuts, reduce to singles, take out fruit that has inadequate room to develop, and aim to have fruit spaced about 4in (10cm) apart. In mid-summer thin again when the fruits are the size of walnuts. The final spacing for nectarines should be about 6in (15cm) apart and for peaches about 9in (23cm).

The laterals that have fruited are cut out immediately after harvesting, well before autumn. Cut them back to their replacements. If the basal replacement has been damaged or has failed to grow, cut back to the reserve.

Top and above: Fan-trained peaches, whether grown in the open or under glass, will only remain fruitful if a proportion of old wood is taken out each year. To produce fruit of good quality it is necessary to thin fruit in 2 stages, in early and then mid-summer.

APRICOTS

The apricot is a hardy deciduous tree that requires frost-free springs and warm summers to produce worthwhile crops. In suitable areas, such as in California and Mediterranean countries, it is grown successfully as a bush or standard tree. It is also possible in much of the north to grow bush apricots by selecting super-hardy cultivars, two being the semi-dwarf 'Moongold' and 'Sungold'. Neither is self-fruitful but each will pollinate the other. In cool areas, however, the apricot does best when fan trained against a sunny wall, and this method of growing makes it reasonably easy to protect blossom against frost.

Several rootstocks of different degrees of vigor are available. One of the most widely used for a moderately sized tree is the semi-vigorous plum rootstock St Julien A. It is likely that compact forms of apricot (in addition to 'Moongold' and 'Sungold') will be available in the near future.

BUSH TREES
To make bush trees about 2½-3ft (76-90cm) high with a goblet-shaped head and a clear stem, apricots are treated in much the same way as plums (see pp.154–55). They need staking for the first four or five years, and the stake should be fixed in place before planting so that its top will be just below the head of the bush.

Formative pruning
Whether starting with an unbranched or a branched maiden, the aim in cutting back the main stem in early spring is to encourage the development of strong laterals that will form the primary branches. Select four of these that are well spaced to give a balanced head, and in early spring of the second year cut each back by a half. As in all stages of the formative pruning, make the cuts at outward-facing buds to establish an open-centered head.

In early spring of the third year select about eight strong, outward-growing, secondary branches to form the enlarged framework. Cut these back by a half to two-thirds of the growth made the previous year. Laterals on the outside of the tree not needed for the framework will carry flowers the following year and do not need to be pruned, but those on the inside need to be shortened to about 4in (10cm).

Pruning the bearing tree
The short spurs that carry fruit develop on two- and three-year-old wood without pruning. On mature trees it may be necessary to take out a proportion of the older laterals every two or three years in late summer to avoid bare unproductive wood. Prune in summer, immediately after the crop has been gathered, or in early spring at bud burst.

FAN-TRAINED TREES
Fan-trained apricots on St Julien A require a minimum wall height of 8ft (2.4m) and will cover up to 12-15ft (3.7-4.6m) laterally. The radiating pattern of ribs growing from a short trunk needs to be supported by a system of wires, which should be fixed to the wall or fence before planting, spaced 6in (15cm) apart, with the lowest one about 1⅓ft (41cm) above the ground.

Formative pruning
The formative pruning for an apricot fan, as illustrated, is much the same as for a peach fan (see pp. 168-70).

Below: In warm temperate regions apricots can be grown as bush trees in the open garden, but in cool temperate conditions they are best fan trained against a sunny wall.

FORMING A FAN

In early spring of the first year cut back an unbranched maiden at a wood or triple bud about 16in (41cm) above the ground. During the growing season train the topmost lateral vertically and a lateral either side at 45°. In mid-summer cut out the vertical lateral.

1 In early spring untie the arms and shorten to 1-1½ft (30-46cm), cutting to an upward bud. Lower their canes by 5-10° and retie, after shortening laterals by half. Cut out any other shoots completely.

2 During the second summer select 4 strong shoots on each arm as ribs of the fan, one extending the original arm, 2 above it and 1 below. Tie these laterals to bamboo canes and cut out any other shoots.

3 At the beginning of the third year the fan should have eight ribs. In early spring shorten each leader by about a third. During the summer select new shoots from each leader to form additional ribs.

4 In the fourth year shorten the leaders by about a quarter in early spring. During the growing season tie in new growth as needed to complete the fan. Retain laterals not needed for the ribs, but thin them to 4-6in (10-15cm) apart.

Pruning the bearing tree

Established fan-trained apricots are pruned in much the same way as fan-trained plums (see p. 158). In early spring rub out shoots that are growing in to the wall or fence and any breastwood. Most fruit, and that of the best quality, is carried on short spurs on two- or three-year-old wood. To encourage the development of these spurs pinch out the tips of new shoots in late spring or early summer.

Extensive pruning is not necessary but, because old wood can become bare and unproductive, in late summer cut out a proportion of the older laterals and sub-laterals that have fruited. This is best done every two or three years.

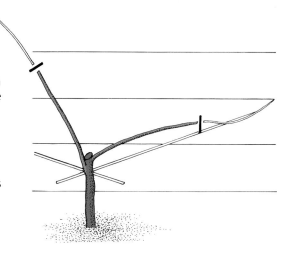

1

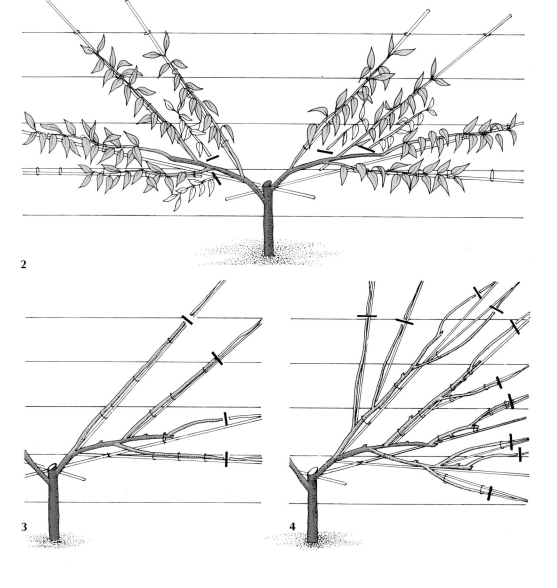

2

3

4

FIGS

The fig is a deciduous tree that is grown in cool temperate areas as well as in tropical and sub-tropical parts of the world. In warm regions two or even three crops may ripen in a year, but in cool temperate areas, although two crops are carried annually, usually only one ripens. A single tree will bear because the type of fig grown can develop fruit without fertilization.

Without root restriction figs grow large, make excessive vegetative growth, and produce little fruit. The most effective way to prevent this is to box in the roots. Figs are particularly prone to a leaf spot disease.

BUSH AND STANDARD TREES

Bush trees are suitable for growing in containers, which allow the plant to be taken under cover in winter. They can also be planted in the open garden, for example in a sunny corner with walls on two sides. Root restriction as recommended for fans is essential to keep the tree to a moderate size. Half-standards and standards, which are sometimes sold as two- or three-year-old plants with the framework partly formed by the nursery, are only suitable for larger gardens. The taller forms need staking in the formative stages.

Formative pruning

In the initial pruning the aim is to build up a well-balanced framework of branches at the desired height, approximately 3ft (90cm) for a bush, 4½ft (1.3m) for a half-standard, and 6ft (1.8m) for a standard. If starting with a young unformed tree, cut out all but one strong shoot, which will become the main stem. In summer train the shoot vertically, either tied to a stake or a bamboo cane. In early spring of the following year cut back the stem at the appropriate height. If forming a standard and the stem is not tall enough after one year, grow on for another year before heading back. Laterals will develop below the cut and four to six that are near the top of the stem should be selected as the primary branches. Remove any other shoots during the growing season. In early spring the following year cut back all leaders by about a half, cutting at outward-facing buds.

Pruning the mature tree

Once the main framework has been formed, trees need little pruning. In early spring cut out any frost damaged growth and deal with crowded and crossing shoots. On mature specimens cut out a proportion of the older wood annually. Cut back to a vigorous young shoot, but where a potential replacement does not exist leave a stub one inch (2.5cm) long. New shoots will develop in summer.

FAN-TRAINING

In cool temperate areas the most satisfactory way of producing fully ripened crops is to fan-train a fig against a sunny wall. Erect a

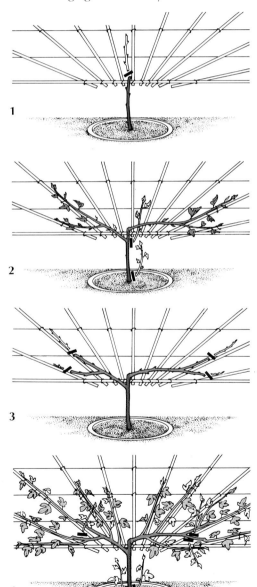

FORMING A FAN

1 Fix wires about 1ft (30cm) apart on a sunny wall or fence and attach to them canes in the pattern of a fan. Plant a young fig in early spring in a sunken container or a pit lined with concrete slabs so that the roots are restricted. Cut back the main stem at about 15in (38cm).

2 Throughout the growing season of the first year tie to the bamboo canes 2 well-placed laterals as the first ribs. Cut out any shoots below these.

3 In early spring of the second year shorten the branches trained as ribs by about half.

4 During the following growing season tie in well-placed young shoots to fill out the fan. Rub out shoots growing towards the wall and pinch back breastwood to 3 leaves. Cut out completely basal growths and any unwanted laterals. Repeat this routine the following year to complete the fan.

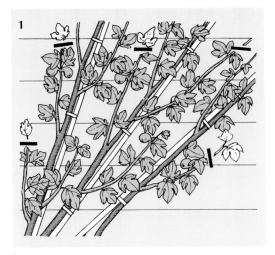

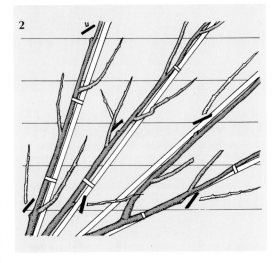

PRUNING A MATURE FAN IN COOL TEMPERATE AREAS

1 In early to mid-summer pinch out the growing points of about half the young shoots growing from the ribs. As shoots develop below the cut tie them to the wires.

2 In late autumn cut back to one inch (2.5cm) about half the shoots on which fruit ripened during the summer. Retain sufficient of the remaining shoots to tie in spaced 9-12in (23-30cm) apart. Cut out any that are superfluous.

Below: In cool temperate areas figs grown outdoors bear 2 crops but only one ripens. The successful crop overwinters as embryo fruit and develops in the following summer. The figs that are produced on the current season's wood are removed in late summer.

permanent system of wires before planting, spacing wires 1ft (30cm) apart to a minimum height of 8ft (2.4m). To restrict the roots dig a pit about 2ft (60cm) square and 2ft (60cm) deep, lining it to an inch (2.5cm) above soil level with concrete slabs or bricks, and filling the bottom 8-10in (20-25cm) with rubble. Another method of restricting roots is to plant in a pot or concrete drainpipe 1½-2ft (46-60cm) in diameter that has been sunk into the ground.

Formative pruning

A fig fan, which may take three or four years to fill the available wall space, is built up in much the same way as a peach fan (see pp. 168-69). Prune in early spring, as the risk of heavy frosts recedes. In the first year, if there are no laterals, cut back the main stem to a bud at about 1¼ft (38cm). If the fig has a pair of suitably placed laterals, cut back to the topmost of these. Remove any other laterals and shorten the ribs by no more than a quarter to upward-facing buds.

Until the wall is covered, in the early spring of subsequent years shorten the leaders by about a half, cutting to upward-facing buds, and during the summer train in the growths to canes attached to the wires.

Pruning the bearing fan

The aim in pruning is to ensure a plentiful supply of young shoots without creating such dense growth that wood and fruit are shaded from sunlight and therefore fail to ripen. The method followed depends on the number of crops that are likely to ripen in a year.

In cool temperate areas embryo fruits develop in late summer at or near the tip of young shoots and, if these pea-sized fruits survive the winter, they stand a good chance of ripening by early summer the following year. The second crop, which develops on new shoots in spring, normally ripens in late summer. By pinching out in early to mid-summer the growing points of all young shoots carried on the framework of ribs, lower buds are encouraged to break. When figs are grown in cold greenhouse conditions shoots are pinched back to the fourth leaf. The shoots produced as a result of pinching back need to be tied in to the wires as they develop. They will harden during late summer and produce embryo figs.

Thinning out of unfruitful stems in mid-summer will let sunlight in to ripen wood and fruit. In late autumn cut back to one inch (2.5cm) about half the shoots from which ripened fruit have been gathered, the aim being to encourage new growth the following spring. The remaining shoots should be spaced about 9-12in (23-30cm) apart. Cut out completely any that are superfluous and tie the others to the wires.

In naturally warm conditions or in a heated greenhouse, where figs may produce three crops between early summer and autumn, a slightly different regime is needed. When the first crop has been picked, cut back to two leaves about half the stems that have carried fruit. Repeat this after each crop is picked.

If on a mature fan-trained fig a framework branch becomes unfruitful, it should be cut out in early spring and a vigorous new shoot from near the base trained in as a replacement. On a neglected fig, where a lot of wood needs to be removed, spread the renovation over two or three years.

RENOVATION OF FRUIT TREES

Although it is often better to take out old, neglected, and mutilated fruit trees that are bearing poorly, their renovation is sometimes possible and worthwhile. Each case must be assessed on its own merits. Grounds for drastic action are old age, the incidence of serious disease such as silver leaf or canker, and stunted growth caused by poor growing conditions. Pruning plays a part in the renovation process, along with pest and disease control and good general cultivation. There are still occasions when the old techniques of bark ringing and root pruning are the most effective ways of dealing with problem trees.

Remedial pruning of neglected trees

Trees that have not been pruned or have been left unpruned for several years may flower profusely but produce fruit that is small and damaged by pests and diseases. Combine measures to control pests and diseases with remedial pruning. As a first step cut out dead, diseased, and damaged wood and remove crossing or rubbing branches. Follow this by pruning branches that spoil the shape of the tree and by thinning overcrowded shoots. On an apple or pear this remedial pruning should be done in winter. Plums and damsons, the trees most likely to be grown on vigorous rootstocks, and any other stone fruits should only be pruned in spring and summer, when there is least danger of infection from silver leaf.

To reduce the risk of infection still further, treat cuts with a wound paint immediately after pruning. In the case of trees where drastic surgery is necessary, it is advisable to spread the renovation over three years.

Remedial pruning of stunted trees

Fruit trees are often stunted because they are competing with weeds or other plants for nutrients and water. Clearing away the competition and applying a fertilizer and mulch are first steps in restoring a tree to healthy growth. Pruning is limited to the thinning of overcrowded spurs and the drastic shortening of any maiden wood. Restake the tree and for a year or two remove all or most of any fruitlets that form so that the tree's energies are not dissipated. Once the tree returns to healthy, fruitful growth, establish a normal pattern of pruning.

Left: Renovation of neglected fruit trees should be staged over several years. The hard pruning of this old apple tree in a single season will probably stimulate a lot of unwanted new growth.

RENOVATING PLUMS

1 Take out any disproportionally large branches and any that are crossing or are badly placed.

2 Remove any remaining dead, diseased or damaged wood, along with suckers and twiggy growths on the trunk.

3 Thin crowded lateral branches and twigs. Repeat this operation the following year.

1

2

3

1 In mid- to late spring (between pink-bud stage and petal fall) remove a nearly complete ring of bark about 3in (7.5cm) in width, leaving a good inch (2.5cm) of the circle uncut.

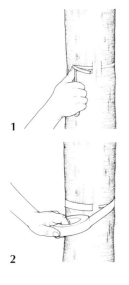

1

2

2 Cover the cut immediately with adhesive tape and, as an additional seal, smear with petroleum jelly. The wound will callous over in the growing season. Remove the adhesive tape in the autumn.

ROOT PRUNING
In late autumn or winter dig a trench about 1½-2ft (46-60cm) wide and 1½ft (46cm) deep just inside the circumference of the branches, cutting through thick and woody roots. Retain fibrous roots and refill the trench. With well-established trees stage the operation over 2 years.

Remedial pruning of over-vigorous trees

Grassing down the area around very vigorous trees is a simple measure that will help check growth. One of the common causes of extreme vigor at the expense of fruit production is a history of excessively severe pruning.

Remedial pruning of apples and pears, the fruits most commonly affected, needs to be spread over two to three years. The removal of dead, diseased, and damaged wood can be carried out in the first winter. At the same time begin the remedial pruning by taking out a proportion of the healthy wood, thinning crossing and congested branches. Cut back to a main branch or to a replacement branch that is not less than half the diameter of the branch being removed.

In all pruning retain, wherever possible, branches spreading outwards rather than those growing vertically, upright branches being less fruitful than horizontal branches. More winter pruning can be carried out over the next two years, but pruning at this time stimulates growth, whereas summer pruning checks it. Laterals of the current season's growth that have become woody at the base and are 1ft (30cm) or more in length can be cut back to five leaves between late summer and early autumn.

Bark ringing of over-vigorous trees

Bark ringing is a technique of last resort to encourage fruiting on over-vigorous apple and pear trees. It might be used, for example, on a tree where the union between the scion and the rootstock has been buried, and the scion has rooted with the result that the dwarfing effect of the rootstock is lost. Complete ringing of a tree is likely to result in its death.

Root pruning of over-vigorous trees

As a general rule the sensible gardener goes to some trouble to avoid interfering with the root systems of fruit trees. However, root pruning is a technique that was widely practiced in the past as a way of encouraging very vigorous trees to form fruiting buds. The availability of dwarfing rootstocks has greatly reduced the reliance on this technique, but it is still occasionally used, more commonly on plums and figs than on other fruits.

If the over-vigorous tree is less than five years old, the simplest method is to lift it in winter, replanting in the same or another site, making sure that the tree's orientation is the same after as before lifting. Retain the fibrous roots, but cut through all thick roots with a spade or hand pruners. The replanted tree must be restaked and kept well watered during dry weather in the following spring or summer.

On older trees the roots are pruned without lifting. With a healthy vigorous tree this operation can be carried out in one season, but with older trees it should be staged over two years. If carrying out root pruning in one season, mark a circle around the tree with a radius of about 5ft (1.5m). The size of the circle may need to be adjusted according to the size of the tree – its circumference should be slightly less than the spread of the branches. Inside this circle dig a trench about 1½-2ft (46-60cm) wide and 1½ft (46cm) deep. Retain the fibrous roots that are exposed but cut through those that are thick and woody, removing them from the trench. To carry out the operation in two stages, trench half the circle one year and the other half the year following. Refill the trench with soil and apply a mulch of well-rotted compost or manure. It is advisable to restake trees and to ensure that they are well watered in the following spring and summer.

OTHER TREE FRUITS

In temperate parts of the world the range of fruit grown is relatively limited. Fruit growers, amateur as well as professional, tend to concentrate on apples and pears and, to a lesser extent, on stone fruit. Because there are many cultivars of these fruits, especially apples and pears, growers can choose plants to suit the growing conditions and to provide a long season of fruit with considerable variation in appearance, flavor, and texture.

There are, nonetheless, a few less commonly planted trees that are well worth growing for the distinctive character of their fruit. These include the pungently aromatic quince, the tangy mulberry, and several nuts. In the case of some of these fruits, home growing is the only way to be sure of obtaining them, for commercial growers rarely trouble with them and the picked fruit is almost impossible to buy. Most of these temperate fruits are easily grown, require relatively little pruning, and often make highly ornamental additions to the garden.

The pruning and training of tropical fruits is beyond the scope of this book, but in addition to the less common temperate fruits this section deals with a few trees that are grown in temperate or subtropical climates. Some of these – including the species, hybrids, and cultivars of *Citrus* – are often grown under glass in cool temperate regions. In general, these plants yield good crops without complicated pruning and training, and are therefore worth including in gardens that can offer the right growing conditions.

Below: Tolerance of drought and preference for hot summers and cool winters has made the olive a major tree crop in many areas around the Mediterranean and in other regions with similar climates. Early pruning to provide a framework of strong branches will produce a tree that has considerable ornamental value.

Above: The quince, grown mainly for its aromatic fruit, makes an attractive small tree that requires little attention once it is established.

Right: Early training and pruning is needed to form a shapely citrus. Left to themselves, these plants make untidy multi-stemmed shrubs.

CITRUS FRUITS

Sweet and bitter oranges (*Citrus sinensis* and *C. aurantium*), lemon (*C. limon*), mandarin orange (*C. reticulata*), and lime (*C. aurantiifolia*) are among the sixteen or so species of *Citrus*, all of which are native to East Asia. They, their hybrids, and numerous cultivars are evergreen and sometimes spiny trees or shrubs that can only be grown successfully outdoors in subtropical and some warm temperate areas.

There is, however, a long tradition of growing them under glass in many temperate parts of the world where they cannot be grown permanently outdoors. Many a noble estate still has its orangery, although it is now often devoted to purposes other than the growing of citrus fruit. Cultivation under glass has often been mainly for ornamental purposes, but trees will fruit readily provided that their requirements for light and temperature are met. By growing them in containers such as the traditional Versailles tub, they can be taken outdoors when all danger of frost is past and brought in again at the end of summer.

Although citrus are easily grown from seeds, this is not a reliable way of raising good plants as seedlings are rarely of the quality of their parents. If the aim is to grow citrus for fruit, start with one-or two-year-old grafted specimens of named cultivars.

Formative pruning and training

If left to themselves, most citrus will develop as rather straggly bushes with multiple stems. The aim of formative pruning is to establish a well-shaped bush on a single clear stem. The best time to prune is in early spring or, in the case of plants needing repotting, in winter once the plant is in its new container.

At planting, in late winter or early spring, remove any shoots below the union on grafted specimens and low shoots above the union. In the first few years establish a clear stem to the required height. In the case of container-grown plants, remove shoots to a height of 1-1½ft (30-46cm). Citrus that are grown outdoors can be trained with a clear stem to a height of 2-4ft (60-120cm), depending on the vigor of the cultivar. If necessary, cut back any strong-growing shoots that spoil the balanced shape. In hot climates the stems of young and old citrus are often white-washed or wrapped with paper trunk band against sun scorch.

Above: In most temperate regions citrus fruits can only be grown satisfactorily if they are kept under glass from autumn to late spring. When grown outdoors in a favorable climate, the lemon, like other citrus fruits, will grow into a small tree. It will flower continuously throughout the year.

Right: Most citrus fruits, including the sour or Seville orange (*C. aurantium*), flower in late winter or early spring on growths made the previous summer. The fruits may take about 12 months to mature.

Pruning the established plant

Most citrus fruits that are grown as one-year-old grafted plants will begin to bear fruit in their fourth or fifth year. The flowers are generally borne in winter or early spring in the leaf axils on growths made the previous summer. However, some citrus fruits, lemons in particular, flower sporadically throughout the year.

Because the fruit takes about 12 months, and sometimes longer, to mature, flowers and fruits can be seen simultaneously. The first crop is likely to be of poor quality and is best removed while the fruits are still immature. In subsequent years it may be necessary to restrict the quantity of fruit carried by container-grown specimens.

Established plants need little pruning and, in general, the less they are pruned the better. If plants are leggy, the central leader and side branches can be shortened to encourage bushy growth. A common problem, particularly in the early life of citrus, is the growth from the main branches of vigorous vertical stems, known as water shoots. These need to be cut out completely because, if left, they become too tall and distort the shape of the plant.

Citrus grown outdoors are much more likely to be damaged by frost when there is a sudden fall in temperature than if the drop is more gradual. Damaged citrus should not be pruned immediately. Wait until the extent of the damage can be assessed which will be after growth has started again. In the case of severe damage, pruning should be delayed for six months.

Left: The grapefruit or pomelo (*C.* x *paradisi*) is fast-growing and makes a dense bush. The fruits generally take more than a year to mature and there are often 2 crops on the tree at the same time.

1

2

PRUNING CITRUS
1 Train citrus fruits as single-stemmed trees, removing low shoots on young plants. It is especially important to remove any shoots that develop below the union on grafted plants because these will develop at the expense of the cultivar.

2 Citrus often produce vigorous upright shoots (water shoots) from the main branches. Cut these out completely to maintain a well-balanced shape.

QUINCES AND MEDLARS

The true quince (*Cydonia oblonga*) is a small, deciduous tree that is grown for its aromatic edible fruits, but it is also an attractive ornamental. It is self-fertile and so a single specimen can bear fruit. It is grown as a vase-shaped shrub or as a standard with an open head. In areas with cool summers quinces are sometimes fan- or espalier-trained, like a pear, against a sunny wall. They have, however, a crooked manner of growth and do not respond well to the heavy pruning that is required when grown in restricted forms.

The medlar (*Mespilus germanica*) is rarely planted in the United States, but can make an attractive small deciduous ornamental. It, too, is self-fertile. The fruits, which look like large brown rose hips, need to be ripened off the tree before being eaten or made into jelly. The medlar is usually grown as a standard or half-standard. The English cultivars 'Nottingham' and 'Royal' are upright growers, but 'Dutch' is of weeping habit.

Formative pruning of a quince standard
Plant quinces in early spring, staking for the first year or two. If starting with a maiden, cut back the central leader to just above the topmost of three to five buds or shoots at a height of 2-3ft (60-90cm). In the summer train the new leader up a stout cane. Keep side shoots cut back to about 6in (15cm). In the second winter cut the leader to a bud at about 6ft (1.8m), or lower for a half-standard, ensuring there are at least four good buds immediately beneath. These will form the primary branches. In the following year remove the lower side shoots to create a clean stem of about 5-6ft (1.5-1.8m). A half-standard will have a clear stem to a height of 4-4½ft (1.2-1.3m).

For the first three or four years prune in winter, cutting back the leaders by about half the previous season's growth at outward-facing buds. Any shoots that are weak or badly placed, including those competing with leaders, should be shortened to two or three buds. Quince trees often produce suckers. Throughout the life of the tree twist and pull off those that form at the base of the tree. Remove completely any shoots that develop on the trunk below the head.

Pruning the established quince
After the fourth year little pruning is required. The fruit is borne on the tips of the previous summer's growth as well as on spurs. Pruning laterals will therefore remove a proportion of the fruit buds. In winter remove any dead or damaged wood but otherwise limit pruning to cutting back vigorous or badly placed laterals and to thinning crowded branches, especially in the center of the tree. Although the spreading and sometimes slightly weeping growth of the head is what gives the tree its distinctive character, long low-lying branches may need to be removed.

Pruning a medlar standard
A medlar standard is grown and pruned in much the same way as a quince. It should be staked at planting and for the first three or four years pruned in winter, the main branches being cut back by about a third to outward-facing buds. Cut back any badly placed or weak laterals to two or three buds.

Established trees usually require very little pruning. To preserve the ornamental character of the weeping cultivars, the branches should be allowed to develop naturally. In winter cut out any dead or damaged wood, but otherwise limit pruning to light thinning and shaping.

Below: The quince is a self-fertile tree and some varieties, including 'Champion', which is illustrated here, begin bearing freely when young. Only light pruning of established trees is necessary to keep the center of the branched head open.

Left and below:
Medlars, like quinces, are small self-fertile trees that are useful as ornamentals. Some cultivars are of upright growth but 'Dutch' is of spreading or weeping habit. Established trees need little pruning.

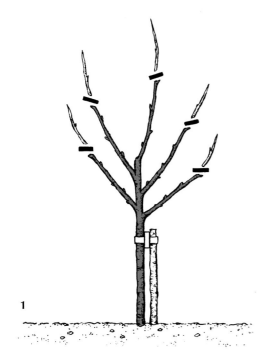

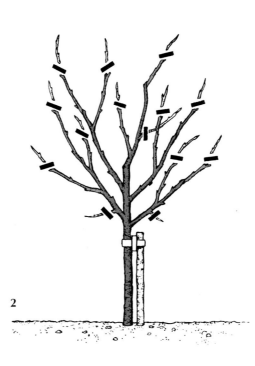

1

2

FORMATIVE PRUNING

1 In the first winter cut back the leaders of a 2-year-old quince by about half the previous summer's growth (of a medlar by about a third), pruning to outward-facing buds. Cut back badly placed and weak laterals to 2 or 3 buds.

2 In the winter of the second and third years, shorten the previous summer's growth of leaders by between a third and a half, and cut back badly placed and weak laterals as in the first winter.

MULBERRIES

The black mulberry (*Morus nigra*) makes an attractive tree, growing up to 30ft (9m) in height and carrying dark red fruits. The fruits have a sweet flavor, but with a pleasant sharpness. Birds take the fruit very greedily and much of the crop of an unprotected tree may be lost to them. Nevertheless, mulberries are generally grown as standards, which may be difficult to net once they are mature. As mulberries are slow to begin bearing – they may take eight to ten years – it is worth buying a three- to five-year-old tree that has already been shaped. In areas with cool summers, training a mulberry against a sunny wall increases the likelihood of fruit ripening fully. Cuts on mulberries tend to bleed, so avoid leaving large wounds and prune in early winter or summer.

Formative pruning of a standard
At planting, between late autumn and early spring, stake the tree. A well-shaped nursery specimen may require no pruning at all. Cut out any dead or damaged wood and, if there are laterals longer than 1ft (30cm) that are not required for the framework, cut these back to four or five buds. In this and subsequent years shorten or remove any shoots that are badly placed or spoil the shape of the tree.

Pruning the established tree
Other than the removal of dead and damaged wood, trees often require very little pruning for many years. The wood on old specimens is brittle and heavy branches are prone to wind damage. Careful thinning can reduce the risk, but often the only solution is to prop up vulnerable branches.

Wall-training a mulberry
This is uncommon and probably only worth considering in areas with cool summers where a long sunny wall is available for planting. However, a wall-trained tree is much more easily netted against birds than a standard in the open garden.

Before planting, erect a system of horizontal wires spaced 1¼-1½ft (38-46cm) apart. The espalier is the most suitable form and the formative training is much the same as for an apple (see pp.148-49). Once the arms have reached the required length, cut them back in early summer, leaving one leaf of the previous season's growth. A week or two after mid-summer prune side shoots to four or five leaves to encourage the formation of fruit spurs.

Above and far right:
The black mulberry is grown for its slightly acid loganberry-like fruit (far right), but is also an attractive small- to medium-sized tree. This young specimen (above) has yet to be trained as a standard. Pruning should be kept to a minimum as these trees are likely to bleed quite heavily.

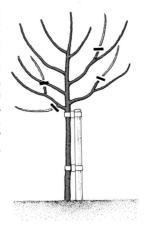

FORMATIVE PRUNING
Nursery-supplied trees often require no pruning. If a newly planted tree has laterals longer than 1ft (30cm) that are not required as framework branches, cut these back in early winter to 4 or 5 buds.

ELDERBERRIES

The common elder (*Sambucus nigra*) and the American sweet elder (*S. canadensis*) are deciduous shrubs or small trees producing edible berries. The common elder, which is native to Europe, western Asia, parts of North Africa, and is also found wild in Canada and the United States, is rarely cultivated. However, although generally considered a vigorous weedy plant, the fruit and flowers are often gathered to make preserves and wine, on their own or with other fruits.

A few useful improved clones of the American elder are available and these are grown in northern parts of the United States and Canada. Two cultivars need to be grown in close proximity, about 10ft (3m) apart, as the American elder will not set fruit with its own pollen.

Elders can be grown as standards with the main stem clear to a height of 2¹/₂-4ft (75-120cm). However, it is much more usual for them to be grown as bushes.

Formative pruning of a bush

The best time to plant is in autumn or early spring. Choose bushy plants and set them at the depth they were grown at the nursery. As a first pruning step, cut out any thin, weak growths and damaged shoots, and if there are suckers it is important to cut these back to ground level.

The aim of the main pruning is to create a well-balanced framework that branches close to the ground. This is done by cutting back main shoots by 2-6in (5-15cm) to well-formed pairs of buds (elderberries have opposite buds and leaves). Bushes will produce little if any flower in the first year, but should start bearing well after that.

Pruning the established bush

The pruning of the established bush, which is carried out in winter, begins in the second year. The aim is to maintain a good shape and encourage the production of new shoots. Begin by removing any dead or damaged wood. About a quarter of the old wood can be cut out each year. Always begin where growth is congested, taking out the oldest branches. Cut back to the base or to vigorous young shoots low down on the bush, and remove unwanted suckers, cutting them off at ground level.

Left: Elderberries can be trained as standards, but are generally grown as large bushes, with formative pruning to encourage the establishment of a strong framework of branches.

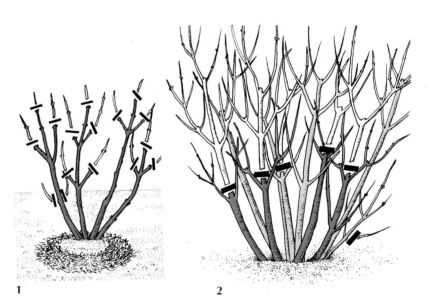

1　　　　　　　　　　　　**2**

Pruning a standard

In the initial pruning of an elder grown as a standard, eliminate all stems other than the strongest and stake this to just below the height at which the head is to be formed, 2¹/₂-4ft (76-120cm) above ground level. Cut back the main stem to shoots or buds that are forming at the desired height of the head. Remove shoots on the main stem below the height of the head and shorten those remaining by 2-3in (5-7.5cm). In subsequent years adapt the pruning recommended for the bush, concentrating in the early stages on building up the head and later cutting out some of the old wood.

PRUNING

1 After planting cut out weak growths and shorten main shoots by 2-6in (5-15cm), cutting to outward-facing buds.

2 In winter of the second and subsequent years cut out dead and damaged wood and about a quarter of the old wood, especially where growths are congested.

HAZELNUTS AND FILBERTS

The hazelnut or cobnut (*Corylus avellana*) and the filbert (*C. maxima*) are deciduous small trees or large shrubs that are widely grown in temperate parts of the world for their edible nuts. Male and female flowers are carried on the same tree, the female flowers being inconspicuous while the male ones are borne in catkins, which release their pollen in late winter or early spring.

In their general cultivation and pruning hazelnuts and filberts are treated in the same way. They are best grown on a short stem 1¼-1½ft (38-46cm) high and maintained as open-centered bushes, 6-7ft (1.8-2.1m) high.

Close pruning is needed to produce regular crops. The nuts are borne on light twiggy shoots and pruning should encourage these, while removing vigorous growths.

Formative pruning

Plant hazelnuts and filberts in late autumn or early spring. Some plants may need the support of a cane for the first year or two. If starting with one- or two-year-old plants, head the tree back at a height of between 1¼-1½ft (38-46cm) and remove any shoots or suckers from the stem or base. The aim is to encourage the development of three or four evenly spaced shoots. If starting with two- or three-year-old plants, select specimens with clean stems to a height of about 1¼-1½ft (38-46cm) on which a head has already been formed. These branches should be pruned after planting.

In the first four to six years prune in late winter, cutting the leaders back by about half to an outward-facing bud, in this way forming a goblet-shaped head with about eight leaders. Any laterals that make vigorous growth should be cut back to three or four buds. Allow trees to build up to a height of 6-7ft (1.8-2.1m). To keep trees at this height it may be necessary to cut back vigorous branches to a lower lateral.

Suckers are often freely produced and need to be removed from around the base by being twisted and pulled out.

Pruning the established tree

A tree planted as a one-year-old is likely to begin flowering four to six years later. It is beneficial to prune in late winter or early spring so that the catkins are disturbed during the operation, resulting in a good distribution of pollen. Cut out dead and damaged wood, and remove old wood where growths are crowded. Cut back vigorous laterals to three or four buds. Do not prune the twiggy laterals that bear the tiny red female flowers.

Additional pruning should be carried out in late summer so that the fruit buds ripen as a result of exposure to light and air. Brutting, the method used, consists of breaking by hand all strong lateral growths about six to eight leaves from the main branch, which are then left hanging; removing shoots with a clean pruning cut would stimulate new growth. The brutted shoots are shortened by 2-3in (5-7.5cm) in late winter or early spring.

Below: The various cultivars of hazelnuts and filberts carry nuts on light twiggy shoots.

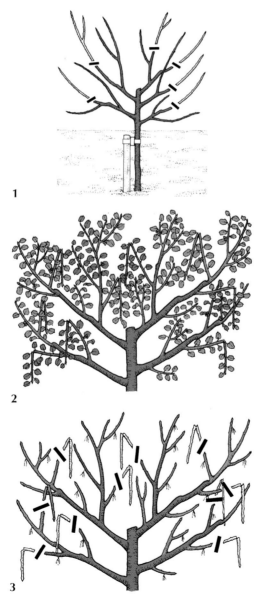

PRUNING

1 For the first 4 to 6 years prune in late winter, cutting back leaders by about half to outward-facing buds. Shorten vigorous laterals to 3 or 4 buds.

2 Once the plant is bearing nuts, in late summer break off by hand strong lateral growths about 6 to 8 leaves from the base, leaving the broken shoots to hang.

3 In late winter cut back the broken shoots to 3 or 4 buds. Do not prune laterals carrying the tiny female flowers.

WALNUTS/PECANS/CHESTNUTS

Walnuts, pecans, and chestnuts all make large ornamental trees, but they will also produce useful crops if grown in suitable conditions. The best way to grow them is as central-leader standards (see p. 49), planted where they are able to develop without being checked. Established trees require little pruning other than the removal of dead or damaged wood and the thinning out of crowded or crossing growth. Branches that form narrow-angled crotches should be taken out.

WALNUTS
Two species that are grown for their nuts are the common walnut (*Juglans regia*), a native of the Middle East and north Asia, and the black walnut (*J. nigra*), an American species. In 20 years they can reach a height of 25ft (7.5m), but in maturity they may be more than 60ft (18m) high with a spread of 30ft (9m) at least.

Pruning and training
Although walnuts can be grown from seed, it is far better to start with a grafted tree of a named cultivar as seed-raised plants very seldom produce good quality fruit. A young plant should be selected as walnuts do not transplant well. Plant in winter, staking for the first year or two. If the leader is lost, as sometimes happens because of frost damage, select and train in a replacement. Very little

pruning is required and only essential cuts should be made, and then only in late summer, as wounds may bleed copiously.

PECANS
The pecan, a species of hickory (*Carya illinoinensis*), thrives in hot humid conditions as are found in its native range in the south-eastern states of America. However, some cultivars are reasonably productive in drier conditions and are grown, for example, in central and western parts of Texas. There are also cultivars that are grown further north.

Pruning and training
Trees are usually bought as one-year-old named cultivars, and at this stage they are about 4-6ft (1.2-1.8m) high. At planting, in winter, cut back the main stem to about 3ft (90cm), the intention being to stimulate the growth of a vigorous leader. Stake the young tree and wrap the stem with hessian or paper to protect it from sun scorch. The wrapping should be maintained for two years.

In the following growing season the topmost shoot may need to be trained in as the replacement leader. The shoots that develop from it form the primary branches. Little pruning is required except to create a clear stem by cutting off the lower branches to a height of about 6ft (1.8m). Their removal should be staged over two or three years, starting after planting.

SWEET CHESTNUTS
The sweet or Spanish chestnut (*Castanea sativa*) may attain a height in excess of 70ft (21m), but in its first 25 years is likely to grow to about 35ft (10.5m). The Chinese chestnut (*C. mollissima*) is smaller, hardier and blight-resistant.

Formative pruning
Obtain a named cultivar as a grafted two- or three-year-old tree. Plant Spanish chestnuts in winter and Chinese chestnuts in spring or autumn, staking for the first year or two. Little pruning is necessary except to create a clear stem to a suitable height, say 5-6ft (1.5-1.8m). Leave the topmost shoots unpruned, but when other laterals are 9-12in (23-30cm) long, cut them back by half. In late summer cut back these pruned shoots to the main stem. In subsequent years repeat this process until the clear stem has been produced.

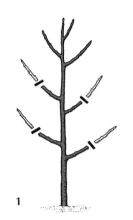

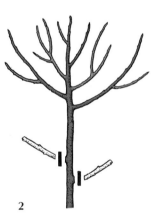

2

1

FORMATIVE PRUNING OF SWEET CHESTNUTS
Walnuts are pruned in a similar way, but in late summer.

1 In the first year cut back by about half the lower laterals when they are 9-12in (23-30cm) in length.

2 In late autumn or early winter of the second year cut the previously shortened laterals back to the main stem.

Left: The English walnut can grow up to 100ft (30m) high.

OLIVES

The olive tree (*Olea europaea*) has been grown for thousands of years around the Mediterranean, the fruits being pickled or pressed to produce a high-quality edible oil. In many other parts of the world this evergreen tree has proved productive, including in California and inland Australia, where warm summers are followed by fairly cold winters. Winter chilling is necessary to induce flower formation, but olive trees are likely to be injured if temperatures fall below 14°F (−10°C). Although the olive is remarkably drought resistant, trees will only yield good crops if regularly watered. Olives are very long-lived, but are slow to become productive, often taking eight years to yield significant crops and up to 20 years to become fully productive.

When grown as an ornamental, the olive requires very little pruning and training and the central leader is allowed to develop naturally. When grown for its fruit, the tree is best trained as an open-centered bush-headed tree, with low spreading branches on a clear stem 3-5ft (90-150cm) high. The aim of this is to encourage trees to fruit freely and to minimize the amount of work involved in harvesting. The bacterial disease known as olive knot can pose a serious problem in some areas, but the risk of infection is greatly reduced by pruning only in summer.

Formative pruning and training
Plant a branched tree in winter, and in early summer cut back the main stem immediately above the topmost of three or four strong shoots that are well placed to form the main branches of the tree. Shorten these shoots by 3-6in (5-7.5cm), cutting to outward-facing buds, and remove any other shoots on the main stem. If starting with a bare-root tree, cut back the main stem at about 3-4ft (90-120cm) above ground level, removing all side shoots. Whitewash the stem to protect it against sun scorch.

In early summer of the following year (a year later if the tree was bare-rooted) reduce the number of shoots on each main branch to two or three, and shorten these by about 4in (10cm), cutting to outward-facing buds.

Right: The olive crop is picked in late autumn. If heavy crops are not thinned in mid-summer the fruit will be small and the tree may develop a pattern of fruiting in alternate years only.

Pruning the established tree
In order to maintain the open center of the established tree, cut out any vigorous upright shoots in early summer. Remove any suckers as they develop (heavy pruning will encourage their growth). On productive trees thinning of fruit is often necessary to maintain size and quality. If they are allowed to carry an excessive amount of fruit, trees often bear in alternate years only. Thin fruit between early and mid-summer, leaving no more than five olives per foot (30cm) of shoot. Some heavily laden shoots can be cut out completely.

PERSIMMONS AND POMEGRANATES

The Oriental or Japanese persimmon (*Diospyros kaki*) and its cultivars and the pomegranate (*Punica granatum*) are only worth growing for fruit in warm climates. The pomegranate thrives in the hot valleys and even desert regions of California. However, the American persimmon (*D. virginiana*) is hardier and is native over a wide area of the Northeast.

PERSIMMONS
American and Oriental persimmons are deciduous trees, the latter growing to a height of about 30ft (9m) and the American species sometimes half as much again. Cultivars of Oriental persimmons are self-fertile, but the American persimmon needs a pollinator to set fruit. If growing Oriental persimmons for fruit, buy trees of named cultivars.

Formative pruning and training
Plant Oriental persimmons in winter, the American species in early spring or autumn, staking the plant for the first year or two. The aim is to establish a clear stem, to a height of about 5ft (1.5m), and three or four strong primary branches with wide crotches. The central leader can be allowed to develop, and shoots that are not wanted to form the primary branches should be cut back to the main stem in late winter.

Pruning the established tree
Persimmons generally start to bear in the fourth or fifth year. Little pruning is required but some annual pruning may be necessary to cut out dead or damaged wood and to keep the center of the tree open. Shortening twiggy growths will help to keep the bearing wood strong.

POMEGRANATES
Although the period when it is without leaves may be short, the pomegranate is a deciduous tree or large shrub. It is self-fertile and can be grown with an open-centered head on a clear stem, when it reaches a height of about 15ft (4.6m). It can also be grown as an arching shrub, and in this form makes a height of about 10ft (3m).

Formative pruning and training
Plant in late winter, staking for the first year or two. Train up the main stem to a height of about 5ft (1.5m) before cutting back in later winter, just above the topmost of four or five well-spaced laterals, and remove any shoots below them on the main stem.

Pruning the established tree
Established plants require very little pruning other than the removal of dead and damaged wood, and the thinning of crossing branches. Remove any suckers that appear.

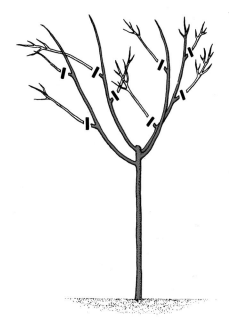

Below left: When ripe, the fruits of the Oriental persimmon turn deep orange. The wood is brittle and narrow-angled branches break easily under the weight of fruit.

Below: The pomegranate is often grown as a tree for its ornamental value as well as for its fruit. It has attractive red flowers, shiny orange to deep red fruits, and the leaves color well in autumn.

FORMATIVE PRUNING OF POMEGRANATES
Train a clear stem to a height of about 5ft (1.5m) and prune in winter to create an open-centered head, cutting out crossing growths and inward-growing shoots.

SOFT FRUITS AND VINES

The shrubs and perennials included in the broad category of soft fruits are particularly useful in the small garden, requiring much less space than tree fruits. As the term suggests, most bear soft, juicy fruit and produce worthwhile crops soon after planting. With a few exceptions, such as the blueberry, most soft fruits belong to one or other of two main botanical groups: the gooseberry family (*Grossulariaceae*) – which includes the gooseberry itself, black, red and white currants, and the worcesterberry – and members of the rose family (*Rosaceae*) including blackberries, strawberries, raspberries and hybrid berries (such as the loganberry). Of the vines that are here combined with soft fruits, the grape is by far the most important and is today one of the most widely cultivated of all fruits.

In general cultivation and in the pruning and training that is needed to produce good yields from healthy and easily managed plants, the kinships between fruits are sometimes relevant. For example, hybrid berries are grown in much the same way as blackberries. However, family connection is not always relevant, one or several regimes being suitable for a particular fruit. In most cases, possible variations of the standard methods are mentioned, but in the case of grapes these are too numerous to cover comprehensively.

Right: The 'Oregon Thornless', a cut-leaved blackberry, can be trained on an arch as well as by the 2-way and weaving systems.

Top right: The best black currant fruits are carried on young wood. The annual cutting back of a third of the bush is to encourage regular replacement growth.

Bottom right: The red currant, shown here in flower, is grown with a permanent framework of branches as an open-centered bush, a cordon or a fan. Pruning aids the growth of fruiting spurs.

Left: Although the basic systems of pruning grapes are limited, there are many variations. Vines grown against walls are usually pruned on the rod-and-spur system.

Bottom left: Summer-fruiting raspberries produce new canes each summer, which bear fruit the following year. Old canes are cut out once they have finished fruiting.

Below: The kiwi fruit or Chinese gooseberry, a vigorous climber, can be grown as espaliers or over pergolas.

GOOSEBERRIES

Right: When gooseberries are grown with a permanent framework of branches on a short stem, pruning should maintain an open-centered bush and counteract the natural tendency of branches to droop.

Below: Gooseberries make attractive short standards, which are pruned in exactly the same way as the bush-grown plants.

The gooseberry is a deciduous thorny shrub that does well in cool temperate regions. Although a favorite abroad, it is hardly known to many Americans. This is partly due to the white pine blister rust, a disease that attacks gooseberries, red and black currants and white pines. To protect white pines, growing these soft fruits in some states and counties is unlawful. The County Cooperative Extension office can tell gardeners whether these fruits can be grown in their region.

Gooseberries are grown with a permanent framework of branches, the fruit being carried at the base of the previous summer's lateral growth and also on spurs that form on the older wood. They are usually grown as bushes, but they can also be trained as cordons, fans, and standards.

BUSH GOOSEBERRIES

Although gooseberries will often fruit reasonably well without regular pruning, free-growing specimens are not easy to manage. Most plants have drooping branches and when these touch the ground they are likely to root, the resulting stools of thorny branches making general cultivation difficult. A tangle of thorny branches also makes picking slow and painful, and crowded growth in the center of a plant may provide favorable conditions for diseases.

The best course is to create an open-centered bush, with six to eight main branches held above the ground on a short clear stem about 4-6in (10-15cm) high. By careful pruning it is possible to counteract

BUSH GOOSEBERRIES

1 At planting prune to leave a clear stem of 4-6in (10-15cm) before the first main branch. Cut back framework branches by half and prune any growth in the center to one bud.

2 In the second winter or early spring cut back by half all leaders and any shoots placed to form permanent branches. Remove any suckers and shoots that develop low down on the stem.

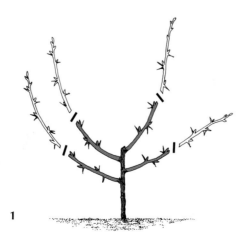

1

2

the drooping tendency of branches. If a branch is weeping, it should be cut to an inward- or upward-facing bud rather than to one that is outward-facing, or alternatively, cut back to an upright shoot.

Formative pruning and training
Planting should be in late autumn or early spring. Before planting a one-year-old plant, the lowest shoots and any suckers at the base of the plant are removed. The aim is to create a clear stem of 4-6in (10-15cm) before the first main branch. Throughout the plant's life any suckers and shoots growing on the stem should be removed immediately. Once planted, the framework branches are cut back by half, and growth in the center pruned to one bud.

It will take a few years to build up the framework. In late winter or early spring, as the bush is coming into its second year, all leaders and any shoots that are well placed to form permanent branches are cut by half. By the following autumn the bush should have six to eight well-spaced branches. Leaders are cut by half to buds facing in the direction that growth is wanted. Any shoots not required for the framework, including those crowding the center, should be cut back to 2in (5cm). The bush should start bearing the following year and from then on should be pruned in summer and winter.

If buying two- or three-year-old plants (which will fruit sooner), select bushes on which strong shoots form a balanced head above a clear stem of the required length, and prune according to age.

Pruning an established bush
Although summer pruning is not essential, it is beneficial, letting light and air into the bush, reducing the risk of disease, and allowing increased spray penetration. It includes the removal of those shoot tips that have been attacked by mildew or aphids.

The aim of summer pruning is to cut back the current season's growth to five leaves, late enough to make secondary growth unlikely, but not so late that the plant will fail to benefit. The timing depends to some extent on growing conditions, but generally is best done two or three weeks before midsummer. Do not prune the leaders unless mildewed, in which case affected tips should be removed.

In late winter or early spring, the growth made by leaders in the preceding summer is cut back by half, or more on older bushes. Thinning will also help to keep the bush vigorous. All dead, diseased or weak growths, unproductive branches and crowded stems are cut out, and the laterals that were pruned in summer cut back. When cutting out unproductive branches leave strong young shoots as replacements. For large dessert fruits two buds should be left, but for heavier crops the pruning should be lighter.

CORDONS
The cordon, which fruits on spur systems, is an easily managed form that allows several plants to be grown in a limited space. The most usual form is the upright single cordon grown to a height of about 6ft (1.8m). A

Below: Cordons are pruned in summer and winter to encourage spur formation.

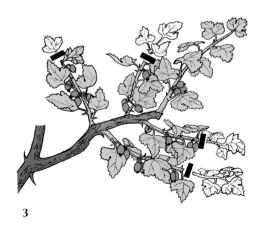

3

4

3 On established bushes prune the current season's laterals in the 2 or 3 weeks before midsummer, cutting back to 5 leaves.

4 In late winter or early spring cut back by about half the current season's growth made by leaders. Remove any diseased or dead wood and crowded growth. Cut back to 2 buds the laterals that were pruned in the summer.

Right: Gooseberries can be grown as multiple cordons, but single cordons are more usual.

Below: The spur systems of cordon-trained plants are built up by pruning laterals in summer and winter.

cordon requires a permanent support system, with each plant being provided with a bamboo cane which is itself tied to wires at a height of 2 and 4ft (60 and 120cm) above the ground.

Formative pruning and training
Like the bush, the cordon should be grown on a clean stem of 4-6in (10-15cm) in length. At planting, in late autumn or early spring, leaders should be shortened by half and laterals cut back to three buds. In the following growing season the leader is trained to its bamboo cane, and, during the next two or three winters, lightly pruned, removing about a quarter of the previous summer's growth.

Pruning the established cordon
Checking lateral growth helps build the spur systems that carry fruit. Summer pruning should begin in the second year. Two or three weeks before mid-summer, the current

season's lateral growth is cut back to five leaves. The leader is not pruned. In winter, the summer-pruned laterals are cut to a bud about 3in (7.5cm) from the main stem, and spurs growing on older cordons shortened at the same time or in early spring.

When the cordon gains sufficient height, it should be cut back in winter or early spring, leaving one to three buds of recent growth.

FANS AND STANDARDS
These forms are attractive ways of growing gooseberries and are well suited to the ornamental kitchen garden. The fan can be grown against a wall or fence that gets plenty of light but little direct sun. Gooseberries grown in these forms are treated in the same way as fans and standards of red and white currants (see pp. 194–95).

Right: An advantage of growing gooseberries as cordons is that the fruit is easily picked, sprayed and netted.

Far right: The spur systems of fan-trained gooseberries are formed in the same way as those on cordons, laterals being pruned in summer and shortened further in winter.

RED AND WHITE CURRANTS

Red and white currants require the same growing conditions, pruning and training as gooseberries. Unlike black currants, they are grown with a permanent framework of branches, the clusters of fruit being carried on short spurs on the older wood and at the base of one-year-old shoots. They are usually grown as open-centered bushes, but can also be trained as cordons, fans and standards. (The growing of currants is illegal in some states and counties. See p. 190.)

BUSH CURRANTS
A currant bush should be a goblet-shaped frame of about eight to ten permanent branches. A short clear stem about 4-6in (10-15cm) high makes for easier cultivation and keeps the fruit clear of the ground. The ultimate height and spread of the bush will be 5-6ft (1.5-1.8m).

Formative pruning
At planting, in mid-autumn or early spring, a clear stem should be created by the removal of shoots less than 4in (10cm) from the ground. Leaders and other branches are pruned by half, cutting to buds facing in the desired direction. Red and white currants droop less than gooseberries, and pruning is generally to outward-facing buds. Center shoots should be pruned to one bud.

Additional shaping may be necessary for the first few years. In winter, leaders and other branches needed for the framework should be pruned by half, cutting to outward-facing buds. To promote spur development, laterals not needed for the framework should be cut to one bud. Prune suckers and any shoots growing on the clear stem.

Pruning the established bush
Once the framework has been established, late winter or early spring pruning consists of taking out any dead, diseased or damaged wood and cutting back the main leaders, leaving about 3in (7.5cm) of the previous summer's growth. If an old, unfruitful branch needs to be taken out, a vigorous young lateral should be left to replace it. Other laterals should be cut back to one bud.

Summer pruning is not essential, but it does help the ripening of fruit and wood by letting light and air into the plant. In mid-summer, the current season's growth should be cut to five leaves except for the leaders.

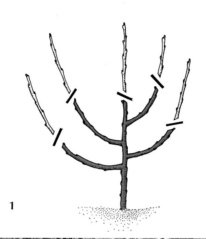

1

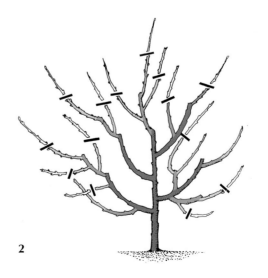

2

BUSH CURRANTS
1 At planting, in mid-autumn or spring, cut branches by half to outward-facing buds. Remove shoots less than 4in (10cm) from the ground.

2 During the second and following dormant seasons, cut leaders and branches needed for the framework by half, to outward-facing buds. Cut other laterals to one bud. Remove suckers less than 4in (10cm) from the ground.

Above left: Pruning of this mature specimen of the red currant 'Jonkheer Van Tets' has created a framework of permanent branches forming a goblet shape.

Above: Red currants are grown on a permanent framework of branches, with the fruit clusters appearing on short spurs on old wood and at the base of 1-year-old shoots.

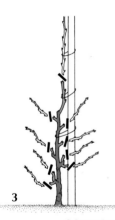

CORDONS

A few red or white currants grown as cordons can be easily fitted into quite a small garden. The single cordon, the most commonly grown form, is described below; while multiple cordons, with two or three stems, differ from the single cordon only in that laterals low on the plant are used in the initial stages to form the main stems.

Formative pruning and training

At planting, in mid-autumn or early spring, the leader of a rooted cutting should be cut back by half. To create a short clear stem, remove all shoots or buds on the bottom 4in (10cm), and cut back all other laterals to one bud. If the plant is older and has already been partly shaped, shorten the leader by a third and prune young laterals back to one bud.

In the following growing season, the leader should be trained to a cane and the current season's side shoots cut back to four or five leaves.

Pruning the established cordon

Each winter or early spring, to encourage the development of fruiting spurs, summer-pruned laterals should be cut back to one bud. For a few years cut back the leader to a bud so that about 6in (15cm) of the previous summer's growth is left. Once it has reached the required height, the leader can then be cut back to leave only one bud of the growth made in the summer.

The leader is not pruned in summer until the required height is reached. From then on the growth it makes is treated in the same way as the current season's side shoots,

CORDON

1 At planting, in mid-autumn or early spring, cut back the leader of a rooted cutting by about half. Remove shoots or buds on the bottom 4in (10cm), and cut other laterals back to one bud.

2 In the first summer train the leader to a cane and in mid-summer cut back the current season's side shoots to 4 or 5 leaves.

3 In late winter or early spring, cut summer-pruned laterals to one bud. Until the leader reaches the required height, cut it back to a bud leaving 6in (15cm) of summer growth.

Right: The best support for red currants grown as standards, such as this example of the cultivar 'Rondom', is a pair of stakes with a crosspiece.

being cut back to five leaves in mid-summer. All suckers and any shoots on the bottom 4in (10cm) of the stem should be removed as soon as they develop.

STANDARD CURRANTS

Nurserymen generally bud or graft a selected cultivar on a suitable rootstock at a height of about 3½ft (1.1m). Red currants, however, are strong enough to form a standard on their own roots and can be trained in this way by the home gardener. White currants, which are of rather weaker growth, are generally not grown satisfactorily this way unless on very good soil.

Formative pruning and training

Start with a rooted cutting or a two-year-old bush which has a suitably placed upright branch. In the initial stages the pruning and training is the same as for a cordon, the leader being taken up a cane. A two-year-old plant will take about two years to develop a strong stem capable of supporting the head. When this stage is reached, the leader should be pruned in winter, cutting to a bud at a height of about 3½ft (1.1m). In the following growing season, select four or five laterals at the top to form the primary branches. As the head develops, firm staking becomes essential. It is best to use two stakes, one each side of the stem, joined by a crosspiece or two figure-of-eight ties. All growths below the head can be removed the next winter to create a clean stem.

Pruning the established standard

The head of the standard is pruned in exactly the same way as the bush, except that it is even more important that the standard maintains a balanced shape. Because there is no risk of fruit trailing on the ground or branches making cultivation near the plant difficult, drooping lower branches can be left to arch over for an ornamental effect. Remove any suckers growing from below ground level or from the stem as soon as they appear.

FANS

Fans can be trained against walls or fences or planted as screens in the open garden. They need about 6-8ft (1.8-2.4m) horizontally, with wire supports rising to a height of about 6ft (1.8m).

Formative pruning and training

Although it is not difficult to build up a fan from a rooted cutting, time can be saved by selecting a two-year-old bush with the potential for making a fan. The ideal is a plant with two strong branches to the left, and two to the right, on a clean stem about 6in (15cm) high.

At planting, in mid-autumn or early spring, all other shoots and branches are cut out and the ribs pruned back by a half to two-thirds, to upward-facing buds. The following summer, train in the ribs and other suitably placed shoots.

Pruning the established fan

It takes several years to build up the framework of a fan, the ribs of which are treated as a number of cordons radiating from a central point. In summer, any laterals that form on the ribs should be shortened to four or five leaves and in late winter or early spring they should be cut back still further, to one bud, in order to encourage the formation of fruiting spurs. When fans are trained against a solid fence or wall it may be necessary to remove growth at the back.

On an established fan the spur systems can become long and branched. When this is the case, it is necessary to shorten them.

Below: The white currant is slightly less vigorous than the red, but is grown in the same way, as a cordon, bush, standard or fan.

Left: The formation of a fan can be speeded up by starting with a 2-year-old bush plant with stems that are suitably placed and angled to become the first ribs. This sequence shows the initial pruning of a specimen of the red currant cultivar 'Jonkheer van Tets'. At planting in the dormant season, the superfluous stems are cut out completely, and the 4 retained as the ribs are shortened by about half to upward-facing buds.

Below: Red currant fans have a permanent framework of ribs with fruit-bearing spurs.

Right: Fruit-bearing spurs are formed through a combination of summer and winter pruning.

BLACK CURRANTS

BLACK CURRANTS

1 Plant in late autumn or early spring, setting the plants 2in (5cm) deeper than they were in the nursery. Prune hard, cutting all shoots to within 4-6in (10-15cm) of the ground.

Below: When pruning black currants in the dormant season it is the older wood, darker in color than younger growths, that should be cut out.

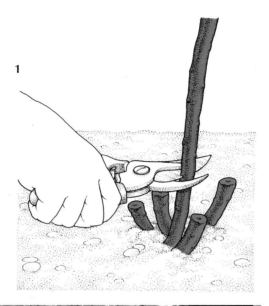

2 Begin regular pruning once the bush has carried its first crop. Preliminary pruning – removing damaged, diseased or weak growths and those shoots close to the ground – can be carried out as soon as the fruit has been picked. The main pruning, in late winter or early spring, consists of removing a third of the oldest wood, cutting to the base or to a vigorous shoot.

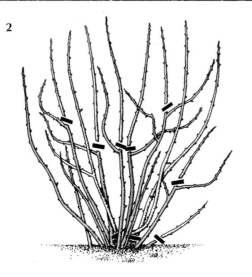

Although closely related to red and white currants, black currants (*Ribes nigrum*) require a different method of pruning. The heaviest crops are carried on wood produced in the previous year, although older wood will also carry some fruit. The initial aim is to establish a good stool system, with shoots growing up from below ground level rather than from a stem. The cutting out of a proportion of the older wood every year, combined with generous feeding in the growing season, will encourage the growth of young shoots.

Black currants are well-known as being alternate hosts to the white pine blister rust (see Gooseberries, p. 190). At least two cultivars, 'Consort' and 'Crusader', are resistant to the disease, as is the jostaberry, a black currant-gooseberry cross.

Formative pruning

Deep planting will encourage the growth of a strong stool system. In late autumn or (in the north) early spring, set the young plants about 2in (5cm) deeper than they were in the nursery (the soil mark on the stems will indicate the original depth). Immediately after planting, prune hard, cutting all shoots to within 4-6in (10-15cm) of the ground. This will mean no crop in the first summer, but the long-term benefit is a vigorous plant with strong young shoots. The pruned shoots will root readily as cuttings.

Provided that strong growth has been made, no pruning will be needed at the end of the growing season and the bush will still bear fruit the following year. However, if the bush has made only weak growth, prune hard again in late winter or early spring. This will mean another year without fruit.

Pruning an established bush

Start the regular pruning program once the plant has carried its first crop. The main pruning is done in late winter or early spring. However, to improve air circulation it is worth cutting out any damaged, diseased or weak growths and shoots that are close to the ground, immediately after picking. The main pruning consists of cutting out about a third of the oldest wood, either cutting right to the base or to a strong shoot near the base. The color of the bark is an indication of age, the young shoots being much lighter in color than three-year-old wood.

RASPBERRIES

Raspberries have a perennial, suckering root system which produces new canes every year. On summer-fruiting raspberries the canes carry fruit in their second year and then die. Autumn-fruiting (everbearing) plants bear fruit on the top part of the current season's canes. After fruiting, the tips are cut back and berries are borne in summer on laterals which then die. The aim in pruning is to regulate the replacement of old canes by young growth.

Support systems
Raspberries need a support system to prevent their tall canes being weighed down by fruit. One method is the single-fence system, with horizontal wires spaced at 2½, 3½ and 5½ft (75, 105 and 170cm). The fruiting canes are laced to the wires and kept well spaced to ensure good exposure to sun. Free air circulation lessens the risk of fungal disease. The young canes can be tied to the lower wires to protect them from strong winds.

The parallel-fence system uses two pairs of wires, at 2½ and 5ft (75 and 150cm) above ground level, spaced 2ft (60cm) apart. The canes are not tied, but kept upright by string or wire cross ties every 2ft (60cm).

The Scandinavian system consists of two parallel wires 3ft (90cm) apart and 3ft (90cm) above ground level. Fruiting canes are grown in a single row between the wires and trained to either side, forming a "V" when the row is seen from sideways on. The canes are twisted around the wires rather than tied.

In a small garden the single-post system can be used with each cane being supported by a stake, to a height of 6ft (1.8m).

SUMMER-FRUITING RASPBERRIES
These raspberries have long canes of up to 8ft (2.4m) tall. These carry fruit on laterals from the early to mid-summer of their second year, and then die.

Initial pruning
Plant certified virus-free plants in late autumn or early spring, setting the canes no deeper than 3in (7.5cm), and with the roots well spread out to encourage the development of suckers. After planting cut each cane to a bud about 9-12in (23-30cm) above ground level. There will be no fruit in the first growing season, and any flowers produced on the stumps should be removed.

SUPPORT SYSTEMS: Single-post system

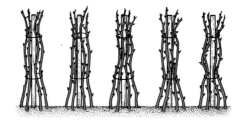

Single-fence system

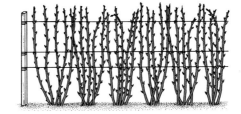

Parallel-fence system

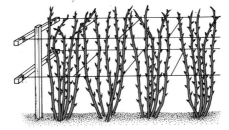

Left: In pruning summer-fruiting plants the aim is to take out canes that have carried fruit, making way for the next season's canes. In this photograph the young canes can be seen on the right.

Above: Vigorous canes
that have been arched
over and tied to the top
wire when grown on
the single-fence system
are tipped back about
6in (15cm) above the
top wire in late winter,
a process that removes
damaged and diseased
ends and stimulates
growth lower down.

SINGLE-FENCE SYSTEM

1 Plant in late autumn
or early spring, setting
the canes no deeper
than 3in (7.5cm) and
with the roots well
spread out. After
planting cut each cane
to a bud at 9-12in
(23-30cm) above
ground level.

2 In the first summer
tie canes 3-4in (7.5-
10cm) apart on the
wires. No fruit is
produced in the first
growing season.

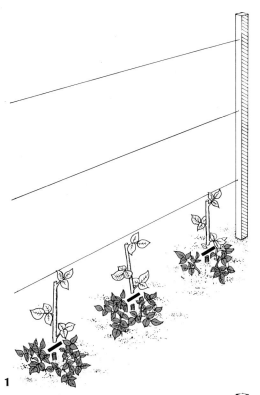

1

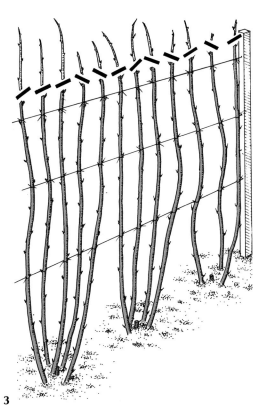

3

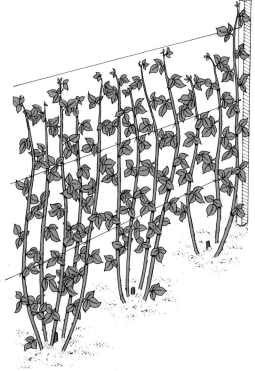

2

4

3 In late winter of the second year cut back dead and weak tips at a height of 5ft (1.5m).

4 In the second and subsequent summers young canes develop as old canes flower and set fruit. In mid-summer remove surplus young canes so that those left are spaced about 4in (10cm) apart.

5 In mid-autumn of the second and subsequent years cut out all canes that have fruited. Loop over and tie to the top wire all long young canes.

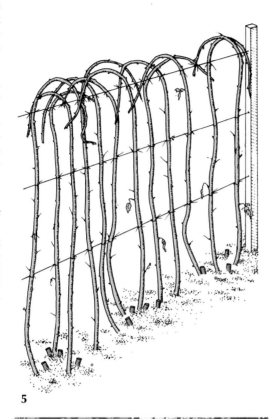

5

Right: Canes of raspberries grown on the single-fence system are tied in to their support. The new canes at the base must be thinned later to provide evenly spaced canes that will carry the next season's crop.

Pruning and training established plants

Using the single-fence system, tie the canes to the wires at a spacing of 3-4in (7.5-10cm) once they have achieved a sufficient height. If using continuous lacing, make occasional knots in case the string breaks. To prevent those canes that are taller than the top wire being damaged by rough winter weather, arch them over and tie again to the top wire. In late winter, cut these canes back to 6in (15cm) above the top wire. Tipping is advisable for all methods of training other than the Scandinavian system, as it removes any growth that has been damaged during the winter and encourages the development of buds that are low on the canes.

With the Scandinavian system, the young canes are woven round the wires in late summer or early autumn, while the current season's growth is still flexible. About four to six canes are gathered together and twisted, as a group, around the wire. Canes should be divided evenly between the two wires and all trained in the same direction. Replacement canes should be allowed to develop freely until those that have carried fruit are cut out. With the Scandinavian system, this twisting should be all the support the canes require. With the single-fence system, new canes should be tied in to the wires as they develop.

Whatever method of training is used, cut old canes that have fruited down to ground level immediately after harvesting. Some thinning of suckers is generally necessary to achieve a spacing of about 4in (10cm) between canes.

AUTUMN-FRUITING (EVERBEARING) RASPBERRIES

'Heritage' is a popular autumn cultivar that does not require support. Other autumn cultivars, useful because of the late ripening of their fruit, between early autumn and the first frosts, include 'Fall Gold' and 'September'. If the tips are cut back after fruiting an early summer crop will follow.

Pruning and training

The initial treatment is the same as for summer-fruiting raspberries. Although the canes will carry some fruit in summer if left for a second season, the crop may be light, and so all canes should be cut to ground level in late winter or early spring. Thin canes to 2in (5cm) apart.

BLACKBERRIES

The wild blackberry is a vigorous rambling cane fruit formidably armed with thorns. In cultivation the quality of the fruit has been improved and several thornless cultivars have been raised. Crosses between blackberries and other *Rubus* species have resulted in a number of hybrid berries, such as the loganberry and tayberry. In general, hybrid berries are less vigorous and less fiercely thorned than blackberries. Even so, a pair of leather gloves is needed when handling thorned blackberries or hybrid berries.

TRAINING METHODS
Most hybrid berries are pruned in the same way as blackberries, cutting out the canes when they have finished fruiting in their second year. Some training is essential, to simplify pruning and picking and to keep the plants manageable – left to themselves, blackberries and their hybrids will form a tangled mass of canes. The choice of method depends on the vigor of the plant and the flexibility of the canes, but all systems aim to keep the older canes, which are retained until they have fruited, separate from the younger ones, which will bear the following year. Two benefits of separating the canes are the reduced risk of fungal diseases spreading from old to young canes, and it makes picking easier.

The canes must be supported (although the sturdy canes of 'Darrow' remain erect). Wires

WEAVING SYSTEM
1 In the first summer, train canes to left and right, weaving them in and out of the bottom 3 wires.

2 In the second and subsequent summers, when the previous season's canes flower and fruit, train new canes up through the center and tie them to the top wire.

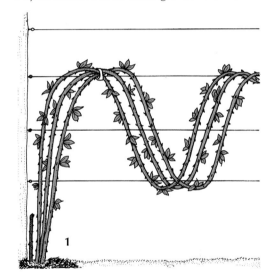
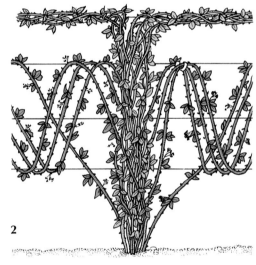

3 In mid-autumn, after harvesting, cut the old canes down to ground level. If there are few new canes, the best of the old canes can be retained.

4 After cutting out old canes, untie the young canes and weave them in and out of the bottom 3 wires before retying.

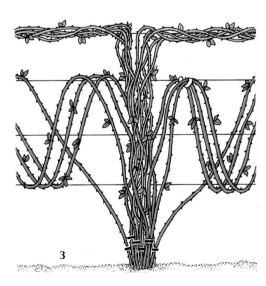

can be fixed to walls or fences or run between posts. Stretch the bottom wire 3ft (90cm) above ground level with three more wires above it, spaced 1ft (30cm) apart.

Several variations of the methods of training outlined below may be used. For example, thornless blackberries and hybrid berries are attractive when grown on a trellis arch. In essence, the method of pruning remains the same.

Initial pruning
Plant certified virus-free stock in spring. Cut all canes down to a height of about 10in (25cm) above the ground. Plants will not fruit until their second summer.

Weaving system
This system requires a lot of handling and is best suited to cultivars with long, flexible canes – for example, the thornless 'Boysen' and the very vigorous blackberries, such as 'Jerseyblack' and 'Thornfree' – as a way of making them more compact. Less vigorous growers need about 8ft (2.4m) horizontally, the most vigorous about 15ft (4.6m).

Each plant produces several canes in its first summer. As they develop, canes should be trained to left and right and woven in and out of the bottom three wires. In the second summer, as the previous season's canes fruit, the plant produces new canes. These should be trained up through the center of the bush and tied to the top wire. After harvesting, old canes should be cut to ground level. The young canes on the top wire are then untied, woven in and out of the three bottom wires, and retied. There should be plenty of new canes but, if there are not enough, one or two of the old canes can be retained. In late winter or early spring any weak growth at the end of canes should be tipped.

The fan and the two-way rope system
Fan training is suitable for the less vigorous hybrid berries, especially those with rather rigid stems, such as 'Smoothstem'. It is a less space-consuming method than most, but 8-10ft (2.4-3m) is needed for lateral spread.

In the first summer canes are trained evenly to left and right, forming an open-centered fan or "V". In late autumn or early spring, canes are tipped back to about 5½ft (1.7m), just above the third wire (this allows 6in (15cm) of cane above the wire for tying).

While the old canes are flowering and fruiting in the second summer, new canes should be trained, as a column, up through the central gap and, if long enough, tied to left and right along the top wire. After harvesting, the old canes are cut to ground level. The new canes, which will fruit in their second year, can then be untied and repositioned to form the "V"-shaped fan.

A variant of this method is the two-way rope system. With cultivars that have thin flexible canes, such as the tayberry, canes in their final position are trained outwards along the bottom three wires of the support, three or four canes per wire, rather than as a fan. As with the fan, the young canes are initially trained as a column.

Left: 'Himalaya Giant' is a very vigorous and thorny blackberry. It can be kept reasonably compact by growing it on the weaving system, but this involves a lot of handling. Handling is reduced to a minimum when the 1-way rope system is used, but this method requires a generous allowance of space.

Left: The tayberry, one of several hybrid berries derived from the blackberry, has light flexible canes and is often trained on the 2-way rope system.

THE FAN
1 In the first summer, train the canes as an open-centered fan or "V", distributing them evenly to left and right.

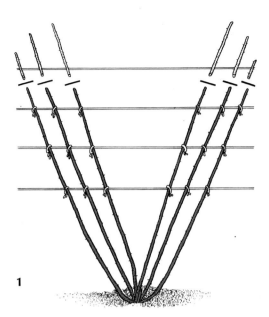

1

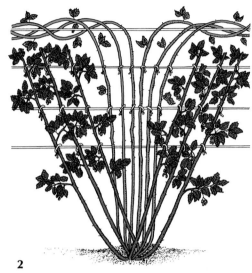

2

2 In late autumn or early spring, tip canes back to about 5½ft (1.7m), just above the third wire.

3 In the second and subsequent summers, when the old canes are flowering and fruiting, train the new canes through the center and tie them to right and left along the top wire.

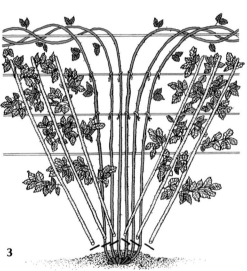

3

One-way rope system

This system requires minimal handling and is therefore useful for heavily-thorned plants, such as the 'Himalaya Giant' blackberry. However, as individual plants require about 15ft (4.6m), this is not a method for the small garden. In the first year, all canes are tied in along the wires to one side of an imaginary central vertical line. The following summer, when these canes flower and fruit, the new canes are trained, three or four to each wire, in the opposite direction. With this alternating program, the replacement canes do not need to be retied when the old canes are cut out in mid-autumn.

If two plants are being grown side by side, ensure that the young canes grow towards each other and are not in contact with older canes, which may pass on fungal diseases.

1-WAY ROPE SYSTEM

In this system the canes of one year are all trained one way, and while these are fruiting the next season's canes are all trained in the opposite direction. The advantage of the system is that canes need be handled only once before being cut out after fruiting, but considerable space is needed to make this a viable option.

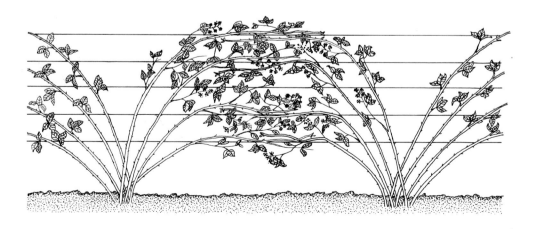

BLUEBERRIES AND CRANBERRIES

A number of ericaceous species of *Vaccinium* bear edible fruits which are used for desserts and in jams. Although the fruits of some species, such as the bilberry or whortleberry (*V. myrtillus*), are often gathered, the yields are generally considered too low to warrant cultivation. The species known collectively in the United States as low bush blueberries, including *V. angustifolium*, come into this category. However, in the blueberry barrens of the eastern United States and Canada large areas are commercially managed. Burning every two or three years in winter is used to clear away old growths and competing plants, and to encourage vigorous shoots to develop from the base. When cultivated, hard pruning every two or three years is used to stimulate this new growth, but to maintain continuity only half the plants are pruned in any one year.

High bush blueberries (mainly *V. corymbosum* and its cultivars) and cranberries, especially cultivars of the American species *V. macrocarpum*, are the most widely cultivated of the ericaceous fruits and do well on the acid soils that suit many heaths and heathers.

HIGH BUSH BLUEBERRIES
These plants are easy to grow on moist but well-drained, very acid soils, either as informal hedges or in mixed plantings of rhododendrons, azaleas and other related shrubs. They grow into spreading bushes 6ft (1.8m) or more in height.

Formative pruning
Plants are usually sold as two- or three-year-old container-grown specimens. At planting, preferably in early spring, little pruning is required other than to trim any damaged shoots. In the next two or three years no other pruning is needed unless plants fail to branch freely, in which case cut back the longest stems by about a third in mid-spring.

Pruning the established bush
As stems age the quality of the fruit they carry deteriorates. After the third year thin bushes annually. Between late winter and early spring cut out two or three of the oldest stems, pruning back to ground level. At the same time take out any dead, diseased or damaged branches, and any stems pulled to the ground by the weight of snowdrifts.

PRUNING BLUEBERRIES
In the third and subsequent years prune bushes annually between late winter and early spring. Take out dead, diseased or damaged wood and cut back 2 or 3 of the oldest stems to ground level.

CRANBERRIES
These plants, which grow to about 2in (5cm) high, but with a spread of up to 1½ft (46cm), need a moist acid soil. Commercial growers often grow them in artificial bogs where the water level can be controlled.

Pruning
At planting, between mid-autumn and early spring, no pruning is generally necessary. Rather than cutting off long stems, they should be partly covered with soil and pegged down to encourage rooting along the whole length. Trim upright and wispy growths on established plants in early spring.

Above: Blueberries, which require acid soil conditions, fruit on side shoots, the flower buds being borne on the growth of the previous year.

GRAPES

Above: The grape, one of the most widely grown of all fruits, lends itself to many forms of training. Here, a fine specimen of a *Vitis vinifera* cultivar has been grown on the rod-and-spur system.

The extensive planting of grapes in many regions of the world is proof of the extraordinary versatility of a fruit that has a long history of cultivation. In Europe and in many other areas the vines grown are almost exclusively cultivars of *Vitis vinifera*. In cool temperate regions most cultivars require very favorable conditions to do well, such as against a sheltered sunny wall, and choice grapes are sometimes grown in greenhouses.

Grapes derived from species other than *V. vinifera* are also grown, principally on the North American continent, and include the American or bunch grapes (most of which have *V. labrusca* in their parentage) and the more tender muscadine grapes derived from *V. rotundifolia*. There are also French-American hybrids, hardy and well-flavored.

All grapes are more or less vigorous deciduous climbers that carry fruit on shoots growing from one-year-old stems. Unless vines are regularly pruned and trained, they develop into a tangled mass of young growths mixed with woody and dead stems, and only small bunches of poorly developed fruit are produced. There are many methods of pruning, all based on providing a permanent framework and promoting the annual production of new wood.

The main pruning of *V. vinifera* cultivars should be carried out in early winter. This reduces the risk of bleeding (an excessive flow of sap from pruning cuts) which can weaken the vine and make it vulnerable to pests and disease. Main pruning of bunch grapes and French-American hybrids is best done in early spring, while the vines are still dormant but when there is little risk of frost damage. Muscadine grapes are pruned in winter. The severity of the pruning may need to be adjusted to the vigor of the cultivar.

Grapes are sometimes grown on their own roots, but cultivars of *V. vinifera* are also commonly grafted on to rootstocks that are resistant to *Phylloxera*, the aphid-like insect that in the nineteenth century devastated the vineyards of Europe. On grafted vines the union must not be buried at planting.

VITIS VINIFERA: THE GUYOT SYSTEM

In Europe, one of the most widely used and successful methods of growing the cultivars of *V. vinifera* outdoors is known as the Guyot system, of which there is a single and double form. In the double form, the more commonly used of the two, the fruit-bearing laterals are trained vertically from a pair of arms of two-year-old wood, each about 2ft (60cm) long, which are trained to left and right of a short stem. Above the junction of the arms three main stems are allowed to develop each year. Two of these are brought down in the autumn to replace the arms that have carried fruit-bearing laterals, and the third is cut back leaving buds to produce replacement shoots the following year.

The single form has only one arm. The two forms are often grown in combination, the single Guyot completing a row.

Vines trained on the Guyot system need permanent support. In the open, use posts and wires, with single wires at 1¼ft (38cm) and 1¾ft (53cm) above ground level and double wires at 3, 4 and 5ft (90, 120 and 150cm). A similar spacing of wires is suitable for individual plants grown against walls or fences. Each vine should be supported by a strong bamboo cane or stake at planting.

Formative pruning and training

Initial hard pruning of a strong young vine will encourage vigorous growth. At planting, between mid-autumn and early spring, cut the vine back to within 6in (15cm) of the

THE GUYOT SYSTEM

1 After planting, between mid-autumn and early spring, cut the vine back to within 6in (15cm) of the graft union, leaving 2 good buds. In the following growing season allow one shoot to develop, training it up a cane. Pinch back any other shoots to one leaf.

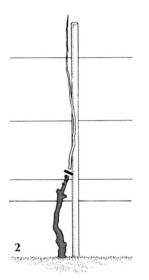

4 In late autumn of the second year tie down to left and right 2 of the shoots that have been trained vertically, arching them between the bottom and second wires. Shorten them to about 2-2½ft (60-76cm) and at the same time cut back the remaining shoot, retaining 3 good buds.

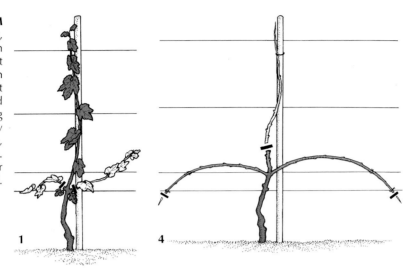

2 In late autumn cut the rod back to about 1¼ft (38cm) from ground level, retaining at least 3 good buds.

5 In the growing season of the third and subsequent years grapes will be carried on laterals trained vertically from the 2 arms. As they develop tuck these laterals through the double wires and cut them back to 3 leaves above the top wire. Train 3 replacement shoots in the center vertically, pinching any laterals back to one leaf.

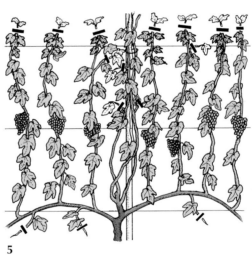

3 From spring to summer in the second year train 3 shoots vertically, pinching back laterals and superfluous shoots to one leaf.

6 In late autumn cut out the 2 horizontal bearing rods and tie in replacement shoots to left and right. Shorten these to about 2-2½ft (60-76cm) and cut back the third vertically trained shoot, retaining 3 good buds.

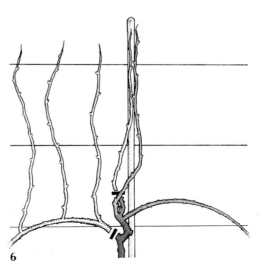

graft union or, if the vine is on its own roots, to 6in (15cm) from the ground, leaving two good buds. In the first summer retain only one shoot, training it up the cane, and pinch back any other shoots to one leaf. In late autumn of the same year cut the vine back to a bud just below the bottom wire, making sure that there are at least two more good buds left.

In the second summer train three shoots vertically, pinching back any laterals to one leaf. Two of these shoots are the first pair of arms, but they are not tied to the bottom wires until late autumn. When tied down, arching between the bottom and second wires, they are shortened to about 2-2½ft (60-76cm). At this stage cut back the

Guyot system
To prune the establised vine in the late autumn, the horizontal bearing rods arched between the bottom and the second wire are cut back to the center.

Two of the shoots trained vertically at the center in the previous growing season are tied to arch between the bottom and second wires, one to left and one to right. These are replacements for the horizontal bearing rods.

The third shoot trained vertically in the previous growing season is cut back, leaving 3 good buds.

remaining shoot, leaving three good buds, which will develop as the replacement shoots the following year.

Pruning and training the established vine
Under normal conditions the vines will begin bearing fruit in the third year, the grapes being carried on the laterals that develop from the arms tied in to the bottom wires. As the laterals develop, slip them between the double wires. Remove any sub-laterals and eventually cut back the laterals to three leaves above the topmost wire. The replacement shoots, limited to three, must also be trained vertically, any blossom on these shoots being removed and sub-laterals pinched back to one leaf.

Although a mature vine can carry one or more bunches per lateral, young vines will be weakened if they are allowed to carry heavy crops. In the first fruiting season keep two or.three bunches only and the next season four or five. In subsequent years a strong healthy vine can carry a full crop.

In late autumn each year cut the two horizontal, bearing rods back to strong young shoots at or near the center and then repeat the cycle of tying down two shoots as replacement arms and cutting back a third upright shoot as described above.

VITIS VINIFERA: THE ROD-AND-SPUR SYSTEM
Under glass, this system is the most widely used for cultivars of *V. vinifera*. The permanent framework is provided by the rod, that is the main stem, fruit-bearing laterals growing from spurs spaced along the main stem about 9in (23cm) apart. The pruning and training described below is for a single rod, but several variations on this are possible, for example with two or more rods to a single plant or with a branched rod.

A system of wires is needed to support the vine or vines. In a large lean-to greenhouse, in which the vines are planted side by side and trained upwards parallel with the glass, run the wires the length of the structure, about 1½ft (46cm) from the glass to allow for good air circulation and to reduce the risk of foliage scorching. Space the wires 9in (23cm) apart, with the first at 3ft (90cm) above the ground. A small greenhouse can probably accommodate only one vine and in this case the best planting position is at the end opposite the door, with the vine trained along the length of the ridge. Allow at least 1ft (30cm) between wires and glass.

Formative pruning and training

Vines can be planted inside the greenhouse or just outside and trained in through a hole in the greenhouse near to the ground. Although container-grown vines can be planted at any time of the year, planting in late autumn or early winter has the advantage that the initial hard pruning can be carried out immediately. Cutting back the previous summer's growth by two-thirds will encourage vigorous growth during the following summer. Any remaining laterals should be cut back to one bud. Vines planted during the growing season should be left unpruned until leaf-fall for, if cut, the bleeding of sap may weaken the plant.

In the following growing season allow the main stem to grow unchecked, tying it and any laterals loosely to the wires or ideally to a cane tied to the underside of the wires. A vigorous plant is likely to make about 10ft (3m) and will produce laterals over most of its length. Cut the laterals back at five or six leaves and pinch out sub-laterals at one leaf. At the end of the season, as soon as the leaves have fallen, cut back the main stem by two-thirds and prune the laterals that remain, leaving one plump bud.

In the second year a new extension leader will develop from the topmost bud of the main stem. Train this and the laterals as in the previous season, but two laterals can be allowed to fruit. Pinch these back to two leaves beyond the flower bunches, but cut back other laterals when they have five leaves.

Pruning and training the established vine

Regular pruning of the established vine is started in the third year. The precise timing will depend on the heating of the greenhouse and the cultivars grown. The aim should be to keep the greenhouse cool and freely ventilated once the crop has been harvested to help the wood ripen.

Immediately the leaves have fallen, cut back the main stem, by about half in the third year and to within an inch (2.5cm) of the old wood in subsequent years, unless growth is required for extension or replacement. At the same time, cut back all laterals to within two buds of the main stem. Only one lateral will be allowed to develop but the second bud may be required as a reserve should growth from the first be damaged.

Left: *Vitis vinifera* trained by the rod-and-spur system.

THE ROD-AND-SPUR SYSTEM

1 In late autumn or early winter cut back two-thirds of the previous summer's growth. Cut back laterals to one bud.

2 In the first summer allow the main stem to grow unchecked, tying it and laterals to the wires. Cut the laterals back at 5 or 6 leaves and pinch out sub-laterals at one leaf.

3 In late autumn or early winter cut back the main stem by two-thirds. Prune laterals to one good bud.

4 In the second growing season train the new extension leader and laterals as in the previous year. If allowing 2 laterals to fruit, pinch these back to 2 leaves beyond the flower clusters. Cut back other laterals to 5 leaves. In early winter shorten the leader by half and cut back laterals to spurs with 2 buds. (Cont. p. 208)

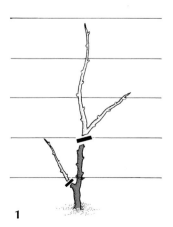

1

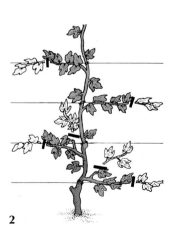

2

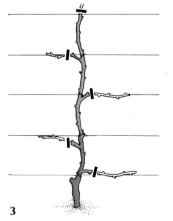

3

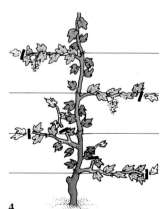

4

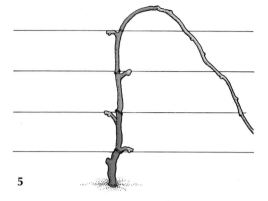

5 Annually, in late winter, starting at the end of the second year, undo the ties above the bottom third and allow the rod to hang down. When the buds on spurs begin to grow, retie the rod.

5

6 On the established vine allow only one lateral to grow from each spur, pinching the weaker back to 2 or 3 leaves. Carefully tie down the retained lateral. Pinch back the laterals to 2 leaves beyond the flowers and on barren laterals at 6-8 leaves. Pinch sub-laterals back to one leaf and remove all tendrils.

6

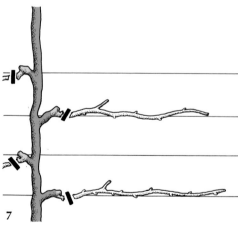

7 In early winter cut back the main stem, leaving an inch (2.5cm) of new growth and cut back laterals to 2 buds at the spur.

7

Right: This spur on a grape growing under glass has been cut back to leave 2 good buds.

In late winter undo the ties above the bottom third so that the stem hangs down, almost touching the ground. If the rod is not lowered, there is a tendency for the topmost buds to develop at the expense of those lower down. When all spurs are showing growth, retie the rod to the wires.

When the shoots are about 4in (10cm) long, pinch back the weaker at each spur to two or three leaves. The retained lateral will grow vertically unless tied down, but care is needed to avoid snapping off young brittle growth. Use a running noose to bring the lateral down gradually once it has become slightly fibrous. Lower a little every other day when the growth is turgid.

The flower trusses will be clearly visible by the time the laterals have made about 1½ft (46cm) of growth. Pinch the laterals back at two leaves beyond the flower trusses or, if there are no flowers, at six to eight leaves. All sub-laterals should be pinched back to one leaf and all tendrils should be removed as soon as they develop.

It may be necessary to reduce the number of bunches that are allowed to develop. The general rule is to allow a pound of fruit for every foot of rod (450g per 30cm), but in the first two years of bearing start with two or three bunches, rising to four or five before full bearing.

When the main stem has reached as far as the height of the greenhouse will allow, pinch out the growing point and, after harvesting the grapes, cut laterals back by about half.

VITIS VINIFERA: THE ROD-AND-SPUR/ CORDON SYSTEM

The rod-and-spur system can be used for cultivars of *V. vinifera* grown outdoors and allows for considerable variation in the training of the rod. A simple option is to plant and train a series of single, vertical cordons supported by posts and wires in the open garden or wires run along a fence or wall. More elaborate is the multiple cordon, with two, four or six uprights per vine, with the rods spaced about 4ft (1.2m). Another possibility is a horizontal cordon or even an espalier. Spur pruning of vertical and horizontal cordons permits considerable flexibility; vines grown on a house wall can be trained around doors and windows. A vine can also be trained up with a bare stem and then run over a supporting framework to make a leafy canopy to an outdoor room. The same principles apply to spur pruning outdoors as under glass.

VITIS VINIFERA: STANDARD VINES

Where space is a problem, one of the most satisfactory ways of growing *V. vinifera* grapes and also American and French-American hybrids is as standards, that is with the main stem supporting a head of shoots that are spur pruned. Grapes can be grown in this way outdoors, either planted directly in the ground or grown in a container, and the pot-grown standard is a convenient way of growing a vine in a small greenhouse. The vine can be taken outdoors after fruiting so that the wood is ripened and the exposure to cold results in satisfactory dormancy.

The following method of pruning and training relates to pot-grown standards, but is easily adapted to the open garden.

Formative pruning and training

Start with a year-old vine, and in its first year grow it in a 7in (18cm) pot. In late autumn or early winter cut the main stem back to a strong bud about 6in (15cm) above soil level or above the union of a grafted vine. In the following growing season train the vine in to a cane. Pinch back laterals to one leaf.

At leaf-fall, cut the main stem back to a bud at 3-5ft (90-150cm), depending on the height of standard that is wanted. Transfer the vine to a 1¼ft (38cm) pot and remove all side shoots.

In the second growing season allow four or five shoots to develop a head, but pinch them back when they have made five or six leaves. Remove all other growths from the stem and, in the unlikely event of flower clusters forming, remove these also.

In late autumn or early winter begin forming the spur systems by pruning each lateral back to one bud. Transfer the vine to a 1½ft (46cm) pot, which, provided the soil is regularly top-dressed and the plant fed, will not need to be changed for many years. The vine will need a strong support.

Pruning and training the established vine

In the third summer the vine can be allowed to produce two bunches of grapes. Pinch out the growths at two leaves beyond the bunches. Pinch other laterals back to five

leaves and sub-laterals to one. In subsequent years the vine can carry more bunches without being weakened. The routine pruning remains the same.

BUNCH GRAPES: THE KNIFFIN SYSTEM

The four-arm Kniffin system is a method of renewal pruning that is widely used in the cultivation of bunch grapes. To support the vines two wires should be run between stout stakes, 11-gauge at 2½ft (76cm) and a 9-gauge top wire at about 5ft (1.5m).

Formative pruning and training

At planting, in early spring, retain the strongest stem only and cut it back to two strong buds. Tie it to the bottom wire or, if not long enough, to a 6ft (1.8m) stake. When the shoots from these buds are about an inch (2.5cm) long, rub off all other shoots and train the two up the stake. In early spring of the second year select the stronger of the two shoots as the main stem and tie it to the top wire, cutting it back to just above the wire, and cut out the other completely. If the stem does not reach to the top wire, tie it to the bottom wire and let it extend during the following growing season.

Above: Grapes grown on the rod-and-spur system outdoors need the support of horizontal wires and vertical canes.

In early spring of the third year select four vigorous shoots as the fruiting arms, training them so that an arm extends either side of the main stem on the top and bottom wires. These arms, stretched out and tied to the wires, should be cut back to leave about ten buds. To provide for the replacement of these arms in the following year, cut back to two or three buds a shoot close to each. All other growths should be removed.

Pruning and training the established vine

In early spring cut out the arms that carried fruit the previous summer and tie in replacement shoots that have grown from the renewal spurs. Cut back a second shoot growing from the renewal spur to two buds. This will provide the replacement shoot the following year. Remove all other growths.

One method of calculating the number of buds to leave on the shoots is to weigh the amount of wood removed from a vine. First prune, leaving a few more buds than will be needed, say 12 to 15 per arm. Weigh the wood removed, and for the first pound (450 grams) leave 30 to 40 buds on the vine, divided equally between the four arms. Leave eight more buds for every additional pound of wood removed.

Umbrella Kniffin

In a variant of the Kniffin system the main stem is trained to the top wire but carries only two arms, which are trained in an umbrella shape, hanging over the top wire and slanting down to extend one bud below the bottom wire, to which they are securely tied. The method of renewal pruning is the same as for the Kniffin system. A high standard of cultivation is needed to produce good-quality grapes.

Other systems of grape training exist: consult County Extension specialists for regional advice.

MUSCADINE GRAPES

Muscadine grapes are rampant growers and for this reason are often trained on arbors. A strong support system is necessary for the main stem, which is taken up to a height of 6-7ft (1.8-2.1m), and also for the arms that spread out horizontally from the head of the vine. A system of wires spaced about 2ft (60cm) apart can be used to form the roof of the arbor. Once the main stem has been trained up to the required height, train out fruiting arms so that they are well spaced. The fruit are borne in small clusters from spur systems. Muscadine grapes can also be adapted to the Kniffin system.

Annual pruning of the established vine should take out dead wood and superfluous shoots. It is desirable to renew the fruiting arms systematically. Take out one or two a year, training in a vigorous young shoot as a replacement.

THINNING BUNCHES

Especially for *V. vinifera* dessert grapes, thinning is essential if the bunches are to be well shaped. This should be done in early to mid-summer. Use long-bladed scissors and avoid touching the berries for this will remove the protective bloom. Check bunches regularly after thinning and remove any berries that are damaged or diseased.

4-ARM KNIFFIN SYSTEM

In the formative pruning train up a strong stem, cutting it in the second spring just above the top wire.

1 In spring of the third year choose 4 vigorous growths to form 2 pairs of arms. Shorten them to leave about 10 buds on each and train them along the wires to left and right of the main stem. To form renewal spurs cut back a growth near each of the arms to 2 or 3 buds. Remove all other growths.

2 In the spring of the fourth and subsequent years cut off the arms that carried fruit in the previous growing season. Tie in growths that have developed from the renewal spurs and shorten these to about 10 buds. To form new renewal spurs cut selected growths back to 2 or 3 buds. Remove all other growths.

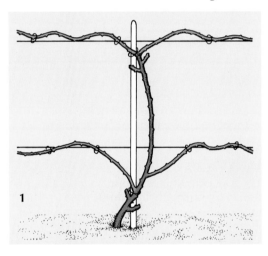

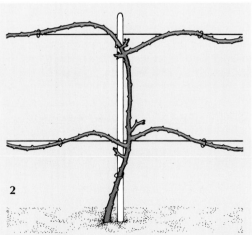

PASSION FRUIT

The passion fruit (*Passiflora edulis*), a vigorous evergreen climber, is a native of southern Brazil. It is grown for its egg-shaped fruits (technically berries), which contain a slightly tart aromatic pulp. The more familiar form has deep purple fruits, but there is also a form with yellow fruits.

Although in the tropics and in warm temperate regions the passion fruit is grown outdoors, in many temperate parts of the world it can only be grown satisfactorily in a greenhouse in which the minimum winter temperature does not fall below 7-10°C (45-50°F). It can be planted directly into the greenhouse border, but can also be pot grown. Root restriction can help to check over-vigorous growth of plants grown in rich soils, but the pot size should not be less that 10in (25cm).

A support is essential and this should be fixed in position before planting. Plastic netting – a 2in (5cm) mesh is ideal – is easy to erect and in the greenhouse should extend from the ground up to within 6in (15cm) of the roof glass. Another method is to use the sort of support that is suitable for greenhouse grapes, with wires run horizontally spaced about 9in (23cm) apart. For plants grown in pots use three or four canes about 6-8ft (1.8-2.4m) tall. These should be set in the pot, equally spaced round the rim, and the passion fruit trained round them in a spiral.

Formative pruning and training
At planting, in early spring, the tip should be taken off any plant with a single stem in order to encourage branching growth. After training two shoots on to the support, the plant is left to develop naturally, although any wayward growths are guided so that the tendrils attach themselves to the support. If main stems make considerable growth without producing laterals, their tips should be pinched out when 2-3ft (60-90cm) long. Passion fruit normally produce little or no fruit in their first year.

Pruning and training established plants
Established plants need to be cut back to encourage the development of new wood. However, hard pruning will result in excessive leafy growth and plants will carry few flowers and fruit. The first reasonable crop will probably be carried in the second summer. In the following winter, all stems

that have carried fruit are cut out at their junction with other branches of the framework. The new growth that is made in spring should be guided on the support, but otherwise the plant can be left alone.

Below: The passion fruit is a vigorous evergreen climber that attaches itself to supports by tendrils.

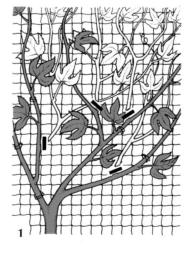
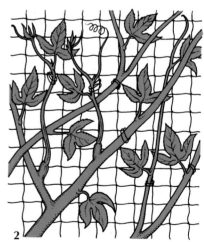

TRAINING
Plastic mesh makes a convenient support for passion fruit grown under glass.

1 In winter cut back stems that have carried fruit to the stems that form the framework.

2 In spring train in new growth to the support but allow the plant to develop naturally.

KIWI FRUIT

Above: The kiwi fruit is a vigorous grower and needs the support of a sturdy pergola or system of wires. Most fruiting cultivars need to be pollinated by a male plant.

The kiwi fruit (*Actinidia deliciosa*), known as the Chinese gooseberry until skilfully marketed by New Zealand growers, is a very vigorous vine most commonly grown in warm temperate areas. Although it can be grown in most areas where European grapes flourish, young growths are easily damaged by spring frosts and the fruit, which ripens over a long period, can be damaged by autumn frosts. The hardy *A. arguta* bears smaller fruit but is hardy in the north.

The principal difficulty in growing kiwi fruit is the amount of space required, partly because the vine is so vigorous, but also because most plants are dioecious, having male and female flowers on separate plants. The recent development of self-fertile cultivars is promising, but a female cultivar such as 'Hayward' will only produce fruit if a male cultivar, such as 'Matua', is planted nearby. In commercial orchards the normal ratio of male to female plants is one to seven. Male plants are usually cut back more severely in summer after flowering.

ESPALIER SYSTEM

For the home gardener this method, which can be used outdoors or in a greenhouse, is probably easier than the renewal system used by commercial growers.

Formative pruning and training

Kiwi fruits are planted between late autumn and early spring, spaced about 10-15ft (3-4.5m) apart. Each plant should be provided with a bamboo cane attached vertically to the wires. To encourage vigorous growth, the plant should be cut back at planting to about 1ft (30cm) above the ground.

In the first and second growing seasons a main stem should be trained vertically and tied to the cane so that it does not twist around it. The aim is to train strong shoots to left and right of the main stem at each wire, all unwanted shoots being pinched out. When the main stem has passed the top wire and the horizontal shoots are about 3ft (90cm) long, the tips should be pinched out to encourage the formation of laterals. Fruit-bearing spur systems are formed by stopping at five leaves the laterals growing on the horizontal shoots. Any sub-laterals should be taken out completely.

Pruning the established plant

The plant will generally begin bearing fruit in its third growing season. The vigorous growth that is made must be checked to keep the plant manageable and to give the fruit the best chance of ripening. All fruit-bearing laterals should be pinched back to seven leaves beyond the last fruit. Pinching barren laterals back to five leaves will encourage the formation of fruiting spurs. Pinch out all superfluous laterals and sub-laterals.

The aim in winter pruning is to strike a balance between maintaining existing spur systems and renewal pruning that will encourage the formation of replacement laterals. All vigorous spurs are cut back to two buds beyond where the last fruit was borne. Some spurs should be cut back to a dormant bud close to the horizontal shoot, especially where growth is crowded. The growth from this bud is subsequently pruned to form a replacement spur.

RENEWAL SYSTEM

When kiwi fruit are grown on pergolas, the aim is to create a permanent framework consisting of a single main stem trained to the height of the pergola – for ease of working commercial growers train to a height of about 6ft (1.8m) – and two leaders trained horizontally along the pergola in opposite directions. The fruiting arms, which are regularly replaced, are also trained horizontally, at right angles to the leaders. The pergola holds up the fruiting arms, but the laterals that bear the fruit hang down.

Formative pruning and training

Planting takes place between late autumn and early spring, with plants spaced at 18-25ft (5.5-6.7m) apart. An alternative that is less space demanding, but also less productive, is to plant male and female cultivars close together. One method is to train the male plant as a cordon about 1ft (30cm) above the female plant. Another method is to allow only one horizontal leader to develop from each, the two leaders being trained in opposite directions. Each plant is provided with a cane on which it can be trained up to the height of the pergola. After planting, the leader is cut back to about 1ft (30cm) to encourage vigorous growth.

In the first growing season a strong shoot should be trained up the cane but not allowed to twist around its support. Some side growths may be allowed in the early stages, provided they do not come from below the union on a grafted plant, to help the development of a strong root system. When the plant reaches the height of the pergola, the growing point should be pinched out. Two strong shoots (or one, if male and female plants are being grown close together) should be selected and trained horizontally in opposite directions. Once these leaders are growing vigorously, remove any shoots on the main stem. Some thinning is essential to create a well-spaced canopy of fruiting arms.

Pruning and training the established plant

Pruning several times in the summer is essential to control the vigorous growth. At the same time, replacement fruiting arms must be selected to bear fruit in the succeeding year. These should be formed from strong shoots arising near the leaders, which are left unpruned throughout the summer. Unwanted growth should be removed, upright shoots cut back to a short stub, and the fruiting laterals pinched back to six leaves beyond the fruit.

The aim of winter pruning, which in areas subjected to occasional severe frosts is best carried out late so that frost-damaged shoots

are removed, is to leave a well-spaced canopy of one-year-old wood. The arms that carried fruit in the preceding summer should be cut back to their replacements, the new arms being spaced about 1 ¾ft (51cm) apart on either side of the leader.

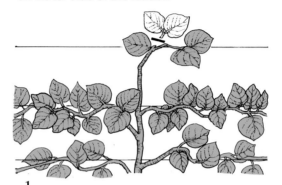

1

2

3

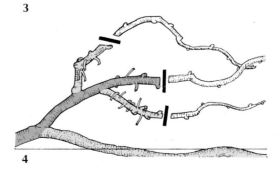

4

ESPALIER TRAINING

1 In the first year or two after planting train the main stem vertically and in early summer, when growth has passed the top wire, pinch out the tip to encourage the formation of laterals.

2 Train laterals horizontally, pinching out the tips when the available space is filled. In summer stop laterals at 5 leaves in order to form fruit-bearing spurs.

3 Plants usually bear fruit in their third year. In this and subsequent years pinch back laterals that are carrying fruit to 6 leaves beyond the last fruit.

4 In the winter of the third and subsequent years cut back laterals to 2 buds beyond where the last fruit was borne. On older plants cut back a proportion of 3-year-old laterals to dormant buds.

TOOLS AND EQUIPMENT

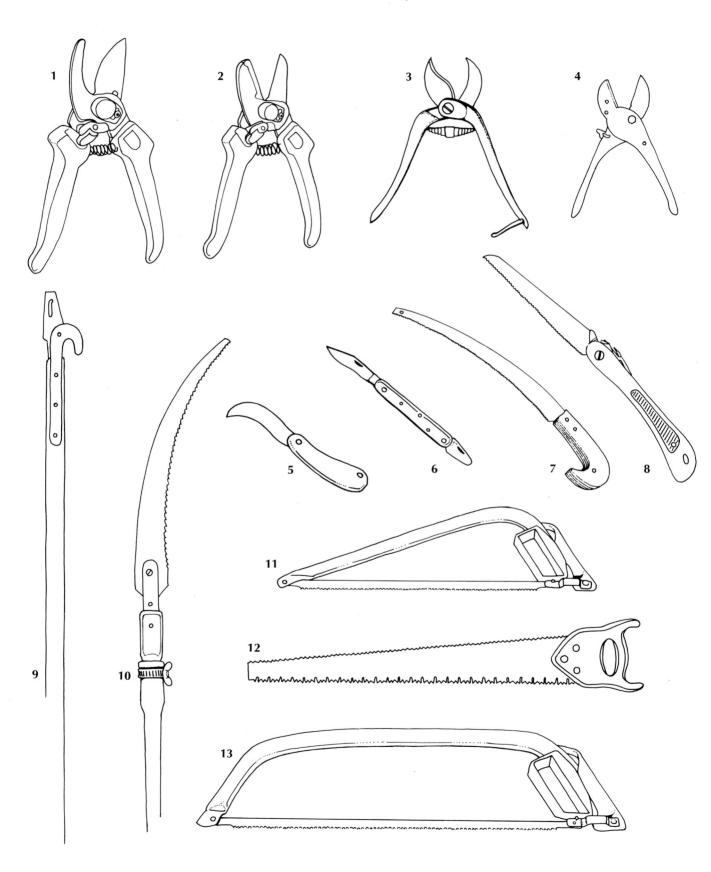

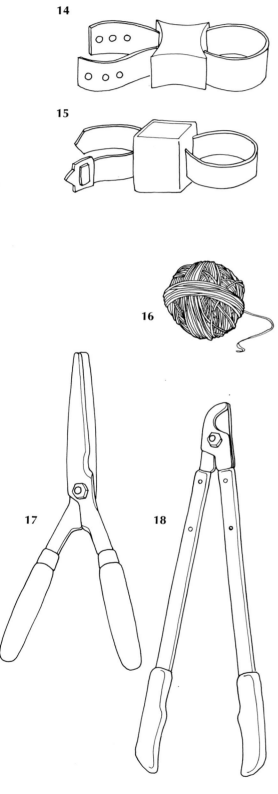

14

15

16

17   18

Very few tools are needed for normal garden pruning and an investment in good quality pays in the long term. It is important to keep all tools sharp, well-oiled, and stored in a dry place away from children.

The most important item is a good pair of hand pruners with a comfortable grip. Three main kinds are available – anvil, by-pass, and parrot-bill – with various models offering additional refinements. All pruners should have a safety catch that locks the blades in the closed position. The anvil type has a straight-edged cutting blade that cuts down on a bar of softer metal or plastic; the by-pass pruner has a convexly curved blade that cuts against a curved fixed blade; while the parrot-bill pruner has two curved cutting blades, cuts with a scissor-like action and is particularly useful for detailed work. All of these pruners will give good results if kept sharp and used for cutting branches that are within their scope. Avoid using the tips of the blades as there is a risk of the pruners being twisted and strained.

Long-handled pruners or loppers are useful for cutting thick stems that cannot be managed with hand pruners, the arms giving extra leverage. They also make it possible to work at a distance, for example while cutting out stems from the base of thorny plants such as roses.

Many gardeners find it useful to carry a knife for general purposes in the garden, but it requires considerable practice to use a pruning knife with the dexterity of the expert. Pruning knives normally have a curved blade, but a straight-bladed grafting knife can be used for removing twiggy shoots.

Saws that can cut green wood without clogging are necessary for dealing with larger branches. The Grecian saw has a curved blade while the English pruning saw has a tapered blade with teeth on both edges. A small folding saw is a particularly useful tool and can be used in confined spaces.

Long-bladed hedging shears will be needed for hedges and topiary and, for detailed work on the latter, one-handed shears are useful. Where there are long lengths of hedge to be cut, it is probably worth investing in a hedge-trimmer, which can be powered from a battery, a generator or by electricity from the house. When using the latter, be careful not to cut the cable: this can prove fatal.

The items illustrated here include basic tools such as hand pruners, saws, long-arm pruners, and hand shears. Other tools can be useful in meeting special needs. The pole saw, for example, can be used to remove high branches without the use of a ladder. Twist, ratchet, and ring ties are useful supplements to twine for tying in young flexible growths.

Hand pruners
1. By-pass
2. Anvil
3. Parrot-bill
4. Lightweight anvil

Knives
5. Pruning
6. Grafting

Saws and pruners
7. Grecian curved blade
8. Folding pruning
9. Long-arm pruners
10. Pole
11. Triangular bow
12. English (two-sided) pruning
13. Bow

Other equipment
14. Tree tie (nail-on)
15. Tree tie (buckle)
16. Twine
17. Hand shears
18. Long-handled pruners

GLOSSARY

ADVENTITIOUS Used of parts of a plant that develop in unexpected positions. Adventitious buds are unlike normal growth buds in that they arise without any relation to the leaves, usually in response to a wound.

AERIAL ROOTS Roots that develop above soil level and, in the case of several climbers such as the common ivy (*Hedera helix*), attach themselves to supports.

ALTERNATE Used to describe the arrangement of buds, leaves, and shoots placed one above the other at different heights on either side of a stem.

ANGLE OF ATTACHMENT The topmost angle at which a branch joins a stem or trunk. A narrow angle forms a much weaker junction than a wide angle.

APEX The tip of a shoot, from which extension growth is made.

APICAL Adjective from APEX. Uppermost, as in apical bud and apical shoot.

APICAL DOMINANCE The control exerted over the development of the lateral buds by the terminal (apical) bud of a shoot, the growth of lateral buds being inhibited while the apical bud grows more rapidly.

ARCURE A restricted method of training apples and pears in which the branches form a series of arches alternating to left and right in the same plane.

AXIL The upper angle formed by the junction of a leaf with a stem.

AXILLARY Adjective from AXIL. Located in the angle between leaf and stem, as in axillary bud and axillary shoot.

BARK-RINGING The removal of a segment, normally a nearly complete ring, of bark from an over-vigorous fruit tree that is bearing poorly with the intention of stimulating flower-bud production by checking vegetative growth.

BARRIER ZONE An internal boundary of cells resistant to pathogens formed in sapwood by trees or shrubs after injury to isolate the damaged part.

BASAL At the lowest part of the plant or of a stem, as in basal cluster (the closely spaced leaves at the base of an apple or pear shoot), basal growth, and basal shoots.

BIENNIAL BEARER A fruit tree that bears good crops of blossom or fruit in alternate years only.

BLEEDING The loss of sap from a cut or other wound on susceptible trees.

BLIND SHOOT A shoot which does not develop fully, used especially of shoots on roses that do not develop a terminal flower bud.

BRACING The use of straps and guys as an alternative to staking to give a young or transplanted tree support while it becomes established.

BRANCH COLLAR The swelling that is usually conspicuous on the underside of the junction between branch and stem.

BRANCH BARK RIDGE The line of generally rough bark angled back from a crotch that marks the junction of branch and trunk cork cambium. The ridge also indicates the angle of an internal barrier to decay between the branch and trunk.

BRANCHED HEAD The arrangement of branches on a tree in which there is no central leader shoot.

BRASHING The forestry practice of cutting off the lower, often dead, branches of plantation-grown coniferous trees.

BREAK The development of lateral shoots on a stem, often as a result of the growing point being stopped or pinched out.

BREASTWOOD Shoots that grow outwards from a plant that is trained against a support.

BUD An embryo shoot (growth bud) or flower (flower or fruit bud). Flower buds are generally fatter and rounder than growth buds.

BUDDING A method of grafting in which a single growth bud rather than a shoot is united with the stock.

BUSH TREE A tree pruned to a dwarf form with a clear stem 2-2½ft (60-75cm) in height.

CALLUS The corky tissue which forms naturally at the margin of a wound, often eventually covering it.

CAMBIUM A layer of actively dividing cells between bark and wood (vascular cambium) that increases the girth of stems. A layer of cells in the bark (bark cambium) that produces outer bark cells.

CENTRAL LEADER The vertical and dominant stem at the center of a tree.

CLEANING OUT The removal from a tree or shrub of dead, damaged, and diseased wood and weak growths.

CLONE A group of plants propagated asexually from a single parent, all with characteristics that are identical to those of the parent.

COPPICING A traditional method of managing woodland in which trees and shrubs are regularly cut to near ground level on a short rotation of years to produce crops of poles and firewood. The regular pruning to near ground level of ornamental trees and shrubs, chiefly to enhance the effects of foliage or colored stems.

CORDON A restricted form of fruit tree with one or, less commonly, several main stems bearing spurs, the stem or stems being trained either obliquely or vertically.

COSMETIC PRUNING Minor pruning to keep a plant tidy and to maintain a balanced shape.

CROTCH The upper angle formed where a branch or twig grows from a trunk, branch or stem of a shrub or tree.

CROWN THINNING Opening up the crown of a tree by the selective removal of secondary and small branches.

CROWN REDUCTION The reduction in the overall height of a tree while retaining the natural outline of the crown by careful cutting back of selected branches to laterals.

CROWN LIFTING The removal of branches from the lower part of a tree to form a clear stem beneath the crown.

CROWN The upper branches and foliage of a tree.

CULTIVAR A cultivated variety produced by horticultural or agricultural techniques and not normally found in natural populations.

DARD An old term for a short shoot that develops into a fruit-bearing spur on apples and pears.

DEADHEADING The removal of faded flowers to prevent the development of seed, often with the intention of encouraging repeat flowering, or to make a plant tidier in appearance.

DEBLOSSOMING The removal of individual flowers or flower trusses.

DECIDUOUS Used of trees and shrubs that lose their leaves annually at the end of the growing season.

DECURRENT Of a tree with a spreading crown and several main branches.

DEFOLIATION The removal of leaves.

DEHORNING The drastic cutting back of main branches, applied especially to this operation when carried out on fruit trees.

DISBUDDING The removal of flower buds or growth buds that are just beginning to develop, generally with the intention of directing a plant's energies to selected buds that are retained.

DORMANT PERIOD The stage in the annual cycle, usually autumn and winter, when a plant makes no growth.

DORMANT BUD A bud which, although formed normally, only becomes active as a result of an injury to the shoot or branch.

DOUBLE-WORKING A grafting technique employed to overcome incompatibility between some cultivars and rootstocks. The selected cultivar is first grafted or budded on to a compatible cultivar, which is then grafted on to the rootstock.

DOUBLE LEADER Two shoots competing as leaders on a tree, each trying to assert apical dominance.

DROP-CROTCHING Another term for crown reduction.

DWARF PYRAMID A restricted form of fruit tree pruned to form a pyramid shape about a short central leader.

EPICORMIC SHOOT A shoot from an adventitious or dormant bud on the main stem or on a branch of a shrub or tree, usually stimulated into growth by a wound or cut.

ESPALIER A restricted form of tree, especially fruit tree, with a vertical main stem and tiers of horizontal branches.

EXTENSION GROWTH Shoots that develop from the apical bud of a stem.

EYE A growth bud, a term used particularly of roses and vines.

FAN A form of shrub or tree grown against a wall, fence or other support in which the main branches are trained to radiate out like the ribs of a fan from the top of a short stem.

FESTOONING Arching over supple branches of fruit trees to encourage the formation of fruit buds.

FLUSH CUT A cut that removes a branch as close as possible to a stem. Formerly widely recommended, flush cuts are now generally considered damaging to trees and shrubs on account of the injury done to the stem above and below the branch.

FRAMEWORK The permanent "skeleton" of

main branches, either formed naturally or, as in the case of the ribs of a fan-trained fruit tree, deliberately manipulated to a particular shape.

GRAFTING The technique of uniting a shoot or single bud of one plant (the scion) with the root system and stem of another (the stock or rootstock).

HALF-STANDARD see STANDARD
HEADING BACK Cutting a stem, especially a central leader, back to a bud or shoot.
HEARTWOOD The central core of hardened lumber containing no living cells which results from the normal ageing process.
HOLDFAST The attachment by which some climbers (e.g. *Parthenocissus tricuspidata*) attach themselves to surfaces.
HOOPING A method of growing fruit trees, especially plums, in which the main stem is bent down to encourage the formation of fruiting spurs.
HYBRID A cross between two or more species or forms of a species.

INCLUDED BARK Bark that has turned in at the junction of branch and trunk or of codominant stems and is a source of structural weakness.
INTERNODE The section of stem between two nodes or joints.

LATERAL A stem or shoot growing from a larger stem.
LAYING A traditional method of renovating a farm hedge by partly cutting through stems, laying them near the horizontal, and weaving them through uprights to form a stock-proof barrier.
LEADER The growing shoot that terminates a branch and extends it.
LOPPING Crude cutting back of the large branches of a tree.

MAIDEN A one-year-old tree or shrub. Used of fruit trees to describe one-year-old growth.

NICKING Cutting into the bark immediately below a bud to reduce the vigor of the growth from the bud. This technique is sometimes combined with NOTCHING in the shaping of young fruit trees.
NODE The joint on a stem where leaves, buds, and side shoots arise.
NOTCHING The removal of a small wedge of bark immediately above a latent bud to stimulate it into growth. The combination of this technique and NICKING is sometimes used in the shaping of young fruit trees.

OPEN CENTER The branch system of a tree or shrub pruned and trained so that the framework has a clear center with no main branches passing through it.
OPPOSITE Used to describe the arrangement of buds, leaves, and shoots that are opposite to one another on a stem or branch.
ORNAMENTALS Plants grown primarily for their decorative value rather than for their commercial usefulness or for the production of crops.

PALMETTE A restricted form of fruit tree with pairs of laterals trained parallel to a vertical trunk. Also sometimes used as a synonym for FAN.
PARING Cutting the bark at the margins of a wound in the belief that making the surface reasonably smooth speeds callusing. See also SCRIBING.
PINCHING BACK The removal, by cutting out or nipping with finger and thumb, of the succulent growing tip of a shoot.
PITH The cylinder of usually soft tissue in a young stem.
POLLARDING A traditional method of managing woodland in which the branches of trees are regularly cut back to the main trunk on a short rotation of years to produce crops of poles and lumber. The regular pruning back of the branches of ornamental trees and shrubs to the trunk, producing young growths with good foliage or colored stems.
PRIMARY BRANCHES The first branches to develop from the main stem of a tree or shrub.

REGULATORY PRUNING Pruning to remove crossing, crowded, and weak growths.
RENEWAL PRUNING Pruning to maintain a constant supply of young shoots.
ROD The main, woody stem of a vine.
ROOT-PRUNING The severing of the main roots of a tree or shrub to reduce vigor and, in the case of fruit trees, to encourage them to bear.
ROOTSTOCK A plant on which another is grafted or budded.
RUBBING OUT The removal of buds with a simple hand movement.

SAPWOOD Soft and recently formed wood between the bark and the heartwood that contains living cells.
SCAFFOLD BRANCHES The main branches of a tree.
SCION The shoot or bud of a shrub or tree that is grafted or budded on to a rootstock.
SCRIBING The removal of bark and wood at the margins of a wound, often enlarging and shaping the wound in the belief that callusing will be speeded up. See also PARING.
SECONDARY BRANCHES The branches that develop from the primary branches of a tree or shrub.
SNAG A short stump left when a branch is incorrectly pruned.
SPINDLEBUSH A cone-shaped form of fruit tree, usually apple, with a staked central leader. The near horizontal lower branches are permanent, but the shorter upper branches are cut out when they become too dominant.
SPORT An aberrant plant form or mutant that has arisen spontaneously.
SPUR PRUNING A pruning technique applied mainly to fruit trees, but also to some ornamentals (e.g. wisterias), which aims to encourage the development of spur systems.
SPUR A short flowering side shoot, usually part of a slow-growing fruiting branch made up of several spurs (spur system) on fruit trees.
SPUR-BEARER A fruit tree that bears most of its fruit on spurs.

STANDARD A tree or shrub grown with a clear stem. A tree or shrub grown as a full standard has a clear stem of 5-6ft (1.5-1.8m) and as a half standard of 3-4ft (90-120cm). However, as applied to a wide range of fruit trees and ornamentals, these terms are not absolute.
STOCK see ROOTSTOCK
STOPPING see PINCHING BACK
STUBBING BACK Cutting back a lateral that has carried fruit, leaving a short stub.
STUBBING see LOPPING
SUB-LATERAL A side shoot growing from a lateral shoot.
SUCKER A shoot that arises from below or just at ground level, usually from a root system. The term commonly refers to unwanted growths that develop from the rootstock of grafted or budded plants.

TENDRIL A modified stem or leaf that twines around supports, enabling plants that are equipped with them, such as grapes, to climb.
TERMINAL As in terminal bud, see APICAL.
THINNING To reduce the number of buds, flowers, fruitlets or branches.
TIP-BEARER A fruit tree that bears most of its fruits at the tips of one-year-old wood.
TIPPING, TIP PRUNING The pruning away of the apical part of a shoot.
TOP-WORKED Of a standard or half-standard, the root system and stem consisting of the stock, the selected tree or shrub having been grafted or budded at the top of the stock.
TOPIARY The imposition of an artificial shape, geometric or representational, on a tree or shrub by trimming and training.
TOPPING The drastic and usually crude removal of the top portion of the main stem of a tree.
TRUSS A cluster of flowers or fruit.

UNION The junction between scion and rootstock or between two scions.

WATER SHOOT, WATER SPROUT Now deprecated terms for EPICORMIC SHOOT.
WHIP A maiden tree without lateral growths.
WHORL An arrangement of three or more buds, leaves, shoots or flowers arising at the same node.
WOOD The lignified tissue of trees and shrubs but sometimes used as a synonym for growth.

INDEX

The A-Z listings of Roses (pp. 38-9) and Ornamentals (pp. 120-28) are intended to be used in conjuction with the index. For this reason, no reference is made to the entries in the A-Zs on the following pages.

Page numbers in *italic* refer to the illustrations.

FURTHER READING

A number of general books on trees and shrubs as well as those specializing in pruning and training contain valuable information and a selection is listed below. Not all of those selected reflect recent thinking on the pruning of trees as described in the work of Alexander Shigo.

Baker, Harry, *Fruit* (Mitchell Beazley, London, 1980)

Baker, Harry, *The Fruit Garden Displayed* (Cassell Ltd./Royal Horticultural Society, London, 1986)

Bean, W. J., *Trees and Shrubs Hardy in the British Isles* Volumes 1-4 (General Editor: Sir G. Taylor) and supplement (Editor: D. L. Clarke) (John Murray, London, 1970-80, 1988)

Brickell, Christopher, *Pruning* (Mitchell Beazley, London, 1979)

Brown, George E., *Pruning of Trees, Shrubs and Conifers* (Faber and Faber, London, 1972)

Clevely, A. M., *The Art of Clipping Trees and Ornamental Hedges* (Collins, London, 1988)

Halliwell, B., Turpin, J., and Wright, J., *The Complete Book of Pruning* (Ward Lock, London, 3rd edn., 1988)

Harris, R. W., *Arboriculture: The Care of Trees, Shrubs and Vines in the Landscape* (Prentice Hall, Englewood Cliffs, N. J., 1983)

Le Sueur, A. D. C., *The Care and Repair of Ornamental Trees* (Country Life Ltd., London, 2nd edn., 1949)

Lloyd, Nathaniel, *Garden Craftsmanship in Yew and Box* (Ernest Benn Ltd., London, 1925)

Pirone, P. P., Hartman, J. R., Sall, M. A., Pirone, T. P., *Tree Maintenance* (Oxford University Press, New York, New York, 1988)

Shigo, Alexander L., *Modern Arboriculture: Systems Approach to the Care of Trees and Their Associates* (Shigo and Trees, Associates, Durham, New Hampshire, 1991)

ACKNOWLEDGMENTS

Commissioned photography by **Andrew Lawson**: 4-5, 6r, 14r, 17b, 21, 26t, 27, 33b, 34b, 42, 43tl, 43bl, 44tr, 44trc, 44brc, 44rb, 45tl, 45tr, 45bl, 45br, 47, 52t, 52b, 53tl, 53tr, 53bl, 53bc, 53br, 54t, 54c, 54b, 55, 57t, 61tl, 61tr, 63l, 63r, 65l, 65, 65c, 65r, 67t, 67b, 68l, 69l, 69cl, 69cr, 69r, 72t, 72cl, 72cr, 72b, 73t, 73c, 73b, 84l, 89bl, 89br, 92br, 93, 95r, 96, 103, 105t, 106-7, 107t, 107b, 109t, 112bl, 114t, 116r, 129, 129br, 129bl, 130, 131, 133, 137r, 140t, 140c, 142, 148t, 157b, 162, 164l, 175tl, 175tr, 192c, 192l, 192r, 193l, 193r, 195r, 195bl, 195t, 196, 198, 206t, 206c, 206b.

The publishers would like to thank the following organizations and individuals for their kind permission to reproduce the photographs in this book:

A-Z Botanical Collection: 13l; **Heather Angel**: 94t, 167; **Paul Barker**: 56-7/ 75t/95l (York Gate), 83t (Stockeld Park); **Peter Blackburn**: 153tc; **Boys Syndication**: 23t/26b/104b/137t/152b/153b/166/189t (Jacqui Hurst), 28b, 110-11, 114b; **Eric Crichton**: 6l, 12, 15, 16t, 17t, 25, 29t, 29br, 40t, 40br, 40l, 43r, 46, 48l, 48r, 50-1, 51b, 56t, 57b, 59, 61b, 64l, 64r, 66-7, 71r, 80, 80-1, 82, 85, 86, 94b, 97t, 98r, 99t, 100, 101tr, 101b, 105bl, 105br (National Trust), 109b, 110, 111, 112t, 113, 115, 132, 134t, 134b, 135bl, 135br, 145tl, 148b, 149, 152-53, 156, 157t, 180, 181r, 183, 184, 187l, 188t, 189bl, 190t, 192b, 193r; **Garden Picture Library**: 135t (Brian Carter), 16b (Derek Fell), 98l (Vaughan Fleming), 8 (John Glover), 54-5/55 (M. Heuff), 204 (Lamontagne), 121 (Perdereau-Thomas), 6-7/101tl (Brigitte Thomas); **Michael Gibson**: 36l; **Robert Harding Library**: 143 (Christopher Nicholson), 174b, 182b, 188br, 189br, 197; **Jerry Harpur**: 56b, 81c, 92tr/ 96-7 (Villandry), 119 (Ladew Garden, Maryland), 136tr, 153bl (Heale House), 170b, 190b (Barnsley House); **Horticultural Research International**: 145r; **Jacqui Hurst**: 41t; **Insight**: 14l, 33t, 136l (Linda Burgess), 152t (Michelle Garrett); **Favardin C. Jacana**: 78, 171; **D. M. Joyce**: 92tr, 181l; **Marjory Majerus**: 23b, 44l; **S & O Mathews**: 154; **National Trust Photographic Library**: 170t/207t (Rob Matheson); **Phillipe Perdereau-Thomas**: 29bl, 34t, 36r, 62, 71l, 83r, 87, 89t, 90, 99b, 97b, 102, 104t, 108l, 118, 136tr, 159, 186t; **Photos Horticultural**: 11, 13r, 49, 51t, 68r, 74t, 74b, 75b, 81t, 83l, 137c, 144, 145b, 164r, 166l, 177t, 177br, 177bl, 178t, 178b, 179, 182t, 185, 186bl, 186b, 187r, 191, 194, 195bc, 201t, 201b, 204, 209, 211, 212; **Hazel Le Rougete/Biofotos**: 35; **Stephen Robson**: 136; **Harry Smith Collection**: 28t, 81b, 92bl, 106bl, 106br, 137b, 141, 153tr, 199, 208; **Brigitte Thomas**: 108r, 112br, 116l, 116-17, 117; **Wildlife Matters**: 84r, 137l.